MULTICULTURAL EDUCATION SERIES

James A. Banks, Series Editor

continued

Culture, Literacy, & Learning

Taking Bloom in the Midst of the Whirlwind

Carol D. Lee

Foreword by Linda Darling-Hammond

Teachers College, Columbia University
New York and London

Published by Teachers College Press, 1234 Amsterdam Avenue, New York, NY 10027

Grateful acknowledgment is made for use of the following:

"The Second Sermon on the Warpland" by Gwendolyn Brooks reprinted by consent of Brooks Permissions.

Excerpt from *Beloved* by Toni Morrison, copyright ©1987 by Toni Morrison. Used by permission of Alfred A. Knopf, a division of Random House, Inc., and International Creative Management, Inc.

Passages in Chapter 7: Excerpted from *If Beale Street Could Talk* ©1974 by James Baldwin. Copyright renewed. Published by Vintage Books. Reprinted by arrangement with the James Baldwin Estate.

"Caged Bird," copyright © 1983 by Maya Angelou from *Shaker, Why Don't You Sing?* by Maya Angelou. Used by permission of Random House, Inc., and Little Brown,

"The Mask" Copyright 1996 Sony/ATV Tunes LLC, Huss-Zwingli Publishing Inc., Obverse Creation Music Inc., Tete San Ko Publishing Inc. All rights administered by Sony/ATV Music Publishing, 8 Music Square West, Nashville, TN 37203. All rights reserved. Used by permission.

Library of Congress Cataloging-in-Publication Data

Lee, Carol D.
 Culture, literacy, and learning : taking bloom in the midst of the whirlwind / Carol D. Lee; foreword by Linda Darling-Hammond.
  p. cm.-(Multicultural education series)
 Includes bibliographical references and index.
 ISBN-13: 978-0-8077-4749-0 (casebound)
 ISBN-10: 0-8077-4749-1 (casebound)
 ISBN-13: 978-0-8077-4748-3 (pbk.)
 ISBN-10: 0-8077-4748-3 (pbk.)
  1. African Americans—Education (Secondary)—Illinois—Chicago—Case studies. 2. Multicultural education—Illinois—Chicago—Case studies. 3. Urban education—Illinois—Chicago—Case studies. 4. School improvement programs—Illinois—Chicago—Case studies. I. Title.
LC2779.L43 2006
373. 1829'96073-dc22   2006025147

ISBN: 978-0-8077-4748-3 (paper)
ISBN: 978-0-8077-4749-0 (cloth)

Printed on acid-free paper

Manufactured in the United States of America

14 13 12 11 10 09 08   8 7 6 5 4 3 2

In memory of

Gwendolyn Brooks
(1917–2000)

Barbara Ann Sizemore
(1927–2004)

The Second Sermon
on the Warpland

1.

This is the urgency: Live!
And have your blooming in the noise of the whirlwind.

2.

Salve salvage in the spin.
Endorse the splendor splashes;
stylize the flawed utility;
prop a malign or failing light—
but know the whirlwind is our commonwealth.
Not the easy man, who rides above them all,
not the jumbo brigand,
not the pet bird of poets, that sweetest sonnet,
shall straddle the whirlwind.
Nevertheless, live.

3.

All about are the cold places,
all about are the pushmen and jeopardy, theft—
all about are the stormers and scramblers but
what must our Season be, which starts from Fear?
Live and go out.
Define and
medicate the whirlwind.

4.

The time
cracks into furious flower. Lifts its face
all unashamed. And sways in wicked grace.
Whose half-black hands assemble oranges
Is tom-tom hearted
(goes in bearing oranges and boom).
And there are bells for orphans—
and red and shriek and sheen.
A garbageman is dignified
as any diplomat.

Big Bessie's feet hurt like nobody's business,
but she stands—bigly—under the unruly scrutiny, stands in the wild weed.

In the wild weed
she is a citizen,
and is a moment of highest quality; admirable.

It is lonesome, yes. For we are the last of the loud.
Nevertheless, live.
Conduct your blooming in the noise and whip of the whirlwind.

Gwendolyn Brooks
From *In the Mecca*

Contents

Series Foreword

The nation's deepening ethnic texture, interracial tension and conflict, and the increasing percentage of students who speak a first language other than English make multicultural education imperative in the twenty-first century. The U.S. Census (2000) estimates that people of color made up 28% of the nation's population in 2000 and predicts that they will make up 38% in 2025 and 50% in 2050 (El Nasser, 2004).

American classrooms are experiencing the largest influx of immigrant students since the beginning of the twentieth century. About a million immigrants are making the United States their home each year (Martin & Midgley, 1999). More than five million legal immigrants settled in the United States between 1999 and 2004 (U.S. Department of Homeland Security, 2006), most of whom came from nations in Latin America and Asia (Riche, 2000). A significant number also came from the West Indies and Africa. A large but undetermined number of undocumented immigrants also enter the United States each year. The influence of an increasingly ethnically diverse population on the nation's schools, colleges, and universities is and will continue to be enormous.

Forty-two percent of the students enrolled in the nation's schools in 2003 were students of color (National Center for Education Statistics, 2005). This percentage is increasing each year, primarily because of the growth in the percentage of Latino students (Martinez & Curry, 1999). In some of the nation's largest cities and metropolitan areas, such as Chicago, Los Angeles, Washington, D. C., New York, Seattle, and San Francisco, half or more of the public school students are students of color. During the 2003–04 school year, students of color made up 67.5% of the student population in the public schools of California, the nation's most populous state (California State Department of Education, 2006).

Language and religious diversity is also increasing among the nation's student population. In 2003 18.7% of the school-age population spoke a language at home other than English (National Center for Education Statistics, 2005). Harvard professor Diana L. Eck (2001) calls the United States the "most religiously diverse nation on earth" (p. 4). Islam is now the fastest growing religion in the United States. Most teachers now in the classroom and in teacher education programs are likely to have students from diverse ethnic, racial, language, and religious groups in their classrooms during their careers. This is true for both inner-city and suburban teachers.

An important goal of multicultural education is to improve race relations and to help all students acquire the knowledge, attitudes, and skills needed to participate in cross-cultural interactions and in personal, social, and civic action that will help make our nation more democratic and just. Multicultural education is consequently as important for middle-class White suburban students as it is for students of color who live in the inner city. Multicultural education fosters the public good and the overarching goals of the commonwealth.

The major purpose of the *Multicultural Education Series* is to provide preservice educators, practicing educators, graduate students, scholars, and policy makers with an interrelated and comprehensive set of books that summarizes and analyzes important research, theory, and practice related to the education of ethnic, racial, cultural, and language groups in the United States and to the education of mainstream students about diversity. The books in the series provide research, theoretical, and practical knowledge about the behaviors and learning characteristics of students of color, language minority students, and low-income students. They also provide knowledge about ways to improve academic achievement and race relations in educational settings.

The definition of multicultural education in the *Handbook of Research on Multicultural Education* (Banks & Banks, 2004) is used in the series: Multicultural education is *"a field of study designed to increase educational equity for all students that incorporates, for this purpose, content, concepts, principles, theories, and paradigms from history, the social and behavioral sciences, and particularly from ethnic studies and women's studies"* (p. xii). In the series, as in the *Handbook*, multicultural education is considered a "metadiscipline."

The dimensions of multicultural education, developed by Banks (2004) and described in the *Handbook of Research on Multicultural Education*, provide the conceptual framework for the development of the books in the series. They are: *content integration, the knowledge construction process, prejudice reduction, an equity pedagogy,* and *an empowering school culture and social structure.* To implement multicultural education effectively, teachers and administrators must attend to each of the five dimensions of multicultural education. They should use content from diverse groups when teaching concepts and skills, help students understand how knowledge in the various disciplines is constructed, help students develop positive intergroup attitudes and behaviors, and modify their teaching strategies so that students from different racial, cultural, language, and social-class groups will experience equal educational opportunities. The total environment and culture of the school must also be transformed so that students from diverse groups will experience equal status in the culture and life of the school.

Although the five dimensions of multicultural education are highly interrelated, each requires deliberate attention and focus. Each publication in the series focuses on one or more of the dimensions, although each book deals with all of them to some extent because of the highly interrelated characteristics of the dimensions.

This timely and significant book is a singular contribution to the literature on culturally responsive teaching as well as on teaching subject matter content. Lee's work builds upon, extends, and deepens the research and theory on culturally responsive teaching (Au, 2005; Gay, 2000; Ladson-Billings, 1994) by illustrating how teachers can skillfully use the funds of knowledge (Moll & González, 2004) that students bring to the classroom to enrich the teaching of academic subjects. Previous researchers in the culturally responsive paradigm have not demonstrated as explicitly as Lee how teachers can use the cultural knowledge of students to teach challenging and powerful concepts in the academic subjects. Most of Lee's examples are derived from her 3 years of teaching low-income African American high school students to do sophisticated analyses of complex literary works such as Toni Morrison's (1987) novel *Beloved*. However, she also describes compelling mathematics examples from the work of researchers such as Saxe (1991), Schoenfeld (1985), and Moses (1994). As Lee makes clear, the work she describes in this book has significant and helpful implications for academic subjects other than English and mathematics.

Shulman (1986) and his former students and colleagues—such as Grossman (1990) and Wineburg and Wilson (1988)—have done pioneering work on the knowledge and skills that teachers need to teach effectively the academic subjects of history and English. Lee makes a unique contribution to the corpus of theoretical and empirical work done by Shulman and his colleagues by describing—in very explicit ways—how teachers can draw upon the cultures of low-income African American students when teaching concepts, generalizations, and skills in literary analysis. Lee's work, which she calls "Cultural Modeling," is authoritative and visionary because she demonstrates how students who are often written off and marginalized by many educators and much of the wider public can do academic work that is often reserved for students who are considered academically gifted and talented.

Lee's theoretical and empirical work is ingenious, original, and significant. It is also hopeful and inspiring. She begins this book with a moving description of the violence and intractable problems that cast a paralyzing shadow on the lives of the African American students at Fairgate High School. Later in this book, when Lee describes the same students doing sophisticated literary analyses of Morrison's highly symbolic and difficult novel, she uncovers the keen insights and intellectual strengths of students whose talents, commitments, and skills are needed to enrich and to help humanize our troubled and polarized world.

Lee brings a lifetime of dedication, commitment, and work with low-income African American students to this needed and seminal book. She cofounded an African-centered school in 1972 that has produced a generation of students who have achieved academic and cultural success. Since becoming a professor at Northwestern University she has returned to the classroom to work with students and to test her ideas and theories. Lee walks the talk by effectively and creatively bridging the worlds of research and practice. She consequently speaks with an authentic, cogent, and caring voice that deserves to be not only heard but also heeded.

James A. Banks
Series Editor

REFERENCES

Au, K. (2006). *Multicultural issues and literacy achievement*. Mahwah, NJ: Erlbaum.

Banks, J. A. (2004). Multicultural education: Historical development, dimensions, and practice. In J. A. Banks & C. A. M. Banks (Eds.). *Handbook of research on multicultural education* (2nd ed., pp. 3–29). San Francisco: Jossey-Bass.

Banks, J. A., & Banks, C. A. M. (Eds.) (2004). *Handbook of research on multicultural education* (2nd ed.). San Francisco: Jossey-Bass.

California State Department of Education. (2006). *Public school summary statistics 2003–04*. Retrieved April 14, 2006, from *http://www.cde.ca.gov/ds/sd/cb/sums03.asp*

Eck, D. L. (2001). *A new religious America: How a "Christian country" has become the world's most religiously diverse nation*. New York: HarperSanFrancisco.

El Nasser, H. (2004, March 18). Census projects growing diversity: By 2050: Population burst, societal shifts. *USA Today*, p. 1A.

Gay, G. (2000). *Culturally responsive teaching: Theory, research, and practice*. New York: Teachers College Press.

Grossman, P. (1990). *The making of a teacher: Teacher knowledge and teacher education*. New York: Teachers College Press.

Ladson-Billings, G. (1994). *The dreamkeepers: Successful teachers of African American children*. San Francisco: Jossey-Bass.

Martin, P., & Midgley, E. (1999). Immigration to the United States. *Population Bulletin, 54*(2), 1–44. Washington, DC: Population Reference Bureau.

Martinez, G. M., & Curry, A. E. (1999, September). *Current population reports: School enrollment—social and economic characteristics of students* [update]. Washington, DC: U.S. Census Bureau.

Moll, L., & González, N. (2004). Engaging life: A funds-of-knowledge approach to multicultural education. In J. A. Banks & C. A. M. Banks (Eds.), *Handbook of research on multicultural education* (2nd ed., pp. 699–715). San Francisco: Jossey-Bass.

Morrison, T. (1987). *Beloved: A novel.* New York: Knopf.

Moses, R. P. (1994). The struggle for citizenship and math/sciences literacy. *Journal of Mathematical Behavior, 13,* 107–111.

National Center for Education Statistics (U.S. Department of Education). (2005). *The condition of education 2005*(NCES 2005-094). Washington, DC: U.S. Government Printing Office.

Riche, M. F. (2000). America's diversity and growth: Signposts for the twenty-first century. *Population Bulletin, 55*(2), 1–43. Washington, DC: Population Reference Bureau.

Saxe, G. (1991). *Culture and cognitive development: Studies in mathematical understanding.* Hillsdale, NJ: Erlbaum.

Schoenfeld, A. H. (1985). *Mathematical problem solving.* Orlando, FL: Academic Press.

Shulman, L. (1986). Those who understand: Knowledge growth in teaching. *Educational Researcher, 15*(2), 4–14.

U.S. Census Bureau. (2000). *Statistical abstract of the United States* (120th ed.). Washington, DC: U.S. Government Printing Office.

U.S. Department of Homeland Security. (2006). *Yearbook of immigration statistics: 2004.* Washington, DC: U.S. Government Printing Office

Wineburg, S., & Wilson, S. M. (1988). Peering at history through different lenses: The role of disciplinary perspectives in teaching history. *Teachers College Record, 89*(4), 525–539.

Foreword

Carol Lee has written an enormously important book. *Culture, Literacy, and Learning* is a scholarly tour de force, generating new theory about learning grounded in culturally and pedagogically sophisticated practices she used to teach African American youth to engage in literary reasoning in an inner city Chicago school. Lee has brought together knowledge from cognitive science, developmental psychology, cultural studies, and several branches of education research with her own deep understanding of adolescents, African American culture, learning, and teaching practice to illustrate *how*, in fact, all students can learn. And her concern is not just that students learn in the multiple-choice-rote-recall manner that has increasingly replaced serious intellectual standards, but that they learn to think, reason, and demonstrate profound understanding as members of a disciplinary community of practice.

"Nommo" is the term used in Yoruba culture for naming—a powerful act of creation that gives life, in a near sacred sense, to a person or an idea. This book, for me, holds the power of Nommo. It names, vividly and with a resonant truth, how it is that the intelligence we know resides in African American youth—indeed, in all youth—gets missed, and how it can be uncovered and cultivated. With the support of science and the insight born of many years of committed and skillful teaching, Lee illustrates how competence can be constructed at the nexus of students' cultural funds of knowledge and the scaffolding a teacher can provide to support both their academic learning and the development of their identities as capable members of an intellectual community.

Reading a book that speaks truth as one knows it is an exciting and affirming experience. As I read this book, I found myself affirming nearly out loud, "Uh huh, uh huh. Yes! See, that's what I'm talking about." What resonated so profoundly for me were the tacit understandings of learning and teaching that I sensed but could not name when I began my own public school teaching career in an urban high school in Camden, New Jersey. Like Carol, I found that students knew and could do much more than they were credited for, either by the schooling institution or the ever-present standardized tests, that their experiences and capacities had to be recognized, publicly identified, and marshaled to the tasks of disciplinary learning, and that when this occurred, they were able to make astounding progress in their learning. I also found that starting with the texts they cared about and could relate to—and developing their identity as members of a productive scholarly community of readers and writers (and in my classroom, journalists, dramatists, script-writers, and movie-makers)—was critical to their engagement and ultimate success with texts that were much further away from their initial starting points. Finally, I learned that teaching well was substantially based on understanding my students' lives, their amazing resilience, daily challenges, and triumphs, which allowed me to find toeholds from which I could build their sense of belonging, ownership, and competence.

I believe it is not only because I started my career as an English teacher that I thrilled to see how Victor, David, Belinda, and Taquisha—some of Lee's students in the class she taught for 3 years at Fairgate High School—could develop sophisticated analyses of Toni Morrison's novel, *Beloved*. I marveled not only at what *they* learned and could articulate about the complex symbolism of this intricate novel, but even more, what *I* learned from their insights and from the thick descriptions of Carol's expert pedagogical strategies.

In one sense, what Carol Lee describes is not new. The kind of pedagogy she enacts and the bodies of knowledge it draws upon have, for the most part, been identified before. Cognitive scientists have described the kind of cognitive apprenticeships in disciplinary domains that Lee constructs for her students. Education researchers ranging from Katherine Au to Luis Moll have identified the task of drawing on students' experiences and funds of knowledge in developing instruction. And Lee builds from her own earlier work on Cultural Modeling to examine how teaching can build, for example, from the African American tradition of signifying to enable students to translate their existing expertise into understanding of metaphor, symbolism, and other disciplinary tools for linguistic expression and literary interpretation.

Scholars of culture and teaching—Sonia Nieto, Gloria Ladson-Billings, Michelle Foster, Jacqueline Jordan Irvine, Eugene Garcia, James Banks—have identified features of culturally responsive pedagogy that enable learning. These include the use of community and cultural referents and strategies that incorporate familiar participation structures and communication strategies; means for learning about and using students' experiences, concerns, and interests in constructing curriculum; and teaching strategies that use an active, direct approach to teaching: demonstrating, modeling, explaining, writing, giving feedback, reviewing, and emphasizing higher-order skills while avoiding excessive reliance on rote learning or punishment. Developmental psychologists have noted the importance of developing academic identity, psychological security, and resilience in students by affirming and building on student capacities.

What is utterly new is how Lee adeptly integrates all of these areas of research, exploring them theoretically and as they inform her practice. The extraordinary contribution made by this book is in large part due to Lee's boundary crossing—the integration of knowledge across research borders that normally prevent a full understanding of the teaching and learning process. Crossing boundaries across disciplines and methodologies, across communities and cultures, and across ideas and ideologies, Lee provides an insightful analysis of what can prevent and enable learning and shows us how the integration of these viewpoints enables major leaps forward in our understanding.

This ability to look at the world through many lenses and from multiple perspectives, including those of students whose experiences are quite different from those of most researchers and teachers, is essential in developing pedagogies that can reach diverse learners. Whereas much research proceeds by narrowing problems to a small, tightly controlled space within which a single variable can be examined, a deeper understanding of complex phenomena requires the integration and enlargement of perspectives that Lee accomplishes here. This approach is like that of the very earliest universities, which brought together scholars from all over the known world, seeking to create ways to share diverse perspectives from various geographic areas, cultures, and disciplines as the basis for developing knowledge and finding truth. Carol Lee pursues these ideals of knowledge-building and truth-finding by creating a genuine praxis between ideas and experience—by honoring practice in conjunction with reflection and research, helping others reach beyond their personal boundaries to appreciate the perspectives of those whom they would teach as well as the bodies of knowledge that can inform their work.

Critical is Lee's exploration of the life context and everyday practices of low-income African American youth and her articulation of the challenges they must learn to navigate as well as the knowledge resources they bring to the classroom. These resources are accessible, however, only to a teacher who can provide affirmation for students' intelligence, support them in risk-taking, and create culturally connected bridges from what they know to the academic forms of knowledge application expected in school. Supporting students' development of an academic self-concept that enables them to engage in this far journey is not accomplished through empty words or gestures intended to reinforce a superficial sense of self-esteem, but through connections that allow the display and further construction of competence through the serious effort required of deep disciplinary understanding.

Lee portrays in detail the cognitive architecture needed for this task—the foundation, bridges, and scaffolds that need to be built. She also describes the "cultural data sets" that teachers need to have in order to construct this architecture. These data sets provide culturally anchored models for forms of reasoning and performance that are already familiar to students, which the teacher can tap when creating connections to expert models in the academic domain. Just as cognitive scientists have worked to identify common conceptions and misconceptions within domains that help build teachers' pedagogical content knowledge, so Carol has identified the conceptions, modes of discourse, and developed skills learners may carry with them as a function of their cultural experiences. As she notes, conceptualizing the resources students bring with them from their experiences outside of school is a fundamental component of teachers' pedagogical content knowledge. The clear exposition of how teachers can assemble such cultural data sets and the practice that draws upon them is a tremendous contribution to teaching and teacher education.

To enable teachers to use these insights, teacher education must do much more, however. As Lee notes, selecting highly generative cultural data sets, in ways that do not trivialize the connections between everyday knowledge and school-based knowledge, requires both developing a deep understanding of the subject matter and a capacity to overcome deficit assumptions about the nature of these everyday practices and about the students themselves. It means "de-constructing colonizing mentalities and ethnocentric assumptions" that create what Edmund Gordon has called a "communicentric bias" which limits understanding of areas of study as well as of those who are taught.

As Lisa Delpit (1995) notes, "We all interpret behaviors, information, and situations through our own cultural lenses; these lenses operate involuntarily, below the level of conscious awareness, making it seem that our own view is simply 'the way it is'" (p. 151). Teachers concerned with democratic education must develop an awareness of their perspectives and how these can be enlarged. Developing the ability to see beyond one's own perspective—to put oneself in the shoes of the learner and to understand the meaning of that experience in terms of learning—is, perhaps, the most important role of teacher preparation.

One of the great flaws of the "bright person myth" of teaching is that it presumes that anyone can teach what he or she knows to anyone else. However, people who have never studied teaching or learning often have a very difficult time understanding how to convey material that they themselves learned effortlessly and almost subconsciously. When others do not learn merely by being told, the intuitive teacher often becomes frustrated and powerless to proceed. This frequently leads to anger directed at the learner for not validating the untrained teacher's efforts. Furthermore, individuals who have had no powerful teacher education intervention often maintain a single cognitive and cultural perspective that makes it difficult for them to understand the experiences, perceptions, and knowledge bases that deeply influence the approaches to learning of students who are different from themselves. The capacity to understand another is not innate. It is developed through study, reflection, guided experience, and inquiry. Strong programs of teacher preparation construct these opportunities. The guidance Carol Lee offers in this book will be invaluable in this task.

Linda Darling-Hammond
Stanford University
June 24, 2006

REFERENCE

Delpit, L. (1995). *Other people's children: Cultural conflict in the classroom*. New York: The New Press.

Preface

In this book I have several goals. I want to interrogate a set of assumptions that have severely constrained our ability to understand what resources or repertoires young people bring to school settings from their experiences in the world outside of schooling. I am particularly interested in understanding and documenting such repertoires among young people who have been defined in terms of their status as members of ethnic minorities or low-income communities. In addition, I want to understand such repertoires as they are connected to knowledge in academic disciplines. In so doing, I want to situate such discussions not only as questions of what it means to be culturally responsive in teaching and designing learning environments, but also as part of the ongoing dialogues in terms of fundamental questions about how people learn. Across the learning sciences, there are long-standing agreements that prior knowledge helps structure how people tackle new targets of learning, but much less is understood about the significance of the range of prior knowledge in target areas to facilitate—or for that matter, constrain—new learning. I want to help move these conversations into other target domains, such as literary reasoning, since much of this work has been in the areas of science and mathematics. But even in investigations of everyday knowledge in science and mathematics, little research has examined such knowledge in a range of ethnic communities or across communities of different economic and social classes. Thus in this book I hope to engender conversations among those who think about culturally relevant pedagogy and those who consider questions of knowledge representation, transfer, and problem solving within and across particular domains.

Moreover, I am committed in this book to examining learning as ecologically situated cultural practices. I focus not only on the content and structure of knowledge inside everyday practices and school-based practices, but equally on the social processes and interactions through which such knowledge is constructed across time. I understand these social processes and interactions as entailing cognitive as well as social and emotional dimensions. In considering cognitive, social, and emotional dimensions of learning, I am making a commitment to trying to begin to better integrate disciplines that have traditionally not been in sufficient dialogue with one another, namely, the cognitive and learning sciences, fields of human development including studies of emotional development and self-regulation, motivation, resilience, agency, and goal setting. I take the position that learning in situ is complex and always involves making sense of, navigating, and coordinating cognitive attention and processing, emotional self-regulation, social cognition in "reading" other people, settings, and tasks; and through such coordinations and navigations to set goals, to put forth effort, and to sustain engagement. Thus, while there are clearly many methodological and conceptual challenges in trying to understand such coordination and navigation, learning and development are just that complex. While I do not offer any easy answer to these challenges, I try at least to provide examples of what it means to think about these multiple dimensions in context within a line of research.

Finally, the field of education is concerned not only with understanding how people learn but equally, if not more important, how to design and manage robust learning environments that maximize youths' opportunities to learn. This is not only the work of researchers, but also the work of parents, other adult caregivers, and teachers. Many of the conceptual issues with which I grapple in this book emerged from examinations of my own practice as a teacher in the interventions I designed as part of the Cultural Modeling Project. In taking this stance, I have been influenced by the work of researchers like Magdalene Lampert and Deborah Ball in mathematics education, who have demonstrated how careful analyses of educational practices can yield important insights about fundamental questions regarding learning in situ. From these investigations of practice, I also discuss in this book the complex nature of teacher knowledge. Much of the folk beliefs about teaching that inform public policy seem to posit that a restricted notion of content knowledge and a disposition to like children are sufficient for good teaching.

Overall, I hope the issues examined in this book offer useful ways for understanding some of the reasons why there is a persistent achievement gap based on race, ethnicity, and class. I do not believe we have sufficiently powerful conceptions about knowledge as constructed in the everyday practices of Black, Brown, and poor youth; about the multiple demands of learning in school based on both better understandings of academic disciplines as well as the multiple challenges that youth from these communities must learn to navigate; and about the demands of teaching that is intellectually rigorous. This achievement gap is, at least in part, influenced by the limitations of the knowledge base and assumptions that inform decisions about curriculum, assessment, pedagogy, teacher credentialing, and the conditions under which teachers work. Even under these circumstances, we know more than we are willing to do. And we continue to be blindsided by the web of assumptions about White supremacy and class biases that are so endemic to our history as a country. Thus I am not convinced that the expansion of our knowledge base will be sufficient to address the problems, but I hope the expansion of our knowledge base in ways I have tried to address in this book can at least challenge the web of cultural assumptions under which the current educational system operates.

Acknowledgments

There are many people and institutions to thank who have made the work reported in this book possible.

First, I would like to thank the two principals who made my work at Fairgate High School (pseudonym) possible. They are superior educators and administrators, each with a strong and far-reaching vision of what is possible in urban schools with long histories of underachievement. Thanks also to the faculty and staff of Fairgate High School who welcomed me in their presence over the course of the 3 years I worked there. I appreciate greatly their willingness to engage in new practices, put in many additional hours, read new works of literature, and overall expand their repertoires in building an intellectual community within the English Department. I also thank many other teachers in the school with whom I had great conversations and from whom I learned much about the school and what it meant to teach in their disciplines. I thank the security staff and administrative personnel who knew students in the school personally and extended themselves beyond the call of duty. I especially want to thank the students at Fairgate High School, particularly those enrolled in my freshman, sophomore, and senior classes. They taught me many lessons about life and about teaching. They were patient in allowing our team to videotape them daily and to participate in clinical and other interviews. They were valiant in wrestling through the dilemmas of their lives while working diligently to display their intellectual prowess.

This research would not have been possible without the financial support of the Cognitive Studies Program of the McDonnell Foundation, the Spencer Foundation, and the Research Foundation of the National Council of Teachers of English. The McDonnell Foundation took a bold move in funding many projects that would go on to provide a strong empirical base for work in the emerging field of the Learning Sciences. I felt privileged to have been able to share findings with the many colleagues who pioneered that field. I want to thank Roy Pea, who was Dean of the School of Education and Social Policy, for his support in crafting the proposal to the McDonnell Foundation. The Spencer Foundation provided additional core support to the research that allowed me to expand the work and continue analyses beyond the 3 years of original funding. The Spencer Foundation has been very important in my overall intellectual development by allowing me to interact in several roles over the years within the strong network of scholars it supports. Receiving funding from the Spencer Foundation is often an introduction to what many have called the Spencer family. Funds from the Research Foundation of the National Council of Teachers of English allowed me to continue analyses of data from the project. The work of the Research Foundation has been a stalwart source of support for research within NCTE, bridging the worlds of research and practice. Finally, I want to thank the Center for Advanced Study in the Behavioral Sciences (CASBS) at Stanford University for my yearlong support as a Residential Fellow during the 2004–05 academic year and the Spencer Foundation for funding the fellowship. That year at the Center provided me not only the time to reflect and complete most of this manuscript, but also the fellowship of an extraordinary group of colleagues from across a range of disciplines who listened to my ideas and shared their work with me. I feel like a lifetime member of the CASBS family and look forward to a second dose of its retreat.

There were many graduate students who contributed enormously to the research reported in this book, without whom the work simply could not have been done. First, I want to thank Jan Derrick, who was during the project a Ph.D. student in film at Northwestern University. Jan assumed the role of both videographer, documenting my teaching across the 3 years as well as other key events in the field, and ethnographer, taking the initiative to follow and interview students outside of class around issues that I had no way of seeing or anticipating. All of the personal information on students' lives comes from the rich ethnographic field notes and interviews conducted by Jan. Next, I want to thank Kelle Hutchinson, who at the time was a Ph.D. student in performance studies at Northwestern University. Kelle served as my project manager and right hand. She was responsible for coordinating all of our data collection efforts and managing the immense amount of data we collected while working in the field site, and was overall a jack-of-all-trades. I greatly appreciate her friendship and the initiative she showed in our work together. I also want to thank Dr. Yolanda J. Majors. Yolanda came to work with us while still a Ph.D. student in English education at the University of Iowa. Yolanda and her family moved from Iowa City to Chicago specifically to work on the project. Yolanda joined the team during the last year of our work at Fairgate High School, and continued to collect data on her own at the school even after our project had formally come to a close. Yolanda played the main role in data analysis of my teaching in the classroom. She took a giant leap of faith in coming to work with us at Northwestern and worked hard in expanding her repertoire of research methods to accommodate the social science orientation of our work. I view her as probably my foremost collaborator in the extension of this research. We have been able to present together in the United States and abroad on this work and have published several articles together as well. Her own research has taken principles of Cultural Modeling in new directions, from which I am learning a great deal. Another major contributor was Dr. Ama Rivers Thompson (then a Ph.D. student in communication disorders at Northwestern University) who played the major role in analyzing our talk-aloud protocols and who brought methodological resources to the project that greatly expanded what we came to understand from the data. Finally, I want to thank my current Ph.D. students in the Learning Sciences Program at Northwestern University. While these students were not present during the data collection and early data analysis phases of the research, they have played invaluable roles in helping me to think broadly about the implications of the data and the new lines of inquiry that have emerged since we left Fairgate High School: Lauren Banks Amos, Malayana Bernstein, Julia Eksner, Erica Rosenfeld Halverson (Ph.D. 2005), Ruby Mendenhall (Ph.D., 2004), Anika Spratley, and Ellen Wang. All of our thinking about the implications of Cultural Modeling for disciplinary literacies, for understanding the social and emotional demands of academic learning and for conceptualizing the demands of teacher knowledge that is culturally responsive and discipline specific have been directly influenced by the work of these students. Their roles in secondary data analysis, developmental work on new projects, and their own dissertation projects have influenced the content of this book. I also appreciate their careful reviews of the manuscript. They are all stars on the horizon.

I want to thank James Banks for inviting me to publish in his important series on multicultural education, for his precise and informative feedback as editor, and for his persistent yet loving prodding to complete this manuscript on time. It took a bit longer than either of us had anticipated. I also appreciate the support of Brian Ellerbeck and other members of the editorial staff at Teachers College Press for their help throughout the process.

There are many colleagues who have spurred, expanded, and challenged my thinking over the years in ways that have deeply influenced this book. While I cannot begin to name them all, I do want to publicly thank a few: Arnetha F. Ball (Stanford University), Phillip Bowman (University of Illinois–Chicago), Linda Darling-Hammond (Stanford), Gloria Ladson-Billings (University of Wisconsin–Madison), Edmund Gordon (Teachers College, Columbia University), Kris Gutierrez (UCLA), George Hillocks (University of Chicago emeritus), Barton Hirsch (Northwestern University), Joyce King (Georgia State University), Douglas Medin (Northwestern University), Nailah Nasir (Stanford University), Marjorie Orellana (UCLA),

Barbara Rogoff (UC–San Diego), Geoffrey Saxe (University of California–Berkeley), Geneva Smitherman (Michigan State University), Margaret Beale Spencer (University of Pennsylvania), and Beth Warren and Ann Rosebery (TERC).

Finally, none of this would have been possible without the love and support of my family, my respite from academia, the womb that makes me whole:

> My colleagues from the Institute of Positive Education and the Betty Shabazz International Charter Schools in Chicago. I am a cofounder of these institutions. Over the course of more than 35 years, these colleagues have been my friends and have been responsible for the genesis of many of the ideas that have culminated in this book. They are my second family. There are so many to thank, but I will name only Kimya Moyo (my very best friend), Soyini Walton, and Elaine Mosley who continue to teach and to challenge me.

> My mother, Inez Singleton Hall, 86 years old as of this writing, who remains the model of womanhood and personhood toward which I will always seek to achieve, and who is the rock on which I depend now and unto eternity.

> Our children—Laini Nzinga, Bomani Garvey and his wife Janet Hutchinson, and Akili Malcolm—who are my life in the most literal sense. I am so proud of the adults they have become and enjoy learning to be their friend. They keep me grounded. They are the reason I know this work is important, as I want for all children the success in life and work that our children have achieved.

> My husband—Haki R. Madhubuti—who besides being my life partner for more than 35 years of marriage and political struggle continues to be my best intellectual partner, always pushing me to achieve the best and to think critically about issues of the day. In spite of his own international reputation as poet, essayist, and publisher (having authored or edited over 27 books) he continues to go before audiences and spout the accomplishments of his wife (of whom they have never heard).

I dedicate this book to two giants who are now ancestors, but who made indelible marks during their remarkable stays on this earth. Gwendolyn Brooks was a mother figure to my husband, godmother to my daughter, and a dear friend to me. She counseled me in times of need, and I treasure the many beautiful handwritten notes of kindness she sent across the years. Years before this book came into being I had conceived of the subtitle, *Taking Bloom in the Midst of the Whirlwind*, from her profound poem, "The Second

Sermon on the Warpland." Gwen's poetry is pungent with her gift of second sight and perfumed with sometimes lyrical and sometimes sparse language. Every time I sit down to write, I am drawn to Gwen's playing with words, much to the dismay of my editor Jim Banks, since I do not have the skill to accomplish what Gwen did with language.

Barbara Ann Sizemore was a second mother figure to my husband and dear friend to me. Barbara probably accomplished more in turning around the achievement gap in real schools than anyone else I can think of, despite the fact that she had to scratch hard to properly fund her work. I never ceased to be amazed at the keenness of her intellect and the many areas of her intellectual expertise. Anyone who knew Barbara realized that she looked the whirlwind dead in the eye and with rocketlike precision catapulted through the disarray to proclaim and accomplish clarity. She was fearless in her pursuit of academic excellence for those children most in need and had no patience for those who doubted its possibility. For me, Barbara remains the stellar example of what it means to conduct our blooming in the midst of the whirlwind.

Conceptualizing Learning as Cultural Processes

Sirens. Ambulance. Blood in the hall. Cop on stretcher, bandage wrapped around his head, unconscious.[1]

Student 1 (boy): See what happened today. Sh - - ! He knocked that cop out. Those teachers better know that we will do the same to them if they don't act right.

Student 2 (boy): (High five). Yeah, man!

Student 3 (girl): I can hardly wait until I graduate and get out of here. Too much violence.

Student 4 (girl): I'm just glad he didn't have a gun.

Mr. Banks: (Pacing hall. Weary.) Be glad you don't have to be here every day. I wish I didn't have to be. I had to reprimand two boys today. You never know when they're going to come back after you. A student just coldcocked a cop. If these kids aren't afraid of a cop, then why should they respect someone like me?

Mrs. Hill: The kids are very upset today. I love teaching, but I don't know what to do when the students come in, upset about some act of violence. Sometimes we talk about it. One thing for sure, we don't get much accomplished on days like these.

Mrs. Albright: I'm retiring this year. Girl, I can't wait to get out of here. My girlfriend was punched out and thrown over a table at Pearson High School. We're both going to retire and live the country life.

Mrs. Smith: What's going on here is happening everywhere. The student who socked the officer is the same one whose parents are suing Mr. G. for interceding when he started a fight in his class. The teacher pulled him off the other student. I guess he won't be able to make his court date now.

1

Ms. Stockton: I can hardly wait to go home today. I was threatened
by a student today. Emotions are running high. It's one of those
days when you wish you had stayed in bed.

Mrs. Buchanan: I used to love teaching. But it has changed so much
over the years. You have to teach and keep order, but you just
never know what the students are going to do. I'm counting the
days to retirement.

Security 1: This stuff started earlier, in the lunchroom. Johnson and
I were breaking up a fight. Makes you feel like it might be
better to just let them keep going at it and kill each other. It's
better than killing us for trying to protect them from each other.

Security 2: I know guys who work for the Department of Correc-
tions. When a cop beater comes in they show him no mercy.
And the judge isn't going to show him mercy either. He may
think he's a bad 17-year-old man now but he'll be an old man
or a girl when everybody finishes with him.

This is an account of what actually happened on February 5, 1998, at
Fairgate High School. Incidents this bold are not the norm, but the tensions
inherent in the scene are: a strong gang presence, a pressure on young men
and women to affiliate or at least show deference, an overarching sense of
insecurity by youth and adults in the community. Although this school has
a leadership—principal and teachers—who care deeply and work very
hard to sustain this educational institution as a safe place where high academic standards are achieved, it has been difficult to accomplish these goals
for many reasons. While there are wonderful teachers at Fairgate, there are
also teachers who do not believe these low-income African American
youngsters can learn; and it is difficult in the system to remove tenured
teachers or to recruit really excellent teachers, in part, because the pool of
such people is very small. In addition, there is a continual reinvention of
procedures and accountability measures that are constantly shifting expectations and constraining innovation. Something as simple as ordering books
can entail a plethora of time-consuming administrative procedures.

The students who enter this school have to manage a host of difficult
life circumstances that their more affluent peers do not. For example, Yetu
was in my freshman class. He is quiet and intensely inward. He is extraordinary bright and offers profound insights into the literature we read. By
his sophomore year, Yetu is dating Mary, a senior. Mary becomes pregnant and they have twins. By his junior year, one of Yetu's twins dies. By
the spring of his junior year, Yetu is kicked out of school for selling drugs.
I met Yetu's parents during that freshman year. They were actively interested in Yetu's future. When our ethnographer, Jan Derrick, interviews Yetu

in 1998 after the death of his child, Yetu is stoic and withdrawn. He says he plans to finish high school. We don't know.

Raquel was in my senior class. She was quiet and very smart. She worked hard in class, had excellent grades, and made important contributions to the intellectual work of the class. She had earned a scholarship to a historically Black college in the fall and was looking forward to going. She lives in her grandmother's house with a total of 12 people. Her mother is single with three children, including Raquel. Her aunt, uncle, and their five children also live in the house and the grandmother has custody of the five children. Financial resources are limited. At one point, Raquel and her family lived on the streets. Her boyfriend is older, has been in prison, and is now on probation. Raquel finds out she is pregnant. Her boyfriend has agreed to pay for an abortion, but by the time they are able to gather the money, Raquel is far along in her pregnancy. When I found out about Raquel's situation, I talked to her mother. Raquel was finally able to get the abortion, but there were complications. With grit determination, Raquel was able to go away to college.

Victor was also in my senior class. Jan first met Victor when he was a junior. The following transcript is from Jan's field notes and interviews:

> I met Victor in the fall of 1996. He was a Junior in Mrs. Hayes' class. Victor put his head on the desk when I was photographing, as did many of the other boys. On the third day he and a group of six boys were sitting on a stoop near the building when I was coming in for work. When I passed them they followed and encircled me.
>
> "What do you boys want?"
>
> "We wanna know, what do *you* want?"
>
> One of the boys was over six feet, menacing, and resembled some eerie grotesque in a nightmare, incapable of being bruised or evaded, but, I remembered, he was a boy. Through a jagged gash in his teeth his voice boomed.
>
> "We don't want you here. Whenever we see a camera, we know it means trouble."
>
> Another boy sidled up to me and with a shrill clamor drilled into my ear, "Yeah, we think you should leave."
>
> I beamed at the boys serenely. "Who do you think I am?"
>
> The boy with the designs in his hair was at my eye level. He retorted, "The police."
>
> "The police?"
>
> "Or maybe the F.B.I.," one boy yelped. "And we don't want you here."
>
> "Are you boys threatening me?"

"Not exactly," said Victor in a cool, dry voice. "We just want to know you're not threatening us."

"Okay, I understand where you're comin' from. First, if I were the police I would have arrested all of you by now. You have the audacity to come up to me, trying to intimidate me with the smell of marijuana reeking from your clothes. Does that answer your question?"

"Who are you?" Victor picked his teeth with a toothpick.

"I tell you what. You take out your ID and show me who you are and I'll take out mine and show you who I am." Victor pulled back his jacket. I pulled back mine. Twelve eyes examined my ID.

"You're a student too. But why are you here?"

"Just doing my job for a research project at Northwestern University."

"But you need our permission."

"Tell you what. I'd be happy if you'd talk with Dr. Lee or Mrs. Hayes."

"Okay, maybe we will."

I walked toward the building. There were many mornings like that in fall of 1996. Curiously, students never questioned the men who were "shooting" (i.e., videotaping or taking photographs). The students spoke with Mrs. Hayes and she asked me to discontinue photographing the next day.

In the spring I noticed Victor in the hall. I walked up behind him and put my arm around his neck.

"What's the 411, Victor? O-o-oh marijuana awfully strong today."

Usually Victor would laugh and say, "I'm sorry. I'm trying, Miss Derrick." But this day he sighed and closed his eyes. "My brother was killed yesterday."

"Oh, Victor, I am sorry."

He bound up with a one-sentence cry that cracked with anxiety and impotence. "I tried to protect him, Miss Derrick, but I couldn't." He looked into my eyes searching for some reassuring word.

"There isn't anything I can say that will ease the pain. You couldn't save your brother, but it would be a tribute to his memory for you to save yourself. I've watched you this past year. You're intelligent. You can do anything you want. But you're letting the streets eat you up the way your brother was eaten up."

"I'm gonna try, Miss Derrick."

"I hope so."

"I care about you, Victor. And there are many who care about you. Just live, Victor."

"I'll try, Miss Derrick."

In 1997 Victor was assigned to Dr. Lee's world literature class. I was exhilarated. He would have the opportunity to expand his horizons with someone who is interested in helping him achieve all he can.

Victor was a good student although he admitted to me that he could have been a better one if he had applied himself more. Victor graduated in 1998.

I've kept in touch with Victor vis-à-vis my nephew who worked with Dr. Lee in 1997. Victor is not planning to go to college. He's earning his living in the streets. I am concerned about his survival. How to intervene?

Jan often saw a side of the school and of students that were not visible to me in the classroom. I offer these brief vignettes of students for several reasons. First, you will meet Victor, Raquel, and Yetu in this book. You will see them in class, offering rich insights into complex literary texts, and in many instances providing observations about the texts that I never noticed. I learned from each of them about the texts we read together, about the demands of learning, and about what it means for an adolescent to figure out how to manage these multiple challenges simultaneously. I also offer these vignettes as examples that difficult life circumstances do not in themselves inhibit learning; rather, it is the nature of supports available that influence whether rigorous learning takes place: supports for coping with loss, for resisting negative influences, for persisting in efforts to learn when the tasks are difficult and appear on the surface abstracted from everyday life, to "read" people and respond in ways that move positive life course goals forward. I offer no panacea suggesting that schools can address all the challenges that students and communities face. However, students spend a lot of time in school, and African American students place great value on their relationships with teachers (Ferguson, 2002b; Graham, 1994). Schools need to be supportive communities for students as well as teachers. The responses of the veteran teachers to the violence described above attest to the fact that they have difficult jobs and understandably can get worn down. I used to say to the principal of Fairgate High School that the school needed a rite of passage program for its students and a church for its teachers. The idea is how schools can be sites of renewal for all its members.

Typical of too many urban high schools, the majority of Fairgate High School students entered ninth grade scoring well below grade level for reading in 1995 when we began working with the school. While a majority of teachers certainly wanted the best for their students, virtually all wrestled with how they could support students in meeting high academic standards. Chicago Public Schools were in the midst of an intense accountability program. Fairgate High School was already on probation because of low scores in reading comprehension on the Test of Academic Proficiency (TAP). In an English Department meeting I attended the year before the intervention, teachers were discussing ways to entice students to come to school the day the TAP was given. As is common in many underachieving schools, the English Department was seen as the site for efforts to improve reading comprehension. The most common configuration for English classes was that students would read selections from a literature anthology, most of which were very old. Generally, only students in the one honors class per grade level were assigned novels. To address the problems of low achievement in reading, the Cultural Modeling Project introduced an intervention to reorganize the curriculum of the English department and to reinvent the fundamental nature of instruction in that department. I am a faculty member in the School of Education and Social Policy at Northwestern University, but as part of the intervention, I taught one high school English class at Fairgate during each of the 3 years of the reform.

In this book I try to help the reader get inside these classrooms in order to deconstruct the very cultural nature of face-to-face interactions to support complex, discipline-specific forms of reasoning. Like Magdalene Lampert (2001), I want to put a public face on the microlevel problems of teaching, illustrated within a specific subject matter and population. All of the students at Fairgate High School were African American, largely low-income, predominantly speakers of African American English, and overall low-achieving. These are the students who are usually the target of educational interventions in urban school systems and of local, state, and national debates over educational policy. They are also the inheritors of the legacy of African enslavement, legalized segregation, and U.S. racism (Bell, 1992; Frederickson, 1981; Mills, 1997; Patterson, 1998; Woodward, 1974). They are members of a pivotal generation who at the turn of the twenty-first century must wrestle with fundamental changes in the African American community: stark class differences resulting in differential access to social and economic networks (America, 1990; Massey & Denton, 1993; Wilson, 1987), public positioning that threatens historical cultural continuities (Irvine & Irvine, 1983; McCoy, 1999; Nobles, 1974, 1985; Siddle-Walker, 1993, 1996) , an overwhelming percentage of its young male population involved at some level in the criminal justice system (Madhubuti, 1990; Parenti, 1999; Sentencing Project, 1997), and health challenges beyond their proportion of the population (Byrd & Clayton, 2000).

There are many publications that either capture classroom processes in urban school settings (Bloome, 2005; Cazden, 2000; Forman, 1998; Green, 1998; O'Connor, 1993), argue for the importance of culturally responsive instruction (Ball, 2002; Delpit, 1986, 1988, 1995; Foster, 1997; Gay, 1993, 1995, 2000; Gutierrez, Baquedano-Lopez, & Tejeda, 1999; Ladson-Billings, 1994, 2001; McCarty, 2002; Murrell, 2002; Nieto, 2002; Perry & Delpit, 1998), or document the inequalities in urban schools serving low-income and minority populations (Ladson-Billings & Tate, 1995; McDermott, 1987; Noguera, 2003; Oakes, 1985, 1990; Varenne & McDermott, 1998). My work clearly stands on the shoulders of this important work in education. However, I do something complementary in this book: I use the examination of instruction in African American classrooms as a case for interrogating fundamental propositions about the nature of learning and the design of environments that promote learning. This task is important because in the fields of educational research and of psychology, certainly within the United States, there has been a historical tendency to ghettoize studies having to do with so-called minority populations (Graham, 1992; Lee, Spencer, & Harpalani, 2003; McLoyd & Randolph, 1984). Fundamental concepts about learning and development are based on studies of White, middle-class populations. On the other hand, theories of deviance from a presumed norm focus on what I satirically refer to as the "colored people"; and on the more liberal side, colored people are presumed to be cultural while the White middle class are just human. As Barbara Rogoff (2003) has so aptly noted, we cannot understand the range of diversity of pathways to development across the life course of the human species until we have a significant body of research that looks carefully and in detail at diverse populations. I hope this book will help readers see how practices and ways of using language in the world that are typically vilified in academic settings may actually be generative resources for both generic learning as well as rigorous disciplinary reasoning.

Cultural Modeling as a design framework addresses the needs of struggling readers in schools like Fairgate High (Lee, 1993, 1995a, 1995b, 2000, 2001; Lee, Mendenhall, Rivers, & Tynes, 1999; Lee & Smagorinsky, 2000; Shuman, 1995). There is a long history of characterizing the lives of these students as filled with deficits to be overcome (Bereiter & Engelmann, 1966; Bernstein, 1961; Deutsch & Brown, 1964; Hess & Shipman, 1965; Jensen, 1969). Cultural Modeling enters this enduring conversation. The language of these students is considered "nonstandard" and not an appropriate medium of communication in either school or the marketplace (Stotsky, 1999). The activities in which these students routinely engage with their families and friends are viewed as not contributing to their academic development. While there is important research documenting culturally responsive pedagogies, this work takes place largely in elementary schools and does not articulate principled ways of connecting specifically to subject matters. Cultural Modeling, however, is a design framework that aims to provide researchers, curriculum designers, and teachers with guidelines and principles for drawing on what Luis Moll (2000; Moll & Gonzáles, 2004) calls "cultural funds of knowledge" specifically to address the demands of complex problem solving in the various subject matters. In this book I will describe the instantiation of Cultural Modeling in the domain of response to literature at the high school level. However, it has also been applied to elementary school and in other academic domains.[2] I focus on the domain of response to literature as a way of grounding and fully illustrating the application of Cultural Modeling, as well as a way of discussing the complexities of implementing such a design as a full school intervention in difficult urban districts.

CHAPTER 1

The Culture of Everyday Practices and Their Implications for Learning in School

I will never forget the day I first sat in on Mrs. Hayes's senior class at Fairgate High School. It was near graduation and the students were discussing their future plans. James, an articulate African American young man, was very upset. He said, "I've done everything my teachers asked me. I got good grades. But when I took the ACT, I didn't score high enough to get into Morehouse." James' situation typifies the enduring achievement gap between White students and their African American, Latino, Native American, and a number of Asian American peers.[1] This gap can be found on all national measures of achievement as well as in grade point averages (GPA) in integrated schools, both at the high school and collegiate levels (Perle, Moran, Lutkas, & Tirre, 2005). There have been many reasons offered to explain this discrepancy. One set of explanations focuses on *structural differences* in available school resources, including per-pupil expenditures (Carey, 2004; Education Trust, 2005b; Hill & Roza, 2004), teacher quality (Darling-Hammond, 1985, 1987, 1999b), tracking within schools (Oakes, 1985, 1990), and political as well as economic differences in opportunities within the society and reflected in schooling (Bowles & Gintis, 1976; Kozol, 1991; McDermott, 1987; White, 1982). A second explanation posits *theories of cultural deficits* as the source of the achievement gap. This deficit perspective has a long history in the United States that begins with the enslavement of African people and the attack on the indigenous peoples of this continent. That perspective remained quite explicit in educational policy through the 1970s. It continues today veiled in arguments about what children from families living in poverty who are predominantly Black and Brown do not learn at home that is needed for successful entry to school (Hall & Moats, 1999). These arguments are most often posited in terms of language deficiencies (Bernstein, 1961; Stotsky, 1999). A third explanation for the gap draws on research on learning among ethnic groups in

9

the United States, particularly African Americans, which has consistently argued that such groups display cultural ways of knowing and acting that are often at odds with the demands of schooling (Boykin, 1982; Boykin & Allen, 1988; Delpit, 1986; Perry & Delpit, 1998; Shade, 1982), the *cultural mismatch* theory. A fourth explanation, but related to the third, puts forth a somewhat different point of view, what I'll refer to as *cultural repertoires of practice* (Gutierrez & Rogoff, 2003; Nasir, Rosebery, Warren, & Lee, 2006; Rogoff, Paradise, Mejía-Arauz, Correa-Chávez, & Angelillo, 2003). This explanation contends that all children and adolescents bring important cultural resources from their home and community experiences. It is the job of schools (and of those who research learning and development) to understand those resources and their application to the demands of school-based learning. I stand in the latter camp, but also build from the cultural mismatch research as well. I hope in this book to extend the arguments about the role of culture in learning and development, in part by examining some of the questions that I think prior research has not yet adequately addressed. In this chapter, I will illustrate the usefulness and limitations of each of these explanations and then go on to explicate the Cultural Modeling framework as one attempt to construct a comprehensive explanatory framework that speaks to some of what prior accounts have not addressed.

Both the cultural mismatch and the cultural repertoires of practice explanations share a common focus on the importance of culture in learning. The cultural mismatch orientation implies a level of homogeneity within cultural communities defined by ethnicity. While it is absolutely correct that cultural communities share historically inherited regularities, it is equally true that these historical regularities also change in response to new historical, political, and economic conditions (Cole, 1996; Greenfield, 2004; Nasir & Saxe, 2003; Rogoff, 2003 ; Saxe & Esmonde, 2005). It is also true that all members of a cultural group do not share or share equally that which the literature suggests is characteristic of the group (Gutierrez & Rogoff, 2003; Irvine & York, 1995). In addition, people participate in different ways in multiple communities. The most basic and pervasive are communities defined within families, often through historically inherited practices, institutions, and ways of using language defined by the experience of ethnicity or nationality. The focus on ethnicity is of particular importance for African Americans (Asante & Welsh-Asante, 1990; DuBois, 1968; Herskovitz, 1958; Mufwene, 1993; Vass, 1979). Within the United States, historically and politically, African Americans have been defined by race. However, the very construct of race is problematic (Gould, 1981). Ultimately to define who is and who is not of a particular race, one must revert back to the primitive calculations of percentage of blood, that is, octaroons, quadroons, and so on.[2]

The very idea that race is somehow in the blood harks back to an established literature in U.S. and Western European pseudoscience wherein differences between the races were defined by measures of phenotypic features. This pseudoscience assumed that there were most often clear distinctions between races based on skin color (Gould, 1981; Stanton, 1960). However, there are many instances where such distinctions are highly problematic (Brunsma & Rockquemore, 2002; Hollinger, 2003; Sollors, 1997). For example, there are many people of Sicilian heritage whose skin color is the same as many African Americans and there are ethnic groups on the Indian subcontinent who are darker than many African Americans (Alcoff, 1995; Bamshad et al., 1996; Rajshekar, 1987; Van Sertima, 1987; Van Sertima & Rashidi, 1985). There are plenty of Italians, Greeks, Jews, and African Americans with tight curly hair. So just how much Black or Brown skin and how tight a curl does one need to be Black? Even if based on something like ways of using language, how do we account for the ways that people routinely cross language borders? Do Vanilla Ice and Eminem become Black when they begin to appropriate African American English and cultural forms? Does Kathleen Battle become a White Italian when she sings a Puccini aria in near perfect Italian?

There is no question that race as a construct has grave social, political, economic, and historical realities (Jacobson, 1999; Mills, 1997). In order to understand how the construct of race functions in U.S. society, we need accurate historical and contemporary accounts that focus on how race is operationalized in institutional structures and opportunities. In order to gauge the social distribution of resources and opportunities, we need data by race. In the absence of such data, we will have no way of gauging both opportunities and progress or a lack thereof (Bell, 1992; Ladson-Billings & Tate, 1995).

At the same time, we must also wrestle with the ways that race as a construct limits our views, particularly in the field of educational research and practice (Lee, Spencer, & Harpalani, 2003). To analyze group membership in ways that take history and cultural practices into account, ethnicity is a more powerful and universal concept than race. Ethnicity takes into account history, identity, practices, and beliefs. An ethnic focus will group Blacks as people of African descent. African descent places a people in history. When linked with a practice-based unit of analysis, we are in a better position to understand the persistence of cultural patterns across time. At the same time, because we are looking at what people routinely do (as opposed to the color of their skin, the texture of their hair, and the width of noses and lips), we have a relatively objective measure for placing people in or out of cultural groups. My great-grandfather was Irish and my great-great-grandmother was Native American (Lee, 2002).

However, I engage in no cultural practices connected with being either Irish or Native American (unfortunately, I do not know the tribal membership of my great-great-grandmother). Thus I would argue that not even family lineage in this sense would define me as ethnically Irish or Native American. On the other hand, the ways I use language, cook food, dance, name my children, and participate in religious practices can be linked to West African practices and historically to routine practices across generations in the African American community (and to some degree other African descent diaspora communities such as the Caribbean).

It is also important to note a distinction between membership in cultural groups and participation in cultural practices. One can participate peripherally in a set of practices without being a member of that group. Membership involves both a sense of identity as well as a level of acceptance by other members. In addition, some practices have both a historical relationship to a particular ethnic or national community as well as a transnational or transethnic identity. For example, practices associated with hip-hop culture are historically rooted in African American youth culture, and by extension to other African American cultural forms (Rose, 1994; Spears, 1999). At the same time, hip-hop is also international in scope.

Through this dual lens of ethnicity and practice, it is easy to recognize that cultural groups have both intergenerational stability and also diversity. Diversity within groups is also persistent and emergent. These are very difficult qualities to conceptualize and comprehend, but are crucial if we are to avoid essentializing cultural membership.

I will illustrate using people of African descent in the United States as an exemplar of a cultural group based on ethnicity. Intergenerational stability can be viewed in language use, family structure, religion and spirituality, music, dance, and food, to name a few areas of routine practice. Within the African American community, practices in each of these areas involve intergenerational resources that can be traced to historical African roots (Asante & Welsh-Asante, 1990; DuBois, 1968; Herskovitz, 1958; Mufwene, 1993; Rickford & Rickford, 1976; Vass, 1979). Most people who are descendants of those Blacks who were enslaved within the United States speak some version of African American English . It must be noted that African descent immigrants in the United States from African, Caribbean, and Central and South American countries where the national language is not English may not speak African American English. However, they are likely to speak a version of the national European language of their country of origin that has African influences (e.g., the French of Haitian Creole or of Senegal is not the French of France; and there are African linguistic traces in Cuban Spanish, Puerto Rican Spanish, and Dominican Republic Spanish as spoken by people of African descent in these countries) (Lipski, 2005).

This issue of African influences on European languages is complex. Because of the historical contacts of Africans and other populations, it is common to find linguistic Africanisms in other languages that are used generally within the population (Vass, 1979). These include common words like "tote" and "banana" as well as recent language practices associated with hip-hop. There are other lexicons (vocabulary) and syntaxes that are uniquely used among Blacks. In a personal communication, noted linguist Geneva Smitherman offers *high yella*, *nigga*, and grammatical patterns such as the copula *be* (as in "He be workin' my last nerve") as examples of Africanisms that are uniquely used within the African American population.[3] Using our practice-linked frame, these commonalities are based on people within diaspora communities living in close proximity with one another. If a person is African American, but grew up and lives in a White upper-middle-class community in which African Americans are a distinct minority, and ceases to have extended family and peer social networks within the Black community, that person is not likely going to speak African American English (AAE) or any of its varieties.[4]

Persistent features of AAE relate to syntax and phonology (Mufwene, Rickford, Bailey, & Baugh, 1998) . These syntactical forms are most prominently marked in the vernacular variety of AAE. Orlando Taylor (1986; Taylor & Lee, 1987) has rightly observed that there are both vernacular and more standard versions of AAE. However, across both the vernacular and standard varieties, there are commonalities related to prosody, intonation, speech genres, and aesthetic norms (Baugh, 1983; Labov, 1998; Morgan, 1998; Mufwene et al., 1998; Smitherman, 1977). These features are part of the deep structure of the language. They can be traced to African, particularly West African roots. At the same time, there is diversity in the ways the language is used (Labov, 1998; Smitherman, 1992). For example, there will be differences—especially at the level of vocabulary—based on age cohort, region, gender, class, and combinations thereof.

One illustration of the persistence of deep structure in the midst of emergent patterns is the speech genre of signifying. *Signifying* is a genre of talk that involves ritual insult (Mitchell-Kernan, 1981; Smitherman, 1977). The contexts of its use are very much related to gender and age cohort. Males are more likely to routinely signify and it is inappropriate for a young person to signify on older persons. When I first began my research on educational implications of competence in signifying in 1990, the high school students with whom I worked had never heard of the terms *signifying* or *playing the dozens*.[5] However, when they heard examples of playing the dozens, as in "yo mama so skinny she can do the hula hoop in a Cheerio," they immediately recognized the form. At the same time, my daughter, who was then in high school, began collecting examples for me. My mother, who was

70 at the time, shared with her friends that her daughter was studying signifying and they became another information source. The genre remained stable, but the lexicon for describing it changed. The circumstances under which it could be practiced changed. By 1990, there were radio programs in which people publicly signified on each other, a practice unheard of during my youth or that of my mother. Also, routine metaphors employed and played upon changed. Thus the practice had both a stable and an emergent quality. Other researchers have done similar analyses of stability and emergence in other African-descent cultural practices such as music, dance, food, and spirituality (Asante & Welsh-Asante, 1990; DuBois, 1968; Herskovitz, 1958). These qualities of emergence are often hybrid, incorporating influences from other cultural and historical forces.

This wrestling with what we mean by membership in cultural groups is crucial to inform how we take culture into account in the design of learning environments and management of learning interactions. Confusion around cultural membership has influenced three opposing orientations to teaching and learning. One orientation presumes that cultural differences don't matter at all and that a generic approach to teaching is all that's needed. The vast majority of curriculum and teaching in U.S. schools work from this generic orientation (Elmore, 1995; Levin, 1993; Slavin, Madden, Dolan, & Wasik, 1996). The problem with a generic orientation is that it does not take into account the extensive body of research documenting the ways a presumed generic approach to teaching and learning is differentially implemented with students of color and students from low-income communities (Anyon, 1980, 1981; Apple, 1979; Dreeban & Gamoran, 1986; Knapp & Shields, 1990). Even where teachers say they are trying not to make distinctions among students based on race or ethnicity, the literature on the prevalence and impact of teachers' low expectations is consistent (Baron, Tom, & Cooper, 1985; DeMeis & Turner, 1978; Rist, 1970). Differential access to learning is also structurally embedded in tracking and basic skills orientations to teaching (Guiton & Oakes, 1995; Oakes, Gamoran, & Page, 1992). Under these conditions of low expectations and structural inequalities, the generic orientation does not account for why some students thrive in the midst of these inequalities, why some schools serving predominantly minority and low-income populations "beat the odds" (Langer, 2001).

A second orientation presumes a cultural hierarchy in which belief systems, epistemologies, practices, and ways of using language associated with persons from low-income and so-called minority communities have been deemed deficits that detract from school-based learning (Coleman, 1966; Jencks, 1972; Traub, 1999). During the 1970s there were many educational programs designed to address what were presumed language deficits of

African American children. DISTAR was perhaps the most visible example (Bereiter & Engelmann, 1966). DISTAR involved direct instruction in oral sentence construction, description, and pronunciation as a basis for learning to read. That tradition continues today in the programs of Direct Instruction (DI) that dominate many elementary schools serving Black and Brown students in low-income communities (Adams & Engelmann, 1996; Gersten & Keating, 1987a).

A third orientation presumes there is no cultural hierarchy and that teaching should be tailored to meet specific ways of learning defined by cultural groups. Professional development programs that derive from the learning styles research is one example (Cassidy, 2004; Dunn & Griggs, 2000). In this research, ethnic communities are defined as individualistic or group oriented; or as having a tendency to solve problems by analyzing its parts or by looking at phenomena holistically (Ramirez & Castaneda, 1974; Saracho & Spodek, 1984). However, this third orientation rarely focuses in any specific way on subject matter demands and presumes a level of homogeneity in cultural communities that masks internal diversity within groups.

UNDERSTANDING CULTURAL DISPLAYS IN THE SERVICE OF DISCIPLINE-BASED LEARNING

We need a more complex explanatory model that provides ways of understanding cultural displays related to discipline-based learning. We need a lens through which to understand the relevance of the cultural practices of everyday life—be they based on ethnicity, nationality, class, or age within any of these categories. We need a model that provides a lens for understanding the role of perceptions in influencing actions so that differences between community-based and school-based norms can be negotiated both by students and teachers. Such an explanatory model must be rooted in theories of cognition, motivation, life course development, understanding language functioning in face-to-face interactions, and discipline-specific learning. Cultural Modeling offers one attempt at a more comprehensive explanatory and design framework. Cultural Modeling is a framework for the design of learning environments that examines what youth know from everyday settings to support specific subject matter learning.

Foundations in Mathematics

Some of the most detailed analyses of thinking in everyday contexts related to academic subject matters have been in mathematics. In this area, the research on children with little or no schooling who sell candy on the streets of Brazil has most directly influenced the conceptual underpinnings of Cultural Modeling. The research by Geoffrey Saxe (1991) and Terezinha Nunes, Analucia Dias Schliemann, and David William Carraher (1993) shed nuanced insights into the nature of learning in everyday practice. While there is a significant body of research on everyday thinking (Cole, 1996; Cole, Gay, Glick, & Sharp, 1971; Hutchins, 1995; Lave, 1988; Rogoff & Lave, 1984; Scribner, 1984; Scribner & Cole, 1981), I will focus on the Brazilian candy sellers for several reasons. First, these children represent the oppressed and stigmatized populations that are of interest to me and that continue to represent the problem that educational research and practice have not addressed successfully. Second, in this case everyday practice has direct links to academic knowledge. Third, the longitudinal nature of these studies allows one to look at developmental trajectories for learning in everyday contexts. I base my analysis below largely on the reports by Saxe (1991; 1999; Saxe & Esmonde, 2005; Saxe & Gearhart, 1990). In a sense, Cultural Modeling has been one attempt to take up the implications of this research for the design of curriculum and learning environments.

The children live in Recife, a poor city in northeast Brazil. Their families typically live in shantytowns and struggle to eek out a living. These children either never attend school or drop out early in order to help their families. Children may begin their work as candy sellers around 6 years of age. The sellers must figure out what candy to buy and select from a number of wholesalers. They must compute how to package and price the candy. They must take into account wholesale prices, what the market will bear, and the general rates of inflation in the economy as they typically sell to foreigners. Saxe (1991) argues that in this complex problem solving, the children draw on a number of supports. These include social supports from adult wholesalers, older and more mature street sellers, the structure of the Brazilian currency, as well as the structures and conventions in place to sustain the practice of selling. To engage in this practice at various levels of expertise, the children have to solve problems involving addition, subtraction, estimation, percentage, and ratio. Saxe wanted to understand how children with little education learned to solve such mathematical problems outside of school. He also wanted to understand how such expertise developed over time.

Two ironies of this research are important. First, among second and third graders, sellers performed better than nonsellers on word problems and computation. Among second graders, in word problems involving small and larger numbers, sellers outperformed nonsellers on both kinds of problems. Among third graders, sellers outperformed nonsellers on problems involving small numbers. On problems involving large numbers, sellers also outperformed nonsellers but by a much smaller margin. With further analysis, Saxe (1991) found that sellers in school were better at regrouping and by third grade did not use school-based algorithms as much as nonsellers. Overall, Saxe found that sellers in school did appropriate their practice-linked strategies to school-based problems:

> The evidence . . . shows that sellers as contrasted with nonsellers are more adept at solving school-linked arithmetical problems. Further, the analysis of children's strategies revealed that a source of sellers' success was their specialized knowledge of regrouping, specialized strategic forms that we have seen some evidence of . . . in sellers' bill reordering to solve the currency addition tasks. In their solutions to the school-linked problems, we see the appropriation of these out-of-school cognitive forms and further specialization of these forms to accomplish school-linked arithmetical problems. (1991, p. 172)

Nasir (2000) found similar patterns in a study of what understandings of percent and averages African American adolescent basketball players learned through the practice of basketball. Nasir gave players problems couched in the context of basketball and the same problem as a school-based algorithm. Basketball players were able to use their strategies for calculating percentages to solve both basketball and algorithm-based problems. However, when larger numbers were involved, players were able to use estimation strategies better with larger sets of numbers where they did not have access to the appropriate algorithm in solving basketball-related problems.

In both the Saxe (1991) and Nasir (2000) studies as well as in other related research, several interesting patterns emerge. How everyday practice-based knowledge is used in the solution of academic tasks is influenced by the maturation of the students, the nature of the problems students are trying to solve, the structure of the domain from which the problem comes, and the nature of the supports available as students learn everyday practice. In the studies described above, classrooms were not organized to support in any explicit way relevant out-of-school knowledge. The studies also demonstrate that the ways students were able to transfer out-of-school knowledge to school-based problems was constrained by the structure of knowledge in both contexts and the goals students established for doing problems in both domains. Where basketball players used estimation strategies to calculate percentages, these strategies were most effective when the numbers in the problem set were within the range they would normally meet in basketball. Where child candy sellers used regrouping to solve practice-based problems and school-based word problems, they did not use school-based algorithms as they got older to the same extent as nonsellers. An interesting question is whether explicit instruction that helped students make connections between the demands of specific school-based tasks and their out-of-school practice-based concepts as well as problem-solving strategies would have made any difference. That is, would their depth of understanding of estimating percentages in basketball and school-based problems, or of regrouping in candy-selling and school-based problems, been expanded and rendered as more complex conceptual networks, if such explicit instruction had occurred? This is the hypothesis that Cultural Modeling investigates.

This question addresses the problem of inert knowledge reported by Whitehead (1929). This is a classic problem of *transfer*. An individual has relevant knowledge, yet does not draw on knowledge that is related to the transfer problem (Garcia, 1998; Griffin, Case, & Capodilupo, 1995; Klausmeier, 1985; Luchins & Luchins, 1970; Singley & Anderson, 1989). These are cases where an individual faces a problem that is different from problems tackled before and that he or she does not know how to solve. *Near transfer* involves problems that are more closely related to problems one is used to solving. *Far transfer* involves problems that are more remote from problems one is used to solving. One challenge of transfer is the ability to detect the kind of problem one is trying to solve and figuring out how the structure of that kind of problem and strategies that are relevant to its solution map onto what one already knows. More often than not, educators believe that in contrast to middle-class White students, students of color and students from low-income communities do not bring experiences and world knowledge that are relevant resources for academic learning. Experiences with storybook reading and museum trips are viewed as resources for middle-class students that help to prepare them for school (Hall & Moats, 1999). Because of these assumptions, the question of transfer of knowledge from everyday practice is not front and center when students are African American, Latino, Native American, from particular Asian American communities (such as Hmong), or when the students are poor. One of the goals of this book is to demonstrate how cultural displays of knowledge rooted in everyday practices of ethnic groups and other communities of practice generally viewed as unrelated to schooling can be scaffolded in service of domain-specific academic learning.

This research on cultural displays of knowledge in everyday contexts also relates to the distinction that Vygotsky made between scientific and spontaneous concepts (Vygotsky, 1978, 1981; Wertsch, 1985). Vygotsky argued that spontaneous concepts were constructed out of everyday experience and that knowledge of how to use them is largely tacit. Families of such everyday concepts do not have the same formal taxonomic relationships as scientific concepts. Vygotsky claimed that scientific concepts were learned explicitly in school and knowledge of them was more conscious than tacit. Vygotsky further argued that scientific concepts reflected a level of abstraction from the tangible that was captured in taxonomic systems. For example, in everyday contexts, a dog is an abstract label that captures mutts, German shepherds, and French poodles. At the same time, you can tangibly touch a German shepherd as dog. By contrast, in the scientific context,[6] dog is of the class of mammals, the order of carnivora, the family of canidae, and the genus of canis. The classifications of mammal, carnivora, canidae, and canis are intended as logical representations of a set of relationships between physiological form and species function (such as the presence of mammalian glands in the female of the species with the function of feeding young in the species). They are not intended as labels that point to a physical or other observable entity, action, goal, or internal state. Although, you could physically point to a dog or a human as a case of mammal, it would be viewed as very strange in the everyday context. I don't fully agree with Vygotsky regarding the taxonomic differences between spontaneous and scientific concepts (Lee, 1993, 2000). However, I do agree with the distinctions between largely tacit versus more explicit understandings in the two areas. I am positing tacitness versus explicitness on a continuum. There is certainly research documenting that deeply expert knowledge may be tacit at one level. However, the overall findings of this research suggest that the problem is not so much that the understanding of experts is tacit; rather the problem is with the methodological challenges for researchers to get such experts to make deeply taken-for-granted knowledge explicit (Chi, Feltovich, & Glaser, 1981). Hence, the use of clinical interviews (Clement, 2000; Flower & Hayes, 1981a, 1981b; Piaget, 1975) and talk-aloud protocols (Afflerbach & Johnston, 1984; Newell & Simon, 1972; Pressley & Afflerbach, 1995) are efforts to bring taken-for-granted knowledge to public articulation. I will take up the implications of *tacit* versus *explicit* understanding in more detail in the next chapter where I explore the nuances of modeling relationships between everyday knowledge and academic knowledge.

From the studies of the Brazilian street children, it is clear that researchers needed a detailed understanding of the practices involved with selling candy on the streets, including the kinds of mathematical knowledge being constructed and deployed, the kinds of assistance in learning to do this practice, and the constraints on the practice. Constraints on the practice in computing percentages in basketball might include the range of numbers (i.e., total number of points in a game and the number of points an individual player might accumulate in a given game). Such constraints constrict the range of kinds of problems in the academic domain to which the everyday knowledge can be applied. It is equally clear that if one wanted to figure out ways to help these children better learn the mathematics of school, one would need a clear explication of the demands of the kinds of problems children would be expected to tackle in school arithmetic (Ma, 1999). This is necessary in order to conceptualize what might be connections between the mathematics they learn on the street and the mathematics they are expected to learn in school. These were the lessons I learned from the Brazilian candy seller studies and other studies of everyday learning that I have attempted to adapt in another domain in Cultural Modeling.

A Case of Literary Reasoning

Literary reasoning is the target domain in which my work in Cultural Modeling began. I recognized early on that literary response required a playful attitude toward linguistic detail and an ability to deconstruct figurative language. In the next chapter on modeling, I will explicate a more detailed map of problem solving in the domain of literary reasoning. However, these two foundational orientations toward literary texts informed my original conceptions of potential relationships between the everyday knowledge of many African American students and the knowledge required to tackle canonical works of literature.

One powerful form of everyday knowledge in the African American English speech community is entailed in talk called *signifying* (Mitchell-Kernan, 1981; Smitherman, 1977). As described earlier in this chapter, the everyday practice of signifying has a long history in the AAE speech community. Signifying involves ritual insult. It almost always involves indirection, double entendre and a high use of figurative language. Signifying is a part of a number of prototypical speech events: sounding, toasting, playing the dozens, testifying. Signifying can be used to insult, as in "Your mother is so fat, when she stepped on the scale, it said 'To be continued" (Percelay, Ivey & Dweck, 1994, p. 43). It can be used to persuade, as in the following example:

> A young man has approached the researcher [Claudia Mitchell-Kernan]. She tells him about her research on signifying. He raps (i.e., talks flirtatiously) to her. In the midst of their signifying dialogue, he says, "Baby, you a real scholar. I can tell you want to learn. Now if you'll just cooperate a li'l bit, I'll show you what a good teacher I am. But first we got to get into my area of expertise." (Mitchell-Kernan, 1982, p. 323, quoted in Lee, 1993)

It can be used to inform, as in the following exchange:

> Grace has four kids. She had sworn she was not going to have any more babies. When she discovered she was pregnant again, she wouldn't tell anybody. Grace's sister came over and they had the following conversation.

Rochelle: Girl, you sure do need to join the Metrecal for lunch bunch. [In the 1970s Metrecal was a drink used to lose weight.]
Grace: (noncommittally) Yea, I guess I am putting on a little weight.
Rochelle: Now look here, girl, we both standing here soaking wet and you still trying to tell me it ain't raining. (Mitchell-Kernan, 1981, p. 323, quoted in Lee, 1993).

In each instance, all players must pay careful attention to language details. When volleying a retort in a game of ritual insult, the respondent must pick up the vehicle of the metaphor and extend it in a creative way. According to Winner,

> At the root of every metaphor is some kind of juxtaposition of a topic and a vehicle which are linked by a common ground. . . . The topic is the subject of the metaphor, what the metaphor is about. The vehicle is the means by which the speaker indirectly refers to the topic. Linking them together is the ground, the attributes shared by topic and vehicle. (1988, p. 17)

Consider the following example of playing the dozens, a specialized form of signifying: "Your mother is so fat, she has her own area code" (Percelay et al., 1994, p. 39). The topic is the mother's size (i.e., "fat"). The vehicle is "area code." The ground or attribute shared is enormous size. This is not the syntax typical of metaphor, which in this case would be something like "Your mother is an area code." Or it could be construed as a simile in the form "Your mother's size is like an area code." However, the reasoning required is metaphorical and clearly the typical metaphor syntax or simile syntax would not have the rhetorical impact and humor of the dozens. And in signifying, rhetorical impact and the aesthetics of how language is used are as important as the content of the message.

Both the producer and those listening must be able to distinguish between that which is literal and that which is figurative. In milliseconds, they must recognize the root of the analogy on which the metaphor is based as well as the vehicle and ground through which the analogy is constructed. They must also recognize the rhetorical function of each move in the exchange. It has been estimated that up to 90% of African Americans may be characterized as AAE speakers.[7] In addition, the popular media (comedy in television and film; R & B, the blues, and rap in music) is replete with examples of Black people signifying on one another. Thus, taking practice as the unit of analysis, I argue that a lot of Black people engage in the reasoning associated with signifying, but not that using language in this way is somehow an outgrowth of dark skin. It is also useful to note that forms of ritual insult and language play generally can be found among many speech communities (see Deborah

Tannen's [1979, 1989] work on dinnertime conversations among Italian American, Greek American, and Jewish American families or Alan Dundes' [1972] work on ritual verbal dueling among Turkish youth as examples).

In my early work on signifying and literary response, I found that through instruction in Cultural Modeling, students' knowledge of how to detect and comprehend literary tropes changed in fundamental ways (Lee, 1991, 1993, 1995a, 1995b). These changes mapped on to what Geoffrey Saxe (1991) calls a "form-function shift." According to Saxe, a form-function shift involves a transformation of cultural practice in which a concept that took on a particular form and function at one point in time shifts. Such shifts may involve a similar form that takes on a new function. Saxe provides an elegant and detailed explanation of shifts in the form and function of the mathematical concept of "Fu" among the Oksapmin of Papua, New Guinea, over historical time (Saxe & Esmonde, 2005). In the case of signifying, over time students' conceptions of signifying shifted in terms of the form that signifying could take and its functions (Lee, 1993). The underlying structure or form of the literary tropes found in canonical literature were qualitatively different from signifying in everyday contexts. In addition, the function of the tropes also changed from the rivalry of the dozens and were more complex than other typical functions of signifying, such as persuading and informing.

In my instruction I used Toni Morrison's novel *The Bluest Eye* (1970). This book includes examples of a form and function shift in the everyday practice of signifying. Students' abilities to understand such literary signifying represents a form-function shift in their understanding of signifying. It is a story about a young African American girl, ironically named Pecola Breedlove, who is sexually molested by her father and who retreats into a world where she defines her sense of beauty and sense of self using an idyllic vision of a White woman as the norm. In a breadth that is typical of Toni Morrison, this family's tragedy is understood in the broader social, economic, and political contexts that constrain the sense of identity of everyone in this family—the father, the mother, and the daughter. The girl's mother, Pauline, deals with the poverty and the misfortune of her family life by retreating into another White world, and by psychologically aligning herself with the privileged White family for whom she is a servant:

> More and more she neglected her house, her children, her man—they were like the afterthoughts one has just before sleep, the early-morning and late-evening edges of her day, the dark edges that made the daily life with the Fishers lighter, more delicate, more lovely. (Morrison, 1970, p. 109)

I have argued elsewhere that here Morrison is engaging in a kind of literary signifying (Lee, 1993). Pauline's family is alluded to as "the dark edges that made the daily life with the Fishers lighter, more delicate, more lovely." Dark and light are in contrast. These contrasts situated in the larger context of the novel capture the tensions between attributions of beauty to the blonde-haired doll that Pecola clutches and the Jean Harlow image that Pauline reveres in the movies where she escapes her own life. The lighter and more delicate associations with the Fishers parallels the lighter and more delicate hair of Pecola's doll and Pauline's images of the Jean Harlow figures of the movies. The edges of a Black woman's hair on the nape of her neck in African American English Vernacular (AAEV) are called "the kitchen," an ironic reference to the work that Pauline does. Both Pauline's life conditions and her hair as an iconic representation of Blackness are resistant to attempts at change.

No matter how hard Pauline tries not to be Black, she is; no matter how hard the Black woman tries to straighten her hair, the dark edges of nappy will always push themselves forward. This commentary by the narrator is a subtle literary form of signifying that Morrison artistically shouts out in soft tones of innuendo, letting the wise reader know that Pauline cannot escape her Blackness, no matter how hard she tries. I argue that this represents a qualitatively different form and function for signifying that students met in the canonical literature. Before instruction, students saw the figuration in signifying dialogues as a practice of the streets, bearing no relation to the problems of figuration they met in the literature they read at school. After instruction, students attended to the nuances of language play in canonical texts with levels of engagement and attention to details found in the practice of signifying outside of school (Lee, 2001).

Just as children who were unschooled and living in extreme poverty on the streets of Brazil were most often viewed by educational authorities as unknowledgeable and incorrigible, children and adolescents who engage in signifying talk specifically and African American English vernacular (AAEV) generally are often viewed as having language deficits. Such attitudes are based not only on a lack of understanding of the demands of the everyday practice, but also on a limited understanding of relevant target domains of academic knowledge for which many presume AAEV limits participation (see the book *Twice as Less* as an example [Orr, 1987] and Baugh's [1988] critique of Orr).

Applications to Other Domains

This conceptual orientation to the examination of relationships between knowledge in everyday practices and academic knowledge is not limited to fields in literacy, such as my work on educational implications of competencies in signifying. The implications of mathematical understandings in everyday practice has been well explicated in theory, albeit not as much in practice. The Algebra Project has done one of the best jobs of taking up the implications of the mathematics of everyday practice research for the design of school-based instruction for African American and other students (Moses, 1994; Moses & Cobb, 2001; Moses, Kamii, Swap, & Howard, 1989; Silva, Moses, Rivers, & Johnson, 1990). Urban students' experiences in figuring out how to get around on the transit system are used as analogs for understanding integers in terms of directionality rather than simply as quantity. In elementary school arithmetic, children typically understand numbers simply as quantities. Robert Moses (1994), the founder of the Algebra Project, argues that the idea of numbers as indicators of displacements in relation to a benchmark is a foundational construct that marks an important transition to algebra. Displacement is a change in position in a direction that can be positive or negative from a point of origin or benchmark. Conceptualizing displacements is necessary to understand, for example, operations with positive and negative numbers. Moses argues that operations involving positive and negative numbers are often counterintuitive and therefore confusing because students' only models involve numbers as quantities. In the Algebra Project, students create problems that ask how many moves in what direction from a starting benchmark station one needs to get from one point to another on an urban transit line. Thinking about the number of moves in a specified direction from a benchmark is then mapped on to mathematical algorithms and algebraic representations.

In science, the researchers in Chéche Konnen have provided revealing examples of scientific understanding and scientific argumentation in the everyday practices of African-descent immigrant populations—Haitian and Cape Verdeans as two prominent examples (Conant, Rosebery, Warren, & Hudicourt-Barnes, 2001; Rosebery, Warren, Ballenger, & Ogonowski, 2005; Rosebery, Warren, & Conant, 1992; Warren, Ballenger, Ogonowski, Rosebery, & Hudicourt-Barnes, 2001; Warren & Ogonowski, 1998, 2001; Warren & Rosebery, 1996; K. Warren, 1993). In one example, Haitiandescent students were supported in leveraging their knowledge of how to produce sounds on African drums to explore scientific representations of sound. Using English and Haitian Creole, students engaged in scientific argumentation in which they generated complex problems regarding sound, investigating relationships between the medium on which the sound is produced (such as the circumference and material of the drum head) and the method through which the sound is produced (such as the angle at which the hand hits the face of the drum).

These two examples of pedagogy that draws explicitly on cultural displays of knowledge in everyday practices stand in stark contrast to typical instruction. A profound lack of understanding of the cultural displays of knowledge in the everyday practices of minority and low-income students —including students whose first language is other than academic English— has led to a pervasive culture of low expectations, to deficit models of student capacities, and to a myriad of misunderstandings within classrooms. Among teachers serving students who typically underachieve in schools, equally profound low levels of understanding of the demands of subject matter problem solving contribute to a culture of blaming the victims. Ironically, the same case can be made regarding the public's conceptions of and attitudes toward teachers, which assume that if people like kids and know some subject matter they can teach: "You can learn to teach in 6 weeks over the summer." "Teaching is a good will or peace corps type of job that you can do for a few years until you know what you *really* want to do with your life." "The reason kids don't learn is because teachers are not adequately prepared in the universities." All of these fundamentally teacher-bashing orientations underconceptualize the complex demands of teaching and of learning to teach. The consequences of such underconceptualizations are especially dire for students who are Black, Brown, and poor.

A LENS FOR UNDERSTANDING THE ROLE OF PERCEPTIONS IN INFLUENCING ACTIONS

I argue in this book for the crucial importance of understanding cultural displays of knowledge constructed in the everyday routine practices of children and adolescents and the relationship of such displays to targets of academic knowledge. However, while such understandings are necessary, they are not sufficient. We can design curriculum and instruction in a way that helps kids make connections between what they already know and what we want them to learn. This does not mean they will put forth the effort to make those connections. The design and management of learning environments involve more than a cognitive architecture. Complex learning is always risky business. We must consider what is involved in designing learning environments in ways so that differences between community-based and school-based norms can be negotiated both by students and by teachers. These may include linguistic differences, such as differences in norms for verbal interactions, in basic syntactic structures and lexicon,[8] and in assumptions about appropriate gestural language; or other arenas such as in epistemological orientations. If we consider more than the cognitive demands of academic work, some basic questions arise:

What leads to both the formation and the sustenance of goals for academic achievement (Eccles, Wigfield, & Schiefele, 1998; Graham, 1994; Graham & Golan, 1991; Graham & Taylor, 2002; Graham, Taylor, & Hudley, 1998)? What in the nature of the supports in a learning environment increases the likelihood that children or adolescents will persist in efforts to learn and engage in what for them is a new practice? To answer these questions, we must draw on constructs related to perceptions and identity.

Nasir has demonstrated how participation structures in routine practices in everyday contexts are often organized in ways that help young people develop identities as members of that practice (Nasir, 2000; Nasir & Saxe, 2003). She has illustrated this with African American middle and high schoolers' routine participation in basketball and dominoes. We know that too many students, especially in schools in low-income communities serving largely minority populations, disengage from school practices for many reasons that make a lot of sense to them. They feel that they are not respected in classrooms, that the content of instruction does not serve the goals that are most immediate to them, or because they do not understand the subject matter as they experience it in classrooms.

Nasir and Saxe (2003) make a compelling argument for a way of thinking about the problems of resistance to academic achievement. They argue that to understand how students experience tensions in the pursuit of academic goals, researchers must consider how such tensions are constructed in local face-to-face interactions, how such tensions develop and change over developmental time (for example from middle childhood to early adolescence), and how such tensions evolve in social history. According to Nasir and Saxe, the emergence of such tensions in social history includes the social capital associated with a given practice in historical time. They cite the example of domino playing as an activity of the elite in ancient China and as an activity of low-income African Americans in certain parts of the United States today. This analytic framework is relevant to Cultural Modeling. Specific participation structures in Cultural Modeling organize face-to-face interactions in ways that position students as sources of authority and make the structure of complex problem solving explicit. This is one way that Cultural Modeling addresses developmental tasks that students face. Another is in the content of problems. For example, the selection of texts in Cultural Modeling literature classrooms focuses, in part, on tasks with which many African American adolescents living in low-income urban communities wrestle. In this way, Cultural Modeling attempts to structure classrooms as one site in which students can think about the challenges of managing such tensions. Third, Cultural Modeling actively privileges sources of knowledge that the students recognize are devalued by schools. By helping students see the functional relationships between everyday knowledge they possess and school-based tasks, Cultural Modeling repositions what might be historically viewed as vernacular practices as intellectually rich. Many of the texts included in Cultural Modeling literature curriculum are from the African American literary tradition and reposition vernacular ways of using language, for example, as literary representations. Thus Cultural Modeling seeks not only to address ways of understanding cultural displays of knowledge in everyday contexts, but also to structure ways of participating that enhance identity development and therefore engagement and persistence. Cultural Modeling is a tool, not a panacea. As such, the tasks and participation structures in Cultural Modeling act as mediational tools to help students make sense and impose meaning on their pursuit of academic tasks. In thinking about the Cultural Modeling framework as a mediational tool, it may be taken up in many different ways by different students, some with more success than others. Its mediational properties, however, are the structures that make certain kinds of learning possible.

Margaret Beale Spencer takes up this issue of developmental challenge in her focus on perceptions of risk (Lee, Spencer, & Harpalani, 2003; Spencer, 1987, 1995, 1999, 2000; Spencer, Swanson, & Cunningham, 1991). Spencer reframes what on the surface appears to be a matter of common sense: To be human is to be placed at risk. The literature on life course development fundamentally posits that *development* is the process through which over time humans learn how to address the challenges of cultivating and sustaining a sense of well-being and of competence, of nurturing interpersonal relationships first within families and later across wider social networks, and of navigating obstacles. However, if one reads the literature on risk, one would leave with the impression that if you are White, middle- or upper-middle-class, without a physical or mental disability, then your life is normal and without risk. Risk in the academy is what people of color face.

Spencer (1987, 1995, 1999, 2000) has developed a framework for analyzing how the experience and perception of risk are associated with identity development across the life course. She argues that the phenomenological experience of risk is what is paramount; what people perceive to be threatening is what is important. Spencer calls this frame Phenomenological Variant of Ecological Systems Theory (PVEST). In the PVEST model, net vulnerability level derives from the nature of risks in the environment and protective factors. Risks can result from such factors as body type, poverty, health status, gender, and challenging relationships. Such risks can be at the level of the individual or the group (such as the family, the neighborhood, social networks). The source of some risks may be macrolevel policies such as welfare or penal policies that affect some groups and some individuals within groups more than others. Protective factors can include forms of cultural socialization, social networks, and organizational resources. As with risk factors, protective factors can be at the individual or the group level and can emerge in light of macrolevel policies. However, levels of vulnerability do not directly predict how people make sense of and respond to that which makes them vulnerable. James Comer is a distinguished psychologist who grew up in a very large and economically poor family in Indiana during the era of Jim Crow segregation (Anson, Cook, & Habib, 1991; Comer, 1988a, 1988b; Haynes & Comer, 1993). Despite growing up under difficult circumstances, he and all of his siblings went to college. Comer is the founder of the Comer Project, which itself is an excellent example of an educational intervention that addresses the developmental needs of underserved students. Spencer (1999) refers to *net stress* as how people make sense of and respond to *net vulnerability* levels. The experience of stress is based on perceptions that are influenced by the quality of challenges posed and the nature of social supports available to deal with the risk. In reading Comer's biography of his family, *Maggie's Dream*, it is clear that James Comer (1988b) had resources to help him adapt in productive ways to the very real risks posed by the environment of his growing up. Spencer says that people develop patterned ways of responding to their perceptions of risk (i.e., what she calls "reactive coping strategies") that over time become part of an emerging identity which can lead to either productive or unproductive outcomes. I have found the PVEST framework extremely important in the evolution of the design of the Cultural Modeling framework. When I first began conceptualizing Cultural Modeling, I focused on the structure of academic domains and cultural displays of knowledge. However, when I began teaching the Cultural Modeling curriculum on response to literature at Fairgate High School, I realized that the framework had to address the developmental as well as the cognitive needs of students. PVEST has become very instrumental as a lens for thinking about the range of needs that any intervention needs to take into account.

In the chapters that follow, I will illustrate how the organization of instruction in Cultural Modeling classrooms structures supports that reduce risks students face as they engage in new and challenging academic tasks. Understanding the dimensions of risk in a generic sense for this population is a crucial task for teachers, administrators, curriculum designers, and policy makers. The students I will describe are African American, primarily from low-income urban neighborhoods. They largely have histories of low academic achievement as represented by standardized test scores in reading. By most demographic measures, these characteristics place them at risk. The scenarios presented in the Introduction certainly reflect some of the risks they faced. These are adolescents—freshmen struggling with the transitions from elementary to high school, seniors struggling with the transitions from high school to the world of adulthood. We know adolescence is a period in the life course where youngsters are wrestling with consolidating identities and establishing long-term goals. These identities include managing friendships and intimate and sometimes sexual relationships, consolidating their identities as competent learners in different domains in conjunction with establishing long-term goals for work and self-sufficiency.

There are also gender-related identities and risks. For girls, identity development includes risks associated with pregnancy, predatory relationships with males, problems figuring out the basis for their sense of self (physical beauty, outgoing personality, academic achievement, and so on), often influenced by how others respond to them. For males, particularly African American adolescent males, there are issues related to figuring out the basis on which their sense of being a man will be based (physical attractiveness, physical prowess, assertive personality, academic achievement). An African American adolescent male living in a low-income community and attending an underachieving large urban high school is likely to experience both direct and indirect violence, exposure and/or involvement at some level in the criminal justice system, disciplinary problems within the school, and pressure from peers for antisocial behavior and gang involvement.

In addition, because many of the students in our sample have long histories of underachievement or low academic achievement, the demands of high school work are challenging. The content of high school subjects tends to be far removed from everyday experience, certainly the everyday experiences of these students. Two large challenges increase the likelihood that students will not have well-developed identities as competent academic learners: repeated failure or mediocre success in school generally, and subject matter learning goals that are difficult to connect to their lived experiences or hopes for the future. On top of this, in the organizational structure of high schools, multiple teachers often place differential demands for successful participation in classrooms. Under these conditions, learning to be academically successful in high school is not an easy task to manage.

Through a combination of content selection and sequencing, participant structures, and scaffolds, Cultural Modeling aims to provide instructional organization that makes academic concepts, strategies, and habits of mind explicit, that makes ways of engaging in the work of the disciplines familiar, and that provides supports for instances when the learner is unsure. Cultural Modeling provides such structures in ways that explicitly and in detail take into account cultural practices, cultural ways of talking, cultural schemas and belief systems of students who are not White and middle class. I hope in this book to provide a detailed lens to see what such cultural displays of understanding look like, what such culturally responsive structures for learning look like, the kind of understanding that such environments make possible, and the quality and scope of knowledge required for teachers to manage such learning. I will situate these examples in the domain of response to literature with a population of African American adolescents. Both the domain and the population make good cases for several reasons. First, the domain of response to literature at the secondary level is highly underspecified, especially in terms of addressing the needs of underachieving adolescents who enter high school as struggling readers. Second, the problems of African American students, especially those living in low-income communities and attending underachieving urban schools, are devastating and highly represented in the educational literature. Third, African Americans historically and in current times face monumental challenges outside of school due to the persistence of structural and institutionalized racism (Anderson, 1988; Ball, 2002; Bennett, 1964; Bond, 1935; Bowles & Gintis, 1976; DuBois, 1973; DuBois & Dill, 1911; Dundes, 1972; Harding, 1981; Ladson-Billings & Tate, 1995; Lee & Slaughter-Defoe, 1995; Walters, 2003). While I use this domain and population as the exemplar, I argue that the principles that can be gleaned from this book apply (in different ways) to different subject matters, different age groups, and different ethnic populations.

CHAPTER **2**

Modeling as a Multidimensional Cultural Space

In any school setting, learning should be a safe space. Safety here involves more than a lack of violence. As safe spaces, schools and classrooms create environments in which students understand what they are to do, see the work of schooling as relevant to some goals, are able to develop meaningful goals they could not achieve on their own, and are willing to take risks to learn tasks that are difficult. Based on these criteria for safe environments in schools and classrooms, outcome data clearly indicate that most urban schools serving largely low-income and minority students are neither physically nor intellectually and socially safe spaces. The statistics I cite below are indicators of the general milieu of life and schooling that too many of our youngsters face.

The Children's Defense Fund report for 2006 highlights the problems of violence involving children. In 2002 some 2,867 children and teens died from gunfire. The report offers the following stark statistics:

- Firearms are the second leading cause of death among 10- to 19-year-olds, after motor vehicle accidents
- Among children and teens, Blacks are more likely to be victims of firearm homicide and Whites are more likely to commit suicide
- The firearm death rate for Black males ages 15–29 is almost four times that of White males ages 15–19
- The rate of firearm deaths among children under 15 is far higher in the United States than in 25 other industrialized countries *combined* (Children's Defense Fund, 2006, p. 2)

High school dropout rates are another indicator that our high schools are often not spaces of intellectual safety. According to a 2004 National Center for Education Statistics (NCES) report, in 2001, 27% of Latinos, 10.9% of Blacks, and 7.3% of Whites between the ages of 16 and 24 were

31

not enrolled in high school and lacked a high school credential, either diploma or GED (Kaufman, Alt, & Chapman, 2004). During that same year, 43.4% of Latinos between the ages of 16 and 24 who were born out of the United States were high school dropouts. Disaggregated figures are not offered in the report for American Indians because of the small sample size in the data set used. However, Table 2.1, from the report *Losing Our Future: How Minority Youth Are Being Left Behind in the Graduation Rate Crisis* (Orfield, Losen, Wald, & Swanson, 2004), reveals that the picture is much more dire than the NCES report acknowledges. These patterns hold for the vast majority of states. These discrepancies in graduation rates are consistently predictable by the percentage of racial minorities and students on free or reduced lunch in a district. Districts in central cities consistently have much lower overall graduation rates compared to suburbs and rural areas.

Another indicator of the paucity of intellectual rigor in high schools is the percentage of 12th grade students who take Advanced Placement (AP) courses. Figure 2.1, from the U.S. Department of Education, shows the continuing trend in discrepancies based on race and ethnicity from 1999 to 2003.

Students who enter high school with long histories of underachievement often have internalized expectations for what schooling is that are not a useful foundation for complex learning. The practices of classrooms characterized by low expectations are well represented in the research literature (Anyon, 1980, 1981; Guiton & Oakes, 1995; Jimerson, Egeland, & Teo, 1999; Kozol, 1991; McDermott, 1987; McLaren, 1989; National Commission on Excellence in Education, 1983; Oakes, 1990; Oakes et al., 1992; Urban League, 1999). Low-level questioning, use of worksheets that ask

Table 2.1. National Graduation Rates By Race and Gender

By Race/Ethnicity	Nation	Female	Male
American Indian	51.1	51.4	47
Asian/Pacific Islander	76.8	80	72.6
Hispanic	53.2	58.5	48
Black	50.2	56.2	42.8
White	74.9	77	70.8
All Students	68	72	64.1

Source: Orfield, Losen, Wald, & Swanson, 2004, p. 2. Reprinted with permission of the Civil Rights Project at Harvard University.

Figure 2.1. Percentage of 12th Graders Who Took Advanced Placement (AP) Examinations from 1999 to 2003 by Race and Ethnicity

Race/ethnicity	1999	2000	2001	2002	2003
White, non-Hispanic	67.08%	69.32%	68.74%	68.60%	68.26%
Black, non-Hispanic	4.85%	5.14%	5.16%	5.24%	5.45%
Hispanic	8.16%	8.89%	9.19%	9.40%	10.04%
Asian/Asian American	10.64%	10.97%	10.93%	10.90%	10.78%
American Indian/ Alaska Native	0.48%	0.47%	0.44%	0.44%	0.45%
Total Number of Students	349,300	378,540	407,572	440,916	470,398

Note: Total number of students includes racial and ethnic groups not shown in categories listed.

Source: Adapted from data available from the College Board; Advanced Placement Program; *National Summary Report,* 1999 to 2003; and the U.S. Department of Education, National Center for Education Statistics.

only for factual information, inauthentic tasks, direct instruction, and basic skills orientations are the norm. At the same time, suddenly moving from years of basic skills to instruction that is oriented to rigorous problem solving is not easy to accomplish.

Some states, such as Maryland, have switched to more authentic forms of assessment with the assumption that this change would influence the quality of instruction in the state's schools. The problem, however, is not whether basic skills or instruction oriented toward problem solving is better or worse for students with histories of academic underachievement. Rather, there are more foundational questions: What routines can socialize students into being more disposed to persist in the face of difficulty and uncertainty? Regarding a target task to be learned, what are important relationships between facts that are memorized and the ability to recognize patterns that are not obvious but are necessary in the ability to tackle a complex problem? I assume that elements of a direct instruction and basic skills orientation are necessary for learning complex problem solving reflected in most reform curricula. At the same time, I am convinced that a direct instruction and basic skills orientation is totally insufficient. Understanding what aspects of problem solving to make explicit and how to do so continues to be thorny. As the old folks say, the devil is in the details.

Cultural Modeling as a design framework aims to structure learning environments in ways that accomplish the following objectives:

- Socialize epistemological stances toward problem solving that are fundamental to the discipline.

- Focus on the kinds of problems that are generative, in the sense that they have a big bang for the buck; what you can do with this knowledge goes beyond the particular kind of problem being taught.
- Help students draw productively on prior knowledge in order to solve new problems.
- Make strategies for solving complex problems explicit.
- Create routines for face-to-face interactions that create meaningful problem-solving roles for students and a variety of safety nets that encourage them to take intellectual risks.

LEVERAGING EVERYDAY KNOWLEDGE

To accomplish the ends stated above, instruction must be based on curricula that capture what is important to know in the subject matter. In particular, curriculum designers and teachers must have detailed knowledge of the subject matter as well as detailed knowledge of the routine practices in which students engage with their families and peers, and in institutional settings outside of school, along with the belief systems inherent in such practices. Luis Moll calls this understanding the "cultural funds of knowledge" students experience outside of school (Mercado & Moll, 1997; Moll & Gonzáles, 2004; Moll & Greenberg, 1990). The Cultural Modeling framework, however, differs from the Funds of Knowledge framework in several ways. The Funds of Knowledge framework focuses largely on practices of adults in a community, examining the cognitive workload in such practices. The goal is to understand how youth's peripheral participation in these practices can be recruited to support school-based learning. There is a strong emphasis in the Funds of Knowledge Project on working with parents and other adults in a community as important resources for learning in school, including bringing them into the classrooms. There is an additional focus on teachers coming to learn about resources available to their students by physically coming into communities and homes as a way of understanding the social ecologies of students' lives, in particular the resources made available for learning from the social networks of which the families are a part.

My conceptualization of Cultural Modeling has been greatly influenced by the groundbreaking work of the Funds of Knowledge Project. However, the Cultural Modeling framework brings a related but somewhat different set of foci. *First, Cultural Modeling concentrates on the practices in which the youth directly engage out of school, not so much ones for which they are peripheral participants in the activities of adults.* Luis Moll (personal communication) has recently commented that one of the things he wants to do in future work of the Funds of Knowledge Project is to examine the practices of youth themselves, what Thorne (2003) calls the social world of children. *A second intent focus of Cultural Modeling is to address the specific and very different demands of subject matter learning.* This requires not only detailed maps of disciplinary domains, but also a careful analysis of the practices of youth culture. The work of Marta Civil (2006) and colleagues in the Funds of Knowledge Project in mathematics has been one important contribution of this work in terms of subject matter learning.

In order for teachers to be able to see how drawing on cultural funds of knowledge may be useful, they must be attuned to seeing where connections between everyday knowledge and school-based knowledge are most fruitful and for what ends. In addition, they must be astute enough to see in the moment-to-moment performances in the classroom what emergent understandings—sometimes in the form of misconceptions—reveal about what students understand about the topics and kinds of problem solving being taught. This is never easy because students often do not present such emergent understandings in the syntactic forms that teachers expect. Students who do not speak academic English or for whom English is a second language may offer explanations that do not take the form of statements of abstraction that are expected in school.

In Cultural Modeling, the first phase of instruction always involves the use of what we call *cultural data sets*. The examination of such cultural data sets provides opportunities to model what expert thinking looks like. These cultural data sets provide problems whose solutions mirror the demands of the academic task we want students to learn. The examination of cultural data sets provides familiar models on which new learning can be anchored (Clement, 1993; Clement, Brown, & Zietsman, 1989). If we take a purely cognitive view, principled examinations of cultural data sets help students to create connections between the known and the unknown. We know that the brain consists of expansive neural networks. Making connections across relevant schemata or clusters of schematic networks enhance the range of contexts and kinds of problems that one can tackle more efficiently. Making such connections also potentially lessens the divide between the world of schooling and lives of students in their families and communities.

The challenge is to select highly generative cultural data sets and not to trivialize making connections between everyday knowledge and school-based knowledge. This task is made more challenging when teachers and curriculum designers must overcome deficit assumptions about the nature of routine practices and attendant belief systems of students from African American, Latino, American Indian, Asian American/Pacific Islanders, and generally low-income communities, particularly those communities who experience persistent intergenerational poverty. It means deconstructing colonizing mentalities and ethnocentric assumptions. It further means that teachers and curriculum designers must develop what LiPing Ma (1999) calls a "profound understanding" of the fundamental principles that under-lie the subject matter. In mathematics, Ma (1999) calls this a "profound understanding of fundamental mathematics."

PEDAGOGICAL KNOWLEDGE OF ACADEMIC DISCIPLINES

For exemplars of profound ways of thinking about learning and teaching subject matter, I turn to mathematics education. Then I look for parallels to learning and teaching response to literature. In arithmetic, knowledge of basic skills includes number facts, procedures for basic operations of addition, subtraction, multiplication, and division. As decontextualized problems, memorizing number facts and operational procedures are efficient and can result in computation that is accurate and fast. In response to literature, learning such declarative and procedural knowledge might include the following: definitions of literary techniques such as onomatopoeia and alliteration; historical facts about the period in which a literary work was written or the setting of such a work; definitions of such elements of the short story as complicating action, rising action, denouement, characterization, and setting. In both the mathematics and the response to literature examples, the knowledge to be learned is important. It can be learned through memorizing and repetition. While such knowledge is important and in some respects could be viewed as foundational, it is clearly not sufficient for solving complex problems. According to Resnick (1987), *complex problems* are ones for which the solution path cannot be fully specified in advance and for which there may not be simple right and wrong answers.

Mathematics Case

In mathematics, even in elementary arithmetic, complex problems may not be so easy to understand. In a brilliant discussion of complex problem solving, Schoenfeld (1998) describes a problem given to an array of groups, including one of highly knowledgeable adults (see Figure 2.2). In many respects it is a fairly straightforward problem, which one would not view as being particularly complex. As is the case with most problems in mathematics, there is a correct answer. However, Schoenfeld describes at least four solution paths for this problem:

Figure 2.2. Mathematics Problem Used to Elicit Expert Reasoning

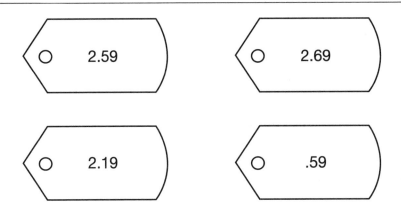

These are the price tags attached to four items you would like to purchase.

Can you make the purchase if you have $7.00 in cash?

Source: Schoenfeld, 1998, p. 303. Reprinted with permission from Lawrence Erlbaum Associates.

1. Add each quantity in sequence: $2.59 + $2.19 + $2.69 + $.59 = $8.06
2. Add one item at a time, starting with the most expensive, and stopping when the subtotal exceeds $7.00.
3. Approximate, first using the whole dollar amounts, which equal $6.00, and then noting through simple approximation that the change exceeds $1.00.
4. Note that two of the items cost more than $2.50 (i.e., $2.59 and $2.69), equaling more than $5.00; so that the next large item will bring the total beyond the $7.00.

Solutions 1 and 2 are procedures typically taught in the arithmetic curriculum. They yield a correct answer from fairly straightforward procedures, although one could argue that the computations involved in such straightforward addition involving carrying across three place values is usually difficult for young children. That may in part be because addition involving carrying across several place values is generally taught as procedures. LiPing Ma's (1999) discussion of such problems demonstrates quite powerfully that to teach carrying in addition and borrowing in subtraction conceptually involves quite rigorous fundamental principles in mathematics, principles that apply to problems beyond simple addition and subtraction. Ma notes,

> Here is a very interesting difference in understanding between the two countries [China and the United States]. In the United States, problems like "5 + 7 = 12" or "12 − 7 = 5" are considered "basic arithmetic facts" for students simply to memorize. In China, however, they are considered problems of "addition with composing and subtraction with decomposing within 20." (p. 16)

Aki Murata explains this conceptual understanding of composing and decomposing within 20 as follows:

> In many Asian countries, for very early number learning, children learn to see and use different chunks within a number. What is particularly important is their emphasis on 10, and children learn to use number partners that make 10 (e.g., 8 and 2, 7 and 3) through different conceptual activities. Using that understanding, when adding and subtracting with totals under 20, children decompose and recompose these "10" partners freely to make a teen number as 10 + another number. For the example above, if the problem 5 + 7 is presented, a child may think 5's partner to make 10 is 5, therefore decompose 7 into 5 and 2, add 5 and 5 together to make 10 and add the 10 and 2 to make 12 (ten-two). For subtraction, similarly, for the problem 12 − 7, a child will think 7's partner to make 10 is 3, therefore decompose 12 into 10 and 2, decompose the 10 into 7 and 3, take 7 away, and add the final two numbers 2 and 3 to find the answer 5. The Chinese language gives implicit support for this thinking as teen numbers are said, "ten-one, ten-two, ten-three" (for 11, 12, 13). This idea of "10" partners will support children's understanding and fluency development as they learn to add and subtract multidigit numbers in the upper grades when they "carry" and "borrow" numbers across different places. (personal communication October 4, 2005)

This pedagogical routine of composing and decomposing operations within 20 represents and promotes a flexible conceptual understanding that moves beyond simple procedures. It provides evidence that flexible conceptual understanding can be explicitly taught (Murata, 2004; Murata & Fuson, in press).

In respect to the original problem in Figure 2.2, Schoenfeld (1998) found that the mathematically adept adults typically used either Solutions 3 or 4. He notes that these are not procedures that are generally taught in the arithmetic curriculum and argues that these adults invented their solutions:

> Methods 3 and 4 are not taught in standard instruction. . . . Each of the mathematically sophisticated adults had, in essence, invented those procedures for him or herself. The invention came as a result of experience with the do-

main. . . . Hence, real expertise, even in domains as simple as that of whole number arithmetic, constitutes a progression from reliance on instructed procedures to the development of personal, flexible, and idiosyncratic methods. It also involves the development of and access to multiple methods. . . . Those who are really good at a task are not simply mechanically good. They do not do the same thing over and over the same way, but have access to a range of methods they can use and may not distinguish among those methods unless the context calls for it. . . . Second . . . features of the materials at hand may have alerted the (knowledgeable) problem solvers to ways of proceeding. This perception of features—or, more precisely, the fact that the features become salient and suggest a particular utilization for the task at hand—is, quite likely, task and context dependent. (p. 304)

In this chapter I demonstrate what I believe are the antecedents to the kind of invention Schoenfeld (1998) describes and illustrate the evolution of such competencies through what happens in the modeling phase of instruction based on Cultural Modeling. Through this book, I illustrate core principles of learning in relation to a specific domain—namely, response to literature—and with respect to a particular population of students—namely, African American adolescents, typically speakers of African American English with histories of low academic achievement—while I continue to argue that the broad principles apply beyond this domain and this group of students.

Schoenfeld (1998) has argued that these mathematically adept adults invented flexible procedures "as a result of experience within the domain . . . a progression from reliance on instructed procedures to the development of personal, flexible, and idiosyncratic methods" (p. 304). I suspect that these adults are persons with a history of high achievement in mathematics, and with that a long-standing sense of efficacy and a sense of personal attachment to the subject matter. Thus their long experience in the domain would be of a particular quality. It was likely that the experience of instruction that started with direct instruction in procedures was always accompanied by explorations of why the procedure was used, what was the essential logic of the procedure, and how a given procedure was related to other relevant procedures. It is likely that these adults also experienced the mathematics curriculum as one of constant efforts to make sense, one of examining alternative explanations and alternative solution paths. Such experiences repeated over the course of many years are likely to socialize participants into a particular kind of epistemological stance. Such an epistemological stance values uncertainty, asking questions, and considering alternative positions (Collins & Ferguson, 1993). It is a stance that fundamentally argues that knowledge is constructed through effort. It is fundamentally different from repeated experience with direct instruction in basic skills that creates an environment that communicates that finding the right answer is paramount, that the sources of truth are in teachers and textbooks rather than a child's mind, and that following prescribed procedures is the way to solve problems.

While there is clear evidence that direct instruction has resulted in high levels of achievement on basic skills standardized tests (Adams & Engelmann, 1996; Baumann, 1984; Gersten & Keating, 1987a, 1987b; Gersten, Keating, & Becker, 1988), it has also had the result of socializing hundreds of thousands of students from low-income communities into kinds of thinking that in the long run hinder their abilities to thrive in school communities that privilege complex reasoning. In a highly prestigious research university, the first African American female to be admitted to the Ph.D. program in mathematics flunked her qualifying exam. After taking courses on theories of learning, she came to reflect on why she had such difficulty in the Ph.D. program in mathematics. In classes, she would use the ways of solving problems that had earned her success in elementary and high school, as well as in both her undergraduate and master's level work at a well-respected historically Black college. She would study textbook solutions and work and rework through prescribed procedures until she achieved the correct answer, which she verified from the back of the textbook. However, the Ph.D program in mathematics privileged a very different orientation to thinking about mathematical problems.

Literary Reasoning Case

Schoenfeld's (1998) observation that "those who are really good at a task are not simply mechanically good . . . but have access to a range of methods they can use" (p. 304) suggests that a fundamental object of instruction is to learn to weigh the affordances and constraints of multiple methods in relation to types of problems. If I try to apply this line of reasoning to the domain of response to literature, I must wrestle with the question of what types of problems students might expect to meet in the range of courses from thematic, genre focused, or chronological literature courses in the typical high school curriculum. It is interesting that questions of types of problems students will meet in learning to interpret canonical works of literature in the high school curriculum are typically not on the agenda of literacy researchers or designers of curriculum and literature anthologies for use in high schools. Earlier researchers such as George Hillocks (Smith & Hillocks, 1988), Alan Purves (1991) and Arthur Applebee (Applebee, Burroughs, & Stevens, 2000) did hypothesize about the kinds of knowledge students needed to interpret literature. Researchers in early literacy have articulated in some detail the kinds of problems young children will meet as they learn to read: problems of phonemic awareness, word recognition, vocabulary, making inferences, and understanding story grammars (Snow, Burns, & Griffin, 1998).

With little empirical evidence, policy makers and school systems want to claim that the low scores in reading comprehension on standardized tests with which too many ninth graders enter high school is evidence that these young people "can't read." Data from the National Assessment of Educational Progress (NAEP) show relative stability in the scores of 13-year-olds over the last 3 decades (Perle et al., 2005). While there has been a trend in reducing the gap between Black and White 13-year-olds between 1971 and 2004, the Black–White gap has been persistent. In 2004, there was a 22-point gap between Blacks and Whites, with Whites averaging a score of 266 and Blacks averaging 244. For Latino students, there is a 21-point gap. These represent qualitatively different levels of reading comprehension according to NAEP performance levels. Figure 2.3 describes NAEP's description of performance levels.

Typically, few students score at levels of 350 or above at any grade level. Only 13% of 13-year-olds and 6% of 17-year-olds scored at levels of 350 or above. For 13-year-olds, the average score of 266 for White students places them as just above a level of being able to interrelate ideas and make generalizations. The score for Blacks of 244 places them as a group below this level of reading ability.

By "can't read," the public and many educators typically mean students have fundamental problems in phonemic awareness, word recognition, vocabulary, and fluency. For students entering high school with reading comprehension scores below fifth grade, this is likely the case. However, this is not the typical case. More low-achieving ninth graders enter high school with grade-level reading scores between sixth and eighth grade levels. This is largely due to heightened accountability measures in most districts and states, including the impact of the No Child Left Behind legislation. Their problems are more complex than simple decoding and word recognition. Vocabulary, on the other hand, is a significant and reliable indicator of comprehension. In addition, formal knowledge of written English syntax is an important stumbling block for many youngsters. With these caveats in mind, the knowledge base needed to tackle complex works of literature cannot be reduced to word recognition and fluency. It is clear from NAEP data for 17-year-olds that even students who are clearly fluent have serious problems understanding complex reading materials across genres and content areas. Among 17-year-olds, the average score in 2004 was 293. The difference between Black and White achievement is even greater for 17-year-olds than 13-year-olds, which suggests that high schools do little to contribute to the academic development in reading of Black

Figure 2.3. NAEP Performance Levels for Reading

LEVEL 350: Learn from Specialized Reading Materials

Readers at this level can extend and restructure the ideas presented in specialized and complex texts. Examples include scientific materials, literary essays, and historical documents. Readers are also able to understand the links between ideas, even when those links are not explicitly stated, and to make appropriate generalizations. Performance at this level suggests the ability to synthesize and learn from specialized reading materials.

LEVEL 300: Understand Complicated Information

Readers at this level can understand complicated literary and informational passages, including material about topics they study at school. They can also analyze and integrate less familiar material about topics they study at school as well as provide reactions to and explanations of the text as a whole. Performance at this level suggests the ability to find, understand, summarize, and explain relatively complicated information.

LEVEL 250: Interrelate Ideas and Make Generalizations

Readers at this level use intermediate skills and strategies to search for, locate, and organize the information they find in relatively lengthy passages and can recognize paraphrases of what they have read. They can also make inferences and reach generalizations about main ideas and the author's purpose from passages dealing with literature, science, and social studies. Performance at this level suggests the ability to search for specific information, interrelate ideas, and make generalizations.

LEVEL 200: Demonstrate Partially Developed Skills and Understanding

Readers at this level can locate and identify facts from simple informational paragraphs, stories, and news articles. In addition, they can combine ideas and make inferences based on short, uncomplicated passages. Performance at this level suggests the ability to understand specific or sequentially related information.

LEVEL 150: Carry Out Simple, Discrete Reading Tasks

Readers at this level can follow brief written directions. They can also select words, phrases, or sentences to describe a simple picture and can interpret simple written clues to identify a common object. Performance at this level suggests the ability to carry out simple, discrete reading tasks.

Source: Perle, Moran, Lutkas, & Tirre, 2005.

students. Seventeen-year-old Black students had an average score of 264, a difference of 29 points in contrast to a difference in 22 points for 13-year-olds. However, Table 2.2 shows that for intermediate levels of difficultly in texts the gap widens; but for the most complex texts (i.e., levels of 350 and above) few 17-year-olds appear capable of such rigorous reading.

Clearly, in the domain of response to literature, conceptualizing the demands of complex literary reading is crucial both for the struggling adolescent readers as well as their peers who are deemed to be better readers. In order to tackle complex canonical literary texts, novices need knowledge in four main areas: plot configurations, character types, archetypal themes, and interpretive problems. *Plot configurations* include typical ways authors organize the causal relationships that hold the events of the plot together, such as mysteries, trickster tales, and the bildungsroman or coming-of-age story. *Character types* capture the prototypical kinds of people readers meet in particular kinds of stories (i.e., plot configurations) and include the detective, the tragic hero, and the mythic hero. *Archetypal themes* include truth, courage, love, redemption, and coming-of-age. *Interpretive problems* include the typical kinds of conundrums readers will meet across a wide range of genres and national traditions: symbolism, irony, satire, and point of view. Each of these interpretive problems involves a disruption of the literal and typically, although not always, involves going beyond understanding the basic plot. Moreover, each of these interpretive problems has subcategories. For example, unreliable narration is only one way in which point of view can be expressed, and there are many reasons why a narrator may be unreliable—the narrator may be a first person character, or one who tells the story but is not a character in the plot. With irony, there is situational irony, dramatic irony, and verbal irony. Irony and satire are very interrelated. Satire may present itself as burlesque, as parody, as gentle humor or invective.

Table 2.2. 2004 NAEP Performance Levels in Reading for 17-Year-Olds by Race/Ethnicity

Performance Levels	Total	Whites	Blacks	Latino	Other	Black-White Gap
250 +	80%	86%	67%	64%	82%	19%
300 +	36%	45%	17%	20%	37%	28%
350 +	6%	7%	1%	2%	5%	6%

Source: Perle, Moran, Lutkas & Tirre, 2005.

Cognitive research discusses the need to characterize the "problem space," that is, to recognize what kind of problem is being presented in order to search long-term memory for knowledge of potentially relevant strategies or heuristics (Newell, 1980). In his description of mathematical problem solving, Schoenfeld (1998) says, "features of the materials at hand may have alerted the (knowledgeable) problem solvers to ways of proceeding. This perception of features—or, more precisely, the fact that the features become salient and suggest a particular utilization for the task at hand—is, quite likely, task and context dependent" (p. 304). The parallel in response to literature is the ability of the reader to recognize typical patterns, to perceive features that signify what Langer (1990) calls a "horizon of possibilities." Such meanings may be drawn from both the world of the text itself and other related texts, but also from the social and natural world outside of the text.

Thus I want to introduce the idea of *access to horizons of possible meanings*. Such access is enhanced by explicit teaching of the kinds of patterns novice readers may expect to encounter and available strategies and heuristics that may be drawn upon to engage the problems these patterns present. Cultural Modeling offers a framework for thinking about these problems in the design of instruction in ways that help students see generative connections between their prior knowledge and the new problems they will meet in the academic domain. How texts are sequenced within and across years of the high school curriculum is paramount if students are to learn to perceive typical patterns. A dose of symbolism at one point and a second dose months later is not an effective intervention.

Induction into the kind of problem solving I have described—recognizing patterns that signify typical types of problems—also involves being able to relate types of problems to strategies for tackling those problems. In mathematics education, this is fairly well specified. Typical instruction in the high school literature curricula, however, will superficially address these problems, but not in a way that helps students recognize patterns. This is in part because of how texts are sequenced. The typical freshman curricula will focus on a very limited conception of genres—types of poetry (sonnet, haiku, and so on), drama, the short story (labeling elements such as character development, setting, plot, and theme, or aspects of plots, such as rising action or complicating action, climax, and denouement). Studying these descriptive elements of genres does not really help novice readers make sense of literary works, but rather it typically leads to students' ability to name these elements. For example, students may learn to detect that a poem is a sonnet without understanding how knowledge of that form can help them understand the text better, as in recognizing that in a sonnet the author will often use the final couplet as a kind of summary or so-what statement. Or a student may recognize a pattern of onomatopoeia in a poem, but not understand how its use creates meaning. Even more important, these curricula ask students to solve problems, such as to describe the theme or explicate the symbolism in works of literature, but rarely provide students with any guidelines as to how to accomplish these tasks. The concept of flexible and multiple procedures or strategies for tackling problems is not evident in either the research, the curricula, or the textbooks.

I looked for places where students were asked to interpret such problems in the McDougal Littell high school literature anthology, *The Language of Literature: American Literature*, 1997. This anthology is considered by many as a reform-oriented series that encourages reader response and is organized to engage students in generic strategies for making sense while reading. Such strategies include asking questions, summarizing, and making predictions. At the elementary school level, these generic strategies are captured in Reciprocal Teaching (Palinscar & Brown, 1984), which has shown very powerful results in improving reading comprehension. While these generic strategies are useful and necessary, they are not sufficient for literary response. This is because particular kinds of questions are privileged in this domain and making predictions is predicated on knowledge of plot configurations, character types, and archetypal themes. For example, once you recognize that a novel is a mystery, you make predictions about the kinds of events to expect and the kinds of people who will inhabit this landscape. In addition, it is unlikely that these generic strategies will focus students' attention on recognizing problems of symbolism, irony, satire, and point of view as they present themselves across canonical works. Particularly for adolescent struggling readers, what I find most problematic is that students are asked to carry out tasks and solve particular kinds of problems with virtually no instruction as to how to go about doing it.

In this regard, consider the assignment for the Iroquois myth "The World on the Turtle's Back" in the *Language of Literature: American Literature* (1997):

> Have students go back through the selection and complete a chart like the one shown here. They can use the left-hand column to jot down objects, events, and characters that they think might be symbolic. In the right-hand column, they can jot down what they think the symbols represent. Emphasize that a symbol may have a variety of meanings. Then set up a chalkboard showing a master list of findings of the whole class. Have a class discussion about which symbols were most important to the overall meaning of the myth. (p. 25)

The problem with what students are asked to do in this assignment is that there are no provisions to help them to recognize when an object, event, action or description is likely literal or likely figurative. Second, there is no instruction about how to go about figuring out what the symbolism might mean once the reader recognizes that he or she should reject a literal interpretation. These are precisely what modeling in Cultural Modeling seeks to accomplish.

There are many attributes of this series that I like very much. There is a clear effort to include literature from diverse ethnic traditions as well as a positive emphasis on helping students make personal connections to the literature. There is a consistent focus on students' attending to when they do and do not understand. In addition, there are no literature anthologies that I know of that are used in the high school curricula that address the needs I have identified, with the possible exception of some of the attention to genre in literacy studies coming out of Australia (Callaghan, Knapp, & Noble, 1993; Callaghan & Rothery, 1988). These Australian studies focus on the functions of the structures of genres, both in terms of literary works as well as student composition.

The idea of teachers or other expert resources (such as software programs) modeling problem-solving strategies, heuristics, and ways of thinking is well-established in the research and pedagogical literature (Collins, Brown, & Newman, 1989; Collins, Brown, & Holum, 1991; Pea & Gomez, 1992; Scardamalia, Bereiter, & Steinbach, 1984; Schoenfeld, 1985; Teasley & Roschelle, 1993). For reading, perhaps the most well known and well documented example of modeling is Reciprocal Teaching (Palinscar & Brown, 1984). In Reciprocal Teaching, initially teachers and later students themselves model out loud what they are doing to make sense of a text, particularly in sections where, as readers, they are confused. The strategies modeled in Reciprocal Teaching include summarizing, making predictions, asking questions, and monitoring comprehension. These generic reading strategies are supported by a wide body of research (Alvermann & Moore, 1991; Pearson & Fielding, 1991; Pressley, 2000). However, Cultural Modeling in response to literature differs from both Reciprocal Teaching and other forms of modeling in several ways: First, Cultural Modeling focuses on discipline-specific kinds of problems and heuristics. Second, since most forms of modeling involve adults modeling for students, especially in the initial stages, such approaches do not usually involve what Moll (2000) calls "cultural funds of knowledge" from the everyday experiences of students, particularly when those everyday experiences and knowledge forms reflect ethnicity or racial identities. In Cultural Modeling, students assume the initial amd major roles for modeling.

In what follows, I will describe how literature units are organized in Cultural Modeling classrooms and how modeling occurs. In contrast to the typical sequence and foci of high school literature courses, Cultural Modeling is based on a reconceptualization of the domain of response to literature for high school novice readers. As I said earlier, the forms of knowledge that readers draw on to make sense of literary works include knowledge of archetypal themes, character types, plot configurations, and key interpretive problems. These forms of knowledge are interrelated. Readers draw flexibly across these kinds of knowledge as they are constructing what Langer (1990) calls a "horizon of possibilities." This horizon of possibilities is a source of predictions of what can happen, hypotheses against which we test the text. Knowledge in these arenas are not isolated facts, but rather configurations of patterns whose features we understand and detect. For instance, if we detect that something bad has happened and we need to find out who did it, we often match those details of the plot to our understanding of the mystery or detective story (i.e., plot configuration). On the basis of reading the plot as a mystery story, we expect certain plot elements to emerge and we expect to meet certain kinds of people, including the detective type. In many respects, our knowledge of plot configurations and character types helps us understand the unfolding of the plot and the internal state of the characters. The details of plot and characterization may be both stated and inferred. A literary reading often involves understanding meanings that are not explicitly stated. This is the terrain of what I have called "interpretive problems," where that which is not explicitly stated involves some reinterpretation of the literal, either through metaphorical attributions in addition to the literal or a reinterpretation that is in tension with or in contrast to the literal (Ortony, 1979; Winner, 1988).

As I said above, interpretive problems include the following families of constructs: symbolism, satire, irony, and point of view. Recognizing the patterned ways these problems present themselves and how they function in literary texts is an important part of the problem-solving tool kit of experienced readers. Symbolism, satire, and irony *all* require that readers reject a literal interpretation. Interpretations that add layers of meaning to the literal are symbolic. Interpretations that stand in contrast to or in tension with the literal may be satire, irony, or problems of unreliable narration. In contrast to most pedagogical approaches, Cultural Modeling articulates heuristics for detecting these interpretive problems and strategies for interpreting these problems. Just as mathematics educators focus on strategies for defining what the cognitive sciences call the "problem space" or on strategies for tackling particular kinds of problems, Cultural Modeling makes a similar case for the domain of response to literature.

What is interesting is that we meet these interpretive problems in our everyday experience. Literature is essentially narratives of personal experience. Turner (1996) has argued that facility in the creation of narratives is a prototypical capacity of the human brain. Bruner and others make the claim that humans construct narratives as a way of imposing meaning on experiences in the world (Bruner, 1990; Champion et al., 1995; Hymes & Cazden, 1980; Miller, Mintz, Hoogstra, Fung, & Potts, 1992; Miller, Wiley, Fung, & Liang, 1997; Nelson, 1989; Polkinghorne, 1988; Scollon & Scollon, 1981; Sperry & Sperry, 1996). Young children and elders across human history and human cultures create and respond to narratives of personal experience. However, the structure of narratives, the functions they serve, the archetypal themes they embody, and the character types who people them will differ by cultural communities and historical contexts. It is not uncommon for authors of canonical literatures to draw in creative ways on scenarios of human experience and ways of using language from the everyday lives of common folk, or what may be termed by some the *vernacular*.

Literature is a generative ground for the marriage of the everyday and the canonical. Gabriel Marquez has said that his writings in the genre of magical realism reflect the stories he heard from his grandmother, a blend of African and South American influences. Until he read the Jewish German writer Franz Kafka, he did not know that stories like his grandmother's could be written: "When I read that I said to myself, 'Holy shit! Nobody'd ever told me you could do this! That's how my grandma used to tell stories, the wildest things with a completely natural tone'" (quoted in Bell-Villada, 1990, pp. 72–73). Wayne Booth (1974) notes that irony can be heard in the streets of Bombay as well in the so-called ivory towers. The voices of vernacular languages abound in writers from almost every national tradition: from Zora Neale Hurston and Ralph Ellison in African American literature to Bernard Malamud and Chaim Potok in the Jewish tradition, to Federico García Lorca in Spanish national literature. Interestingly, Dante Alighieri in the early part of the fourteenth century wrote an essay arguing for the eloquence of the vernacular in literature, *De Vulgari Eloquentia*, making the case for moving beyond the scholastic tradition of only writing in Latin (Dante Alighieri, trans. 1996). In African American literature, the issue of the vernacular in literature is complex, involving not only uses of dialect by writers such as Paul Laurence Dunbar, Sterling Brown, Langston Hughes, and Zora Neale Hurston, but also the structural manifestations of jazz and blues motifs in the works of writers such as Jean Toomer, Ralph Ellison, and Amiri Baraka, as well as the incorporation of folk motives as in Toni Morrison's *Song of Solomon* (G. Jones, 1991). The Black Arts Movement of the 1970s was very much centered on using vernacular language and African American oral and music traditions in literature (Gabbin, 2004; Neal, 1989).

In order for students to build a cohesive body of knowledge about character types, configurations of plot, archetypal themes, and interpretive problems, sequencing texts across the 4 years of the curriculum is of utmost importance. Smith and Hillocks (1988) refer to this as "sensible sequencing"; Applebee (1996) articulates this as coherent "curricular conversations." To learn to detect archetypal themes and understand the range of critical conversations about these themes, students must have repeated experience across the literature curriculum to explore a series of texts within a given unit of instruction where authors engage these themes. Similarly, students must have repeated experiences with texts that are clustered around prototypical configurations of plot. These include, but are not limited to, allegory, particular kinds of myths—such as creation myths—coming-of-age stories, science fiction, and mystery. A Cultural Modeling approach would pair exemplars of such genres from students' everyday experiences with film, television, music, and oral traditions.

To illustrate, a unit on symbolism will begin with rap lyrics (e.g., "The Mask" by the Fugees, 1996), rap videos (e.g., "I Used to Love H.E.R." by Common Sense, 1994) to be followed by the short story "Everyday Use" by Alice Walker (1994), the novel *Beloved* by Toni Morrison (1987), and then selections from *The Inferno* (Dante Alighieri, trans. 1995). The point is for students to be supported in examinations of the range of ways character types and plot configurations may present themselves, from cases that are prototypical to those that are unusual permutations of typical patterns. A basic aspect of all problem solving is *pattern recognition*. A focus on pattern recognition is not for the purpose of isolated description, but rather to help students understand what such patterns suggest to them about meaning: What do you expect to happen once you identify the pattern of unfolding early plot elements as evidence of a coming-of-age story? What do you expect a character will do and feel once you recognize that his early actions and feelings suggest a tragic hero?

The point is not simply to label, but rather to understand more deeply what is happening and what can be expected to happen as the story unfolds. It is important to note that sometimes an author will use conventions in order to tease the reader into a set of predictions that the author will subsequently turn around. To experience the aesthetic quality of surprise, one must first follow where the conventions would typically lead. For instance, all the character attributes of Madam Loisel in Maupassant's "The Necklace" (1992) would lead the reader to expect that the necklace she so coveted was made of expensive jewels. Thus only if one followed Maupassant's rhetorical sign posts would one be surprised at the end to discover the necklace is made of cheap fake jewels. It is through this twisting of expectations that Maupassant creates the irony of what she covets, an irony that constitutes one of the major themes, or what Hillocks (Hillocks & Ludlow, 1984) calls "author's generalizations" (i.e., something the author is saying about the world beyond the text).

Because more has been written about archetypal theme, character type, and plot configurations, I will illustrate Cultural Modeling by focusing on an interpretive problem, and I will illustrate teachable heuristics for detecting and making sense of these interpretive problems. These interpretive problems invite a quality of reasoning that is particularly literary, the terrain on which the flirtations with language play take place, the muddy waters in which literary criticism loves to waddle. It is perhaps the practice that most reveals membership in a worldwide club of lovers of literature, particularly lovers of the canons that can be found in all national literatures. This is the club to which I want most to lure students. Loving to play this game links readers to rich books across a lifetime. By contrast, the net impact for most students—whether in wealthy suburban or low-income urban high schools—is that they learn to hate the literature that English teachers most want them to love. The classrooms that I will describe are ones in which passionate debates about the meaning of symbols and satire abound, in which students feel a deep compulsion to make their interpretations public, and in which the norms for literary arguments are rooted in textual and worldly warrants.

One can identify heuristics for each of the kinds of interpretive problems I have listed. Wayne Booth (1974; 1983) and Michael Smith (1991) have deconstructed the processes for detecting and interpreting both irony and use of unreliable narration. Smith has demonstrated that whether teaching these strategies for irony and unreliable narration are explicit (telling students the rules) or indirect (helping students infer the rules), students are better able to interpret these problems as a result of such instruction. Through a synthesis of literary theory regarding satire, the Cultural Modeling research group has developed a domain map for satire. Based on that domain map, the group developed the strategy described in Figure 2.4 for detecting satire and for reconstructing a warrantable set of claims about the object of the satire.

These "rules of notice," as Rabinowitz (1987) calls them, are teachable. They apply to satire in literature, in essays, in rap lyrics, in film, and in television. We also identified exemplars of kinds of texts—everyday popular texts and literary canonical texts from African American and other traditions—to which students could apply these strategies. Modeling instruction begins with the everyday texts and then moves on to those canonical texts in which the social world is one about which we anticipate students will have greater prior knowledge and then moves on to canonical texts that are further removed from students' prior knowledge and life experiences. Table 2.3 provides samples of selections we developed in 2003. Everyday texts would likely need updating if such a unit were designed today.

Figure 2.4. Rules of Notice for Satire

Satire

1. Notice discrepancies between real-world referent (event, person, institution, typical experience) and description or representation in the text.

   a. This act of noticing can be based on discrepancy between the reader's beliefs and those of a character, or between what the reader believes to be the belief, perspective, or moral stance of the author and that of a character.

2. Determine whether the source of the discrepancy is based on

   a. Exaggeration

   b. Understatement

   c. Humor

3. Is the direction of the exaggeration negative?

4. Based on the above, reason whether the goal of the satire is to

   a. Critique

   b. Make fun of

   c. Change a belief, policy, or an institution

Notes:

It is important to recognize potential relationships among interpretive problems. For example, irony, satire, and use of unreliable narration share similar rules of notice (that is, reasons to reject a literal interpretation). Thus readers face a decision tree once they determine that the literal should be rejected, that the direction of a constructed interpretation will be in contrast to or in tension with the literal; they must then distinguish whether the object of interpretation could be satire, irony, or use of unreliable narration. In addition, it is not uncommon for these three interpretive problems to present themselves together in a single work.

Like these other tropes, symbolism is pervasive in literature and in everyday narrative texts, including songs, film, television, rap videos, proverbs, traditional oral stories, and other genres of everyday talk. In literature, symbolism can be found in poems, plays, short stories, and novels, and across all national literatures. It is precisely because symbolism is prevalent in both everyday life and in canonical literature that Cultural Modeling can help students create linkages between the two. Anika Spratley (2005), a member of the Cultural Modeling research group, has extended my earlier work on heuristics for symbolism by developing a domain map of symbolism. Spratley's graphic, presented in Figure 2.5, is

Table 2.3. Cultural Data Sets and Canonical Works for Satire

Text	Satire
Non-African-American Canonical Works	Bradbury, Ray. (1950). There Will Come Soft Rains.
	Orwell, George. (1936). Shooting an Elephant.
	Orwell, George. (1931). A Hanging.
	Twain, Mark. (1905). The War Prayer.
	Buchwald, Art. For Want of a Teacher.
	White, E.B. (1951). Calculating Machine. In *The Second Tree from the Corner*.
	Swift, Jonathan. (1729). A Modest Proposal.
	Kafka, Franz. (1913). A Common Confusion. In *Meditation*.
	Donne, John. (1598). A Defense of Women's Inconstancy.
African-American Canonical Works	Hughes, Langston. (1961). *The Best of Simple*.
	Schuyler, George. (1931). *Black No More*.
	Reed, Ishmael. (1986). *Reckless Eyeballing*.
	Killens, John Oliver. (1971). *The Cotillion*.
Cultural Data Sets	Common and Q-Tip. (1996). The Remedy. On *Get on the Bus* soundtrack [CD].
	De la Soul. (1989). A Little Bit of Soap. On *3 Feet High and Rising* [CD].
	De la Soul. (1991). Who Do U Worship? On *De la Soul is Dead* [CD].
	Ice Cube. It Was a Good Day. On *The Predator* [CD].
	Ice Cube. (1993). Heaven. On *Lethal Injection* [CD].
	Dead Prez. (2000). Hip-Hop. On *Let's Get Free* [CD].
	MC Lyte. Poor Georgie. On *Act Like You Know* [CD].
	Murphy, Eddie. (1984). Black History Minute. *Saturday Night Live* [DVD].
	Bambi Meets Godzilla [DVD].
	Hollywood Shuffle [DVD].
	Rock, Chris. American Black Progress Charted [TV Episode].
	Mad TV. *No Blacks* [TV Episode].
	Boondocks [Cartoons].

useful for constraining the problem space. It helps us figure out what kind of problem we are meeting in a text, how it might look, what it might do, and where we might look for information to understand the problem. Such a fundamental understanding of the contours of symbolism as a kind of problem we will meet in texts is extraordinarily important. Spratley has used this model in assessing teachers' pedagogical content knowledge of symbolism in literature and in coding the moves made by readers to understand symbolism in literary works.

For purposes of detection, one strategy successfully used in Cultural Modeling classrooms has readers continue reading, filling in the goal structure of the plot as it unfolds, until they come to a stretch of text for which a literal interpretation seems insufficient. This is because the author has done a lot of work drawing our attention to the text. Some description, some object, some event, some action either is repeated a lot or a literal interpretation of it just seems out of place or not particularly believable. In addition, these details may be in a prominent position—a title, an opening, a closing—or are at a critical juncture or turn in the plot. According to these "rules of notice," the reader's attention is drawn to this part of the text.

Figure 2.5. Spratley's Graphic Representation of Symbolism in Texts. Reprinted with permission of Anika Spratley.

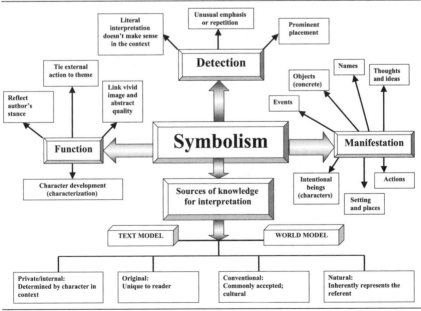

This toolkit of heuristics will suggest that a literal interpretation of this part of the text should be rejected and a figurative interpretation should be explored. This toolkit will also alert the reader that figuration can be in the form of symbolism (or simply metaphor), irony, or satire, or any of the members of the family of each of these tropes requiring a rejection of the literal. Both irony and satire will be based on some level of distrust of the characters or the narrator, but, if there is no reason to distrust the character or the narrator, symbolism may be a candidate.

There is another layer of heuristics that is necessary to tackle problems of symbolism beyond detection, manifestation, function, and sources of knowledge. Once detected, the reader needs strategies for figuring out its possible and warrantable meanings. These processes may be relatively automatic and unconscious for very experienced readers (Graves & Frederiksen, 1996); however, even very experienced readers meet texts with such novelty that they must engage in conscious metacognitive reflection about particular strategies that can help them figure out what is going on. Many readers have been in this position with James Joyce (1922/1993) *Ulysses* or Toni Morrison's (1987) *Beloved*. The strategy I describe here can be taught explicitly to novice readers, especially adolescent struggling readers, but used by more expert readers by simply engaging in a process of self-questioning (Scholes, 1985) that parallels what Figure 2.5 depicts. Once students determine that a stretch of text is both figurative and likely symbolic, they can create a table based on the model shown in Table 2.4. In the first column of the table, students identify the target image, event, character, or action that may be symbolic, using the rules of notice described under the headers "Detection" and "Manifestation" in Figure 2.5. This simply means students are thinking about where tropes may be found and how the tropes might present themselves in literary texts. In the second column of the table, students write down the location or the exact words of the text in which the symbolic target is represented. Such text may be localized in a paragraph or sentence or may be distributed across

Table 2.4. Heuristic for Tackling Localized Problems of Symbolism in Literature

Target	Textual Source	Associations	Generalization
Image, event, character, action	Text selections related to the target	Associations • Real-world • Personal • Textual Deconstruct possible elements or functions of the target	Warrantable interpretation of the symbol

a literary work. In the third column, students begin to brainstorm about associations they make with the target that is deemed possibly symbolic. These associations relate in the labels "Text Model" and "World Model" under "Sources of Knowledge" Spratley's graphic in Figure 2.5 (Kintsch, 1992, 1998; Kintsch & Greene, 1978). Students brainstorm both about real-world associations they make with the target (i.e., "World Model") and also with associations with other texts and authors, including other works by the same author (i.e., "Text Model"). Students then ask themselves what relationships can be drawn between their associations (worldly and textual) and the text. The goal is to infer what generalizations about a particular character, set of events, or the human condition may be warranted from the relationships articulated.

In Table 2.5, I illustrate how students in my senior English class at Fairgate used this heuristic to tackle a problem of symbolism in Toni Morrison's (1987) *Beloved*. This heuristic was originally used with the cultural data sets I have described in this chapter. The target was the image of the protagonist Sethe kneading dough in her kitchen while Paul D caressed the deep scars on her back. Sethe had not seen Paul D for 18 years since they were both enslaved persons on the plantation ironically called "Sweet Home." Using the rules of notice captured in Spratley's Figure 2.5 under the label "Detection," the students hypothesized that the excess detail describing a simple act of making biscuits warranted further attention than what a literal account would explain. In the second column they identify stretches of text in which Morrison creates close descriptions of the act of kneading the biscuit dough. In the third column students identify elements of the act of baking biscuits they felt might shed light on possible generalizations to be drawn about what this act of making biscuits says about the text, in this case the internal states of the two characters. They made real-world associations about each of these elements of baking biscuits. In the final column, they state generalizations they drew from their real-world associations about baking biscuits in terms of what those associations potentially revealed about what was going on internally—and within the context of the text symbolically—with Sethe and Paul D. These generalizations are complex and highly literary interpretations of a crucial symbolic act in this very difficult novel. This is an example of a *horizon of possibility*, which was accessible to these students because heuristics for identifying a possible problem and tackling its solution was an explicit foundation of instruction. This example illustrates what we are trying to accomplish in Cultural Modeling through the examination of cultural data sets.

Such reasoning can lead to what I call a *warrantable interpretation*. A warrantable interpretation is one for which the reader can support claims both from the text in question, knowledge of the world, and knowledge of this author, other authors, and other texts. This idea of a warrantable inter-

Table 2.5. Illustration of Symbolism Heuristic with Toni Morrison's *Beloved*

Notice patterns that signal an image, event, character, or action is not intended only as literal.	→	Identify and analyze **text selections** related to the target.	→	Brainstorm **associations** with the target: • Real world • Personal • Textual Deconstruct possible **elements or functions** of the target.	→	**Generalize** a proposition that is a warrantable interpretation of the symbol based on perceived relationships between target, text, and reader's associations.
Sethe kneading dough for biscuits Paul D massaging Sethe's breasts	→	"fat white circles of dough"	→	**Making Bread** *Ingredients:* Flour, milk, sugar, salt, butter, yeast *Process:* Kneading *Function:* Fill you up	→	**Making Bread and massaging breasts** *Ingredients:* White circles of dough remind us of Sethe's breasts Milk missing from her bread like the milk stolen from her in the rape. *Process:* Paul D massages Sethe's breasts like Sethe kneads the dough *Function:* Sethe kneads the dough to satisfy the hunger of her family (including Paul D), just like Paul D kneads Sethe's breasts to satisfy her need to feel better because of her devastating memories.

pretation is particularly important to the domain of response to literature. Claims about the elements of the plot of a narrative are fairly constrained by the text in terms of right and wrong answers. However, claims about internal states of characters, about goals of characters, about the themes of a work, and about what symbols, satire, irony, and point of view may mean in a text are not subject to simple right and wrong criteria (Fish, 1980; Tompkins, 1980), although typical standardized tests of reading comprehension that include literary samples often assume there are clearly right and wrong answers. I believe that this is one example of how schooling in the United States has very weak measures of competence in literary response [C.D. Lee, in press; Wolf, Bixby, Glenn, & Gardner, 1991]).

A fundamental precept in response to literature is that the reader brings as much to the text as the author, although the fields of literary theory and literary criticism have heated debates about the relative weight of influence of the author, text, and reader (Bloom et al., 1987). The most common claim is that readers bring to a text orientations that influence and constrain what sense they make of what the author provides as food. Peter Rabinowitz's (1987) book *Before Reading* is a rich description of the kind of knowledge readers bring to a text before ever picking up a given book. Applemann (2000) has demonstrated how high schools can teach students to read texts in ways that reflect major critical orientations, such as Reader Response, New Criticism, Feminist, Black Aesthetic, Deconstructionist, Marxist, Structuralist, and Poststructuralist. How to make complex processes explicit is a fundamental challenge of schooling. While important for all students, it is particularly imperative for schools serving students with histories of under achievement, a problem all too common for Black and Brown students and those from low-income communities. I have illustrated in this chapter how such complex problem-solving processes can be made explicit and public in the domain of response to literature. Current academic standards, curricula, and textbooks in response to literature simply do not make explicit how to go about tackling the complex problems readers will meet in canonical literature. I have further demonstrated how making problem solving explicit can and should go beyond the scope of what is typically viewed as direct instruction today, involving much more than memorization.

Making problem solving explicit and public serves more than a cognitive function. Engaging in acts of complex problem solving entail emotional and social commitments as well. Learning is optimized when students understand how to navigate such intellectual spaces and how exerting effort to make sense aligns with their personal goals and senses of identity. When students are grappling with the kinds of life challenges described in the Introduction, it is particularly important that teachers and curriculum designers consciously attend to these multiple, dynamically interrelated dimensions of learning.

CHAPTER 3

Modeling with Cultural Data Sets

In Cultural Modeling, units of instruction, organized around particular interpretive problems, begin with what I call *cultural data sets*. These are texts from students' everyday experience that pose a problem of interpretation similar to what students will meet in the canonical texts they will read. It is important that students experience the cultural data sets as a part of their routine practices outside of school. Generally, students have greater prior knowledge of such cultural data sets than teachers. Typically, cultural data sets represent practices and knowledge that schools not only devalue, but which schools have historically viewed as detrimental to academic progress. Since my work has been with African American students, cultural data sets have included R & B or rap lyrics, rap videos, stretches of signifying dialogues (a genre of talk in African American English Vernacular), as well as film clips and television programs.

The Cultural Modeling research group has made several interesting findings from using cultural data sets in this way. First, the students model for each other how they reason about the interpretive problem in question. The teacher then gives a language to the strategies, a metalanguage of problem solving that applies not only to the text in question but to many kinds of texts. Second, the level of reasoning is very high from the beginning of instruction. This is because they already use such reasoning in their everyday lives, but this knowledge is tacit. Because it is tacit, when they meet similar types of problems in other contexts, such as in canonical works of literature in their English language arts classrooms, they see no connections to what they already know and therefore do not tap into the relevant schemata or organized bodies of knowledge that can help them with the problem. This is the classic difficulty of what Whitehead (1929) called "inert knowledge." Third, the power relationships between students and the teacher about who can serve as authoritative knowledge sources is restructured from the very beginning of instruction. I will illustrate the first two findings in this chapter and the third finding in Chapter 4.

58

CULTURAL MODELING OF SYMBOLISM

In this section I describe a unit of instruction on symbolism, a Cultural Modeling unit taught to all senior English students at Fairgate High School. In each of the texts in the unit, a significant problem of symbolism arises. The symbolism in each text is not an isolated case, but rather is central to making sense of the text as a whole. The primary text is Toni Morrison's (1987) award-winning novel *Beloved*. *Beloved* is a complex novel for many reasons. For one thing, it includes an inverted chronology: Morrison will sometimes move through two time periods in the course of a single paragraph, and the markers for such transitions are rarely explicit. In addition, the novel is clearly in the tradition of magical realism. That means supernatural events occur, but are to be taken as real. They are not like events in horror movies, but rather are representative of cultural worldviews in which the world of spirits and of humans intersect in real ways. It is in this sense that *Beloved* is much more than a ghost story. There are also numerous shifts in point of view. The same event—such as the story of Denver's birth—will be told from more than one point of view. This variation in point of view is not an indicator of unreliability, but rather I think Morrison is saying to the reader that truth is never objective, but always captures multiple perspectives, each with different meanings to the people involved. Finally, the symbolism in *Beloved* is robust. Nearly every chapter poses several symbols that together intersect to carry the subtle themes of this monumental work.

Besides *Beloved*, the following texts were included in this extended unit on symbolism:

Short Stories / Chapters

- John Edgar Wideman. (1998). Damballah (from the novel *Damballah*).
- Jewelle Gomez (1991) "Louisiana" (from the novel *The Gilda Stories*).
- Stephen Crane (1895) "The Open Boat" (from *The Red Badge of Courage*).
- William Faulkner (1950) "A Rose for Emily."
- William Faulkner (1950) "Wash."
- Amy Tan. (1989). "Lena St. Clair: Rice Husband"; Ying-Ying St. Clair: Waiting Between the Trees" (from the novel *The Joy Luck Club*).
- Virginia Woolf (1972) "A Haunted House."

Poems

- Robert Hayden (1966) "Runnagate"
- Frances Harper (1854) "The Slave Mother"

- Emily Dickinson (1863) "Because I Could Not Stop for Death
- John Milton (1667) *Paradise Lost* (selections)
- Dante (1321) *Inferno* (selections)
- Robert Frost (1916) "The Road Not Taken"
- Dylan Thomas (1952) "Do Not Go Gentle Into That Good Night"

Novel

- Ralph Ellison (1933) *Invisible Man*

These are all very demanding texts. The first text taught was Wideman's (1998) "Damballah," from his novel *Damballah*. It shared many of the features of *Beloved*: inverted chronology, magical realism, symbolism, and one of the themes of *Beloved*, resistance to enslavement. After "Damballah," the students read *Beloved*. The texts read after *Beloved* not only presented complex problems of symbolism, but also themes that students met in *Beloved:* guilt, redemption, dilemmas that try the soul, the multiplicative consequences of racism, and complexities of what happens when different worldviews meet.

Note that this is a unit of instruction taught in a high school with a history of underachievement. The vast majority of these high school seniors had reading scores on the Test of Academic Proficiency (TAP) well below the 50th percentile. All of the students were African American, most from families living in low-income communities. (Data on the school are presented in Chapter 1.) This unit was based on the assumptions that these students were capable of much more than their test scores and academic histories implied and that they had robust experiences in the world that were important resources on which they could draw to tackle the problems presented in this unit of instruction. The challenge was to design instruction in such a way that the heuristics and strategies as well as habits of mind needed to attack these problems could be made explicit. (Strategies for symbolism are discussed in Chapter 2.) Since inverted chronology was an ongoing area of difficulty in *Beloved* and other texts that would follow, we provided students with additional cultural data sets that exposed signals for shifts in time. Students also read background information relevant to the setting of the novel, including selections from Lerone Bennett's (1964) *Before the Mayflower: A History of the Negro in America, 1919–1964.* for background information on the historical experiences of the African Holocaust of Enslavement.[1] Reading logs, graphic organizers, and focused questions were used throughout the unit in order to focus students' attention on making sense *while* they were reading. These efforts represent common teaching strategies used across most literature classrooms. However, what was unique was the preparation for these difficult texts through modeling strategies for detecting and interpreting symbolism through cultural data sets that came from the everyday experiences of these African American adolescents.

The cultural data sets used to teach symbolism in this unit were the following:

- Rap lyrics—"The Mask" by the Fugees (1996)
- R & B lyrics—"People Make the World Go Round" by the Stylistics (1990)
- Rap video—"I Used to Love H.E.R." by Common Sense (1994)
- Television minifilm—Julie Dash's "Sax Cantor Riff" (1997) from the HBO series *Subway Stories*

The point of cultural data sets is to provide students with support for making public and explicit the tacit knowledge they possess about how to make sense of a particular kind of problem, to provide them with a language to talk about their problem-solving processes, and to help them make connections between what they already do and what they are expected to do with canonical, school-based problems (such as the literature that would follow). Furthermore, the work with the cultural data sets is intended to establish a culture of inquiry, of argumentation with evidence, of hypothesizing, of intellectual risk taking as norms for participation in class—a redefining of what it means to work in these classrooms. In addition to these habits of mind, the work with cultural data sets is intended to socialize students into using particular habits of mind that are specific to the discipline in question, the particular ways that inquiry, argumentation with evidence, hypothesizing, and risk taking are characteristic of response to literature, mathematics, history, or science.

With respect to response to literature, these habits of mind include the essential disposition of paying attention to language play as an aesthetically pleasing end in itself. It includes a willingness to enter the subjunctive world of an imaginary text. It also includes a disposition to impose coherence even when there seems to be little in the text.[2] The coherence is a construction that the readers make and experienced readers configure that coherence based on beliefs they bring to the text. These may be dispositions to see issues of gender as important (i.e., feminist criticism), to see issues of equity in the structure of societies (i.e., Marxist criticism), to privilege a Black or African view of the world (i.e., Black Aesthetic criticism), or to privilege purely individual and personal connections with the text (i.e., Reader Response criticism). We made a conscious decision to privilege what some might view as something close to—although clearly not—a New Criticism orientation, in the sense that paying close attention to the text as a source of evidence was privileged from the beginning of instruction. We took this stance because I believe that a close reading of the text is the starting point for novices to be able to engage in other critical stances. Regardless of critical stance, good readers read closely.

In order to make tacit knowledge of problem-solving strategies public, a main focus of modeling with cultural data sets is the coordination of what I call *metacognitive instructional conversations*. *Metacognition* has to do with thinking about one's own thinking, monitoring one's understanding, and knowing what to do when comprehension breaks down (Flavell, 1981). Explaining one's thinking is difficult for most people. It is especially difficult for students whose history of schooling has been dominated by a recitation around right and wrong answers where the teacher is the primary source of authority. It is clear from early class discussions that talking about their thinking was both very unfamiliar and very difficult for these students. In addition, it was challenging for me as a teacher to learn how to coordinate such discussions.

Metacognitive discussions as a central pillar of modeling with cultural data sets require that talk address not so much what students know about the meaning of a text as it does about how students come to know. Cultural data sets are ripe for such talk because in most cases the students know more about the meaning of these texts than the teachers. Thus, to merely discuss what the texts mean is somewhat inauthentic, except as the students teach the teacher about the meaning of these texts. That does happen and is an important feature of such modeling.

To illustrate these features of metacognitive discussions I refer to a class taught by Wilma Hayes. Mrs. Hayes (I use her real name with her permission) is an extraordinary teacher. I had the wonderful opportunity to work with her 4 years before the full Cultural Modeling project at Fairgate High School. She always said that teachers should not be asked if they taught a subject, topic, or skill, but rather what did students learn. Mrs. Hayes had an established routine in all of her classrooms of handing responsibility for thinking over to students. She would wait however long it took for students to respond rather than impose her thoughts on the group. Her most repeated question to students was always "How do you know?"

In this class the students have been reading the lyrics of "The Mask" by the Fugees (1996). Each stanza is followed by the following chorus lines:

M to the A to the S to the K,
Put the mask up on the face just to make the next day.
Brothers be gaming, Ladies be claiming.

I walk the streets and camouflage my identity.
My posse Uptown wear the mask.
My crew in the Queens wear the mask.
Stick up kids with the Tommy Hil wear the mask.
Yeah everybody wear the mask but how long will it last.

The particular stanza being discussed is about Lauryn Hill, a popular member of the Fugees, visiting a club in her old neighborhood. She is approached by a young man drinking an Amaretto sour who grabs her. She initially is prepared to rebuke the young man when she recognizes him as Tariq, someone she knew from around her grandmother's house.

I thought he was the wonder, and I was stunned by his lips,
Taking sips sipping Amaretto sour with a twist,
Shook my hips to the bass line,
this joker grabbed my waistline,
Putting pressure on my spine
trying to get L-Boog to wind,
I backed up off him, then caught him with five fingers to his face,
I had to put him in his place,
This kids invading my space,
But then I recognized the smile,
but I couldn't place the style,
So many fronts in his mouth, I thought he was the Golden Child . . .

The students have been working in small groups discussing the meaning of "The Mask." Mrs. Hayes, who does not listen to rap music or attend movies because of her religious beliefs, moves from group to group. She sits with one group that is discussing the reference to the "Golden Child." The discussion of this group follows.

(1) *T*: What does he mean here, "so many fronts in his mouth I thought he was the Golden Child."
(2) *Ellen, Alicia, Fatima*: Gold teeth.
(3) *T*: But . . .
(4) *Ellen*: That's like a big front anyway, cuz he got all this gold, all up in his mouth, and he just makin it his business to smile and let it be noticed.
(5) *T*: But who is "the Golden Child"?
(6) *Fatima*: The golden child that little boy who . . .
(7) *Ellen*: Eddie Murphy played . . .
(8) *Alicia*: In that movie. (laugh)
(9) *T*: So he's referring to something in a movie?

(10) *Alicia*: Yeah. (pause) You know how the golden child had all the power in the movie. (waits for a response) OK. (laughs)

(11) *T*: I'm listening.

(12) *Alicia*: It was the movie. You ever seen the movie *The Golden Child*?

(13) *T*: Umm, umm [no].

(14) *Ellen*: Oh well that's . . . (laughs)

(15) *Alicia*: It was the movie where this little boy he had all the power. But I don't really think that he just directly referring to it. He just indirectly. Everybody know the Golden Child had all the power. But he said that he had all these fronts in his mouth and he's the Golden Child . . .

(16) *Ellen*: Right, Golden Child, except you know he got gold teeth.

(17) *Alicia*: He had all this gold in his mouth like he this Golden Child.

(18) *T*: And what would you have needed to know in order to come to that conclusion? What you just said . . . ?

(19) *Alicia*: I just need to know all the fronts in his mouth. When she said "mouth," I knew.

(20) *Ellen*: Right. Once she said that you knew what that meant.

(21) *T*: And what else would a person need to know in order to come to the conclusion that you just came to? What little bits of information would a person need? And where are you getting your answers from?

(22) *Alicia*: From stuff we already knew.

(23) *T*: So you're using prior knowledge.

(24) *Ellen*: They say in here how they . . .

(25) *Alicia*: We were usin our context clues, we were like when we see the word *mouth* then you know it's automatically it's something that got to do with, got to be in his mouth.

(26) *T*: I'm saying that to you because a piece of my knowledge that's missing is, I don't know anything about the *Golden Child*. So I'm in the same position that you're in sometimes when you approach these novels. I may know what the author's talking about because I can hook it on to something, and that's why if you can prove it, instead of saying there's no right or wrong answer, you have a reason for coming up with that. And I don't know what he's talking about, to be honest with you. That's why I listen to you.

(27) *Ellen*: He just talkin a lot about bringing attention to sayin he got a lot of gold in his mouth. He might not necessarily mean

the Golden Child. Cuz that don't have a lot to do with his mouth.

(28) *T*: So the Golden Child would be like a symbol?

(29) *Ellen*: Right.

(30) *T*: Representing . . .

(31) *Ellen*: But not a symbol as being the Golden Child for his teeth, for having gold teeth.

(32) *Alicia*: It's figurative language. It's like if I be like Ellen, you star bright something, that's another way of sayin she real light-skinned. You know, that's figurative language.

(33) *T*: Umm hmm.

(34) *Ellen*: (Laughs) No, It's all right, it's all right.

(35) *Alicia:* I mean no, cuz you know, so she can understand this. Cuz if you called me little black star, you know . . .

This discussion reveals several important characteristics of discussions around cultural data sets as modeling. First, it is clear from the discussion that the students have more prior knowledge about this text than the teacher. Perhaps because of this, power relationships between the teacher and the students radically shift from the IRE (Initiation-Response-Evaluation) pattern of talk that is very typical in classrooms, particularly in those serving students from low-income minority backgrounds (Cazden, 2000; Mehan, 1979). Although Wells (1995) has accurately noted that the IRE pattern of talk can serve useful functions in classrooms, problems arise when it is the only pattern. The IRE pattern involves teachers having sole control over what responses are allowed in discussion and over who gets to talk. In this interchange, 37% of the turns are held by the teacher, while 63% are held and largely controlled by students. (Turns are numbered in the figures.) When Mrs. Hayes asks in turn 1 the meaning of the phrase "so many fronts in his mouth that I thought he was the Golden Child," and in turn 5 "Who is 'the Golden Child'?" she is posing genuine questions to which she does not know the answer. The students recognize that these are genuine questions. I believe it is this recognition by the students that invites them to take on the stance of teacher in relation to Mrs. Hayes and that opens up structures of talk that they control. The turns of talk after each of Mrs. Hayes's questions involve multiple responses from students and Mrs. Hayes does not control who speaks. The students' assumption of teaching roles bids them to draw actively on prior knowledge that they have and Mrs. Hayes does not.

A second feature of modeling discourse is the focus on students' problem-solving processes. Such modeling represents an interesting instantiation of Vygotsky's (1978) concept of a zone of proximal development. Vygotsky defines the *zone of proximal development* as the distance between what the learner can do on his or her own and what he or she can do with assistance. It is a dynamic zone in the sense that the students are assisting the teacher and the teacher is assisting the students. Neither has full knowledge of the task. Mrs. Hayes's knowledge of the referents in the lyrics is incomplete. The students' knowledge of the task toward which Mrs. Hayes is seeking to scaffold them is incomplete, namely to articulate heuristics for detecting and interpreting symbolism. Although the students bring important prior knowledge to such tasks, their knowledge is both tacit and incomplete. The quality of reasoning that we find the students demonstrating is rarely an object of explicit conversation outside of school. Thus the quality of reasoning we see here is the extension of an emergent understanding that is a result of careful scaffolding by the teacher. The teacher's role in this process is fundamental, and Mrs. Hayes is superb in this work.

It should be noted, however, that there are expert communities of practice within youth culture. Morgan (2002), for example, describes communities of young people who engage in a practice called *wordsmithing*, a poetry-crafting process. Fisher (2003, 2004) also describes intergenerational communities who foster the development of young people in this art. In such communities, explication of popular texts of rap and contemporary youth poetry are a routine practice. Most students in this class are not members of such writing communities.

Most of Mrs. Hayes's turns are directed toward students' articulating their reasoning—how it is that they come to know. In turn 18, Mrs. Hayes asks "And what would you have needed to know in order to come to that conclusion?" In turn 21, she asks "where are you getting your answers from?" It is clear from her repeated formulations of this general question that expressing how they reason is not easy for the students. However, it is revealing to follow the refinement of communication in turns 22, 24, and 25. The first statement, "From stuff we already knew" is accurate, but in a more vernacular register. In turn 24, the student directs attention to the text itself as a source of knowledge. This is an extremely important recognition and is consistent with one of the habits of mind the modeling activities are intended to invoke, namely, that careful attention to the text is privileged. Ellen is not able to complete her sentence because Alicia completes the thought with no pause between turns. In turn 25, Alicia not only makes explicit reference to the words in the text that signal special attention, but also uses a teaching register, "We were usin our context clues." Certainly, Mrs. Hayes has taught them about context clues and named the phenomena. But here, students invoke it and name it without prompting from

Mrs. Hayes. They have invoked the construct and see its application to their explication of these lyrics.

This is an example of students making connections between what they can do with everyday texts and what they can do with canonical texts. In this instance, the rap lyrics are being reconstructed as canonical because they are working on it as they have worked on school-based canonical texts. It represents the beginnings of what Saxe (1991) calls a "form-function shift." In a form-function shift, the form and function of a concept or tool changes from one context to be appropriated in slightly different ways to a new context. It is a particular way of viewing transfer. There are many examples of form-function shifts from these classrooms; I offer this example as representative of a qualitative shift in reasoning in one context to another.

Mrs. Hayes is especially skillful at being explicit about turning responsibility for student thinking over to the students. In turn 26, she makes a powerful connection. Whereas in turn 23, she had revoiced the student's vernacular register (i.e., "from stuff we already knew") to a more disciplinary register (i.e., "So you're using prior knowledge") (O'Connor & Michaels, 1993), in turn 26, she shifts her position back to that of a learner: "I'm saying that to you because a piece of my knowledge that's missing is, I don't know anything about the Golden Child." It is within that turn that Mrs. Hayes makes the brilliant and pivotal move of making explicit how what the students are doing with these rap lyrics is like what they will be doing with the novels that follow: "So I'm in the same position that you're in. . . . I may know what the author's talking about because I can hook it on to something, and that's why if you can prove it, instead of saying there's no right or wrong answer, you have a reason for coming up with that." She thus communicates a powerful conception of reading—that is, even expert readers can be stumped, which implies that not knowing or being confused is not a bad thing. She also labels what the students have accomplished up to this point. They have provided evidence and reasons for their claims. This epistemological stance is continuously restated across class sessions to socialize a culture of inquiry and argumentation based on evidence. It communicates to students that this is what we do here. This is the game we play.

A third feature of Cultural Modeling is the high quality of reasoning that students display from the beginning of instruction. This conversation about "The Mask" occurs very early in the instructional unit. At the conclusion of turn 26, Mrs. Hayes admits, "And I don't know what he's talking about, to be honest with you. That's why I listen to you." The students resume with vigor their mission to teach Mrs. Hayes. The reasoning is brilliant. In turn 27, Ellen articulates what Rabinowitz (1987) calls "rules of notice." These are conventions that the author uses to alert the reader to pay special attention. This heuristic has not been taught to the students. However, in order to teach Mrs. Hayes who the students see as a naive observer of rap, Ellen reveals that the reason the author uses the phrase "fronts in his mouth" is to bring attention to the fact that Tariq has a lot of gold in his mouth. She then goes on to make an insightful distinction between the attention to the gold in his mouth and his being the Golden Child, "cuz that don't have a lot to do with his mouth."

Mrs. Hayes takes up that assertion as implying that the reference to the Golden Child is intended to be symbolic. In a revolutionary response— something we rarely see happening in classrooms, especially in schools like Fairgate—the students correct Mrs. Hayes. Instead of being enticed to follow the reasoning of the teacher as the sole source of authoritative knowledge, the students put forth an alternative explanation. They argue that the reference to the Golden Child is not intended to be symbolic, but rather a way to emphasize the gold in his mouth. Although they do not have the language to label their reasoning, they are arguing that this is a case of hyperbole. Because so much rich reasoning emerges in these modeling discussions, it is a challenge for teachers to always understand the significance of what students are saying. This is because students are communicating their reasoning often by using a vernacular register and contextualizing their claims to the text (i.e., cultural data set) under discussion. The teacher must translate such contextualized statements by mapping them onto her understanding of core constructs, strategies, and heuristics in the discipline. In this case, Mrs. Hayes would need to have understood Alicia's statement in turn 32, "It's figurative language. It's like if I be like Ellen, you star bright something, that's another way of sayin she real light-skinned" as an expression of hyperbole. Mrs. Hayes did not understand the import of Ellen's statement in turn 27 at the time. However, after reviewing the video of this class session, she saw a missed teaching opportunity.

A final feature, which I will discuss in more detail in the next chapter, is the ongoing presence of community-based language practices as an exciting medium of communication. In this case, students are often invoking African American English rhetorical features as the envelope for communication. In turns 32, 34, and 35, Alicia and Ellen are signifying with each other. As I have explained before, signifying is a form of ritual insult that has been used for generations as a form of language play, often involving figurative language and double entendre. Alicia and Ellen are good friends. Ellen is light-skinned and Alicia is dark-skinned. When Alicia offers the example in turn 32, she is using Ellen as her example of using figurative language to emphasize a point, "Ellen, you star bright." Students in the group laugh, and Ellen says "No, it's all right." Alicia then responds, "cuz if you called me little black star, you know . . ." Alicia is playfully insinu-ating that if Ellen called her "little black star," those would be fighting words. This also reflects a long standing conflict in the historical African American community over skin color (Hunter, 2005). It is not a serious argument here, but a playful one, a way of playing games with words (Goodwin, 1990). That such playfulness has a place in the classroom in-vites a level of comfort, of intimacy, of safety that invites students to en-gage and to take intellectual risks. It is one of the features of modeling discourse that makes connections between home/community and school real and meaningful.

RANGE OF REASONING SCAFFOLDED THROUGH CULTURAL DATA SETS

The next set of examples is taken from a senior class that I taught at Fairgate High School. Students are again working in small groups and tack-ling the rap lyrics of "The Mask" by the Fugees as a platform for establish-ing classroom culture and for making explicit tacit strategies for tackling symbolism. In this example, students are discussing a different stanza:

> I used to work at Burger King. A king taking orders.
> Punching my clock. Now I'm wanted by the manager.
> Soupin' me up sayin' "You're a nice worker,"
> "How would you like a quarter raise, move up the register"
> "Large in charge, but cha gotta be my spy,
> Come back and tell me who's baggin' my fries,
> Getting high on company time."
> Hell, no sirree, wrong M.C.
> Why should I be a spy, when you spying me,
> And you see whatcha thought ya saw but never seen.
> Ya missed ya last move, Checkmate! Crown me King.
> Held my 22 pistol, whipped him in his face.
> Hired now I'm fired, sold bud now I'm wired,
> Eyes pitch red but da beat bop my head.

These lyrics illustrate one of the tensions in using texts from youth culture, especially hip-hop. The line "Held my 22 pistol, whipped him in his face" is clearly violent. While I can certainly understand the caution some schools may have about such lyrics, I would argue that the violence committed by Macbeth, a play the students would read later in this unit, is far worse than that depicted in "The Mask." At one level, it may seem ironic that so much of the canonical literature we teach is extraordinarily violent and counter to accepted social norms—Oedipus has sex with his mother (Sophocles, trans. 1977); Raskolnikov in *Crime and Punishment* commits brutal murder (Dostoevsky, 1866/1984). Great literature is not defined by the presence of violence or sexuality or the lack thereof, but by how great writers have the ability to make us think deeply about the dilemmas of the human experience. I would not argue that "The Mask" is a profound statement on the human experience, but it is an accurate one. We all, at one time or another, wear masks to disguise our intentions. Intimate friends, government officials, the rich and famous—all wear masks. While "The Mask" may be an accurate, albeit not profound statement, there are hip-hop lyrics that possess insights into the human experience. Wyclef Jean (1998) a member of the Fugees, communicates a philosophical statement on violence in the world with "Gunpowder." "Don't Go Chasing Waterfalls" by TLC (1994) is more than an argument against unprotected sex, but offers a symbol that has many degrees of freedom, capable of being appropriated for a number of important life lessons. Thus the terrain of the canonical and the so-called vernacular is murkier than we might expect.

Jonetha offers a very literary interpretation of this passage:

(1) *Jonetha*: Oh, I . . . (Class is noisy)

(2) *T*: Shhh. OK, quiet down.

(3) *Jonetha*: I'm saying I think he had a mask on when he was fighting, when he beat him up, because in order for him to have the mask on, he was spying on that person. He was spying on somebody. I don't know who he was spying on. But in order for him to realize that the man was spying on him, he had to take off his mask. In order to realize that the man was saying . . . I don't know! Shoot. (laughter from class).

(4) *T*: Let me try to break this out a little bit. Jonetha give me the words. You're saying . . .

(5) *Jonetha*: I'm saying that the man, in order for him to realize that the other man was spying on him, that he had to take off his mask.

As with the students in Mrs. Hayes's class, these insights are not the result of any explicit preparation by the teacher, no work sheets, no guiding questions, no activating prior knowledge, just discussion. Jonetha's argument is fundamentally as follows: In order for a king to work at Burger King, he must take on a mask of servility because kings don't work at fast food joints. In asking the worker to spy on his colleagues, the manager also assumes a mask to hide the fact that he is trying to use the worker. Thus in order for the king, masking himself as a worker, to recognize that the manager is trying to dupe him, the worker must remove his mask and stand as his true self. Two observations are appropriate here. First, it is clear that as the teacher I am translating Jonetha's words. That is my job. Second, in my process of translating, I am mapping the qualities of Jonetha's interpretation on to my internal representation of the domain of response to literature. Jonetha is clear that the mask is symbolic. She has no illusions that the king disguised as worker or the manager is wearing a physical mask. It is her recognition that a literal interpretation here doesn't make sense that leads her to infer a symbolic significance. She has paid careful attention to the details of the text, noting the meaning of the opening line: a king working at Burger King. She imputes significance to this contradiction and uses that attribution of significance to filter the details that follow. She uses her knowledge of the social world to impute internal states to the worker and the manager, states that must be inferred. This is precisely the kind of reasoning that I will want her to engage in when the class begins reading *Beloved* and the other texts that will follow.

Besides offering a very literary interpretation, Jonetha also demonstrates important habits of mind that are required for literary reasoning. She attends to the details of language play in the text. She does not ignore the salient detail of a king working at Burger King. Further, Jonetha is willing to put forth a hypothesis about which she is not entirely clear. Her wording in turn 3 clearly shows she is still figuring this out. Her frustration is evident when she says "I don't know! Shoot." This willingness to take intellectual risks is absolutely necessary if the students are to wrestle with the complex canonical works that follow. When the problem is really difficult, it is rare that you can be certain of your first efforts to make sense of it. The students about whom I am concerned have generally across their school careers experienced classrooms where intellectual risk taking is not valued, where the name of the game is an immediate right answer. My efforts in turn 4 to get her to restate her claims cues Jonetha and the rest of the class that uncertainty is a good thing.

A continuing challenge in this kind of modeling is to help the students communicate abstractions. Initially, their responses are circumscribed by the immediate context of the cultural data set. The teacher's job is to revoice contextualized claims as general propositions that can be applied across similar kinds of problems. This was clear in the examples of Mrs. Hayes. Sometimes, the statement of an abstraction emerges from students' interactions with one another. Across these class sessions, students' debates were quite heated. This level of intensity transferred to the canonical texts as well. When students perceive a debate as authentic, they have a vested interest in either clarifying or contesting.

In the following example, this same class I taught is discussing the chorus that repeats across "The Mask":

> (1) *T*: OK, "my posse up town wear the mask, my crew in Queens wear the mask, stick up kids with Tommy Hil wear the mask." Who is he talking about here?
>
> (2) *Carl*: So they tryin to say that little kids are stickin up people too with masks on? Is that what they trying to say?
>
> (3) *T*: They actually have masks on?
>
> (4) *Marvin*: No, well basically, they tryin to hide their true identity. Even if they don't actually have a mask, it's like an illusion in a sense, because obviously they don't walk around with a mask on, but they walk around with this cover like, you know how some people try and act like they're hard, but they really not. And they, you know, but that don't mean that they have. They got like a cover, you know a shield over em, but it's not, it's an invisible shield.

It is clear that the student in turn 2 is reading the chorus as a literal statement. To try and push the student's thinking, I ask a question intended to get the student to think about the unlikelihood that a literal interpretation makes sense. Of course it is possible if one lives in a neighborhood with much violence to imagine that someone could stick up (i.e., rob) wearing a mask. However, this student is even misinterpreting the vernacular-based, satirical comment "stick up kids with Tommy Hil," a wry commentary on poor kids on the street wearing Tommy Hilfiger clothing. Without prompting from the teacher, Marvin in turn 4 responds to the teacher's query (directed at Carl from turn 2) with a brilliant explication of why the literal should be rejected. Marvin's explication includes a wonderful abstract claim about the meaning of the mask, "it's an invisible shield." It is evident that these students have begun to play the game of literary reasoning. In fact, it is a game and they recognize that it is playful and thus an enticing world to enter.

Another cultural data set that proved to be quite powerful in eliciting insightful reasoning from the students is the short film "Sax Cantor Riff," written and directed by Julie Dash (1997), who made the beautiful, award-winning film *Daughters of the Dust* (1991). This 5-minute-long film appeared as one of many short films—all of which take place in a New York subway station—in the HBO series *Subway Stories*. The film opens with an African

American saxophonist playing a jazz riff. Then an old man (likely an Eastern European immigrant) is shown admonishing a group of young women of color for taunting him and stealing from his newsstand. All of a sudden, a young African American woman walks down the stairs of the subway, with flowers in her arms. She approaches the pay phone and calls her mother, who is in the hospital. She tells her mother that she doesn't have money for a taxi, but she wanted to talk with her before it was too late. In a voice that resonates through the subway, she begins singing the African American spiritual "Soon I will be done with the troubles of the world." The group of girls watch in amazement, first thinking the woman is crazy, but then determining that something must be wrong. The woman drops the phone, continues singing, and begins walking up the stairs to leave the subway. Meanwhile, the camera zooms in on the scarf around her neck, waving in the wind with images of flowers in its design. She drops the flowers she was carrying and the camera zooms in on the flowers flying in the air while a train goes by. As the train passes, you see clearly a sign that says Church Avenue. As the jazz riff reappears, a Jewish man, likely a cantor, wearing the dark suit and wide brim hat of the Hassidic, comes down the stairs of the subway singing in Hebrew, "Let my prayers, O Lo-rd, be for You at a time of favor; O G-d, with Your abundant kindness, answer me with Your saving truth."[3] Then he and the African American saxophone player face each other from separate sides of the track. They nod their heads toward each other.

This particular cultural data set is good fodder for discussion for several reasons. First, it is replete with symbolism. Student discussions of this minifilm were rich with literary reasoning even though none had seen this film. Second, it provides an opportunity to discuss authorial intent. In our discussions, the director Julie Dash was positioned as the "author" of the text because she intentionally put every image and word into the created product. This recognition of authorial intent, of the conscious craft of the "writer," transferred to discussions of the canonical texts that would come later.

The following exchange took place as part of a whole class discussion after viewing "Sax Cantor Riff":

1. *T*: Do you know why? You think that everything . . .
2. *Sarah*: (inaudible) Try to make money.
3. *T*: So you think that Julie Dash made this film so she could show a saxophone player make money in a subway?
4. *Job*: Yeah.
5. *T*: Remember the question, the question may be why does she, Julie Dash, she is like the author so to speak. She made a film

just to show the guy try and make money in the subway without . . . (inaudible) You think . . .

6. *Trish*: Well what else was she doing?

7. *T*: That's a good question. You think that HBO would have given her all the money it took to make that movie so they would show . . .

8. *Trish*: But that ain't all they was showing.

9. *T*: Okay so what are some of the questions?

10. *Felice*: I don't know what's going on now.

11. *T*: Well that's a question to answer. (Students are talking among themselves.) First thing you need to do is come up with the questions. What are some questions you ask yourself?

12. *Job*: Why were there roses?

13. *T*: Why were there roses on the floor of the subway? (Students were talking all at the same time.)

14. *Marion*: Were they roses or flowers?

15. *T*: Good question.

16. *Felice*: Why did it have to be Church Avenue?

17. *T*: Why did it have to be Church, ooh wow, why did it have to be Church Avenue? That's deep. Haven't noticed that. that's wonderful! David.

18. *David*: Why was the scarf blowing around in the subway?

19. *T*: Why was the scarf blowing around in the subway?

20. *Felice*: Because the wind was blowing.

21. *T*: Is there wind in the subway? (Students were talking at the same time.)

22. *Marion*: They showed it twice.

23. *T*: They showed it twice that meant it was important right? They showed it . . . great. What other questions? Keep in mind that there can be literal questions of everything, right? It's possible that the scarf was blowing because the train was passing and there was some air blowing. But maybe there is something else. It's possible that she dropped the flowers but maybe there is something else. That's what we're looking for. What other questions do you have? (A male student was talking to another male student.) What did you say Victor?

24. *Victor*: I was talking about the scarf because it keep you in mind of because it started off with this and went to that.

25. *T*: Alright let's put some of these questions on the board.

Turns 1–9 are about recognizing authorial intent. They are also about figuring out where one should focus attention in a literary text. It is evident at this early stage that some students do not see the relevance of this point. When Trish in turn 8 alerts the class that the saxophone player is not the only thing being shown, she shows that students have been paying attention to many details of the film. Beginning in turn 9, the teacher asks what questions students have about the film in order to make public the range of details to which they are attending and to determine what may be sources of misunderstanding. Another function is to continue to communicate to the students that asking questions and being uncertain is a good thing. This goal is reflected in turns 10 and 11 when one student says, "I don't know what's going on now," and the teacher responds, "Well that's a question to answer." Their responses indicate that they have attended to the unusual details of the film. Their ability to pay attention to such details in the absence of any direct instruction to what Rabinowitz (1987) calls "rules of notice" is evidence of their tacit knowledge of symbolism and other tropes employed in the narrativization of experience. If these details were not salient to the students, they would not have raised questions about them.

Their responses are revealing. It is important to remember that there was no prompting by the teacher about what kinds of questions were valued. Virtually all of their questions were about why some detail of the film was present. The prevalence of such "why" questions and the particular details they asked about suggest that these students already engage in a kind of literary reasoning, albeit tacit, as they listen to music, watch television and film, and themselves tell stories. They ask why there are flowers, does it make a difference whether these are just flowers or specifically roses, why the sign said Church Avenue, and why the camera zooms in on the scarf blowing in the wind. These are precisely the details that are symbolic, precisely the details that the "author" Julie Dash positioned her camera work on to draw the "reader's" attention. To recognize such details as significant is to use important rules of notice. As typically happens across the instructional unit, the students notice details that the teacher had not. For example, in turn 16, a student has noticed the sign Church Avenue. The teacher responds in turn 17 showing that she is moved by the observation, "Why did it have to be Church, ooh, wow, why did it have to be Church Avenue? That's deep. Haven't noticed that. That's wonderful!"

Besides revealing the students' attention to symbolic details, the discussion also involves descriptions of why they paid attention to particular details. Again, because the students see the discussion as authentic, they act as if it is important to clarify misconceptions that others have. This happens without prompting by the teacher. In turn 18, David asks, "Why was the scarf blowing around in the subway?" In turn 20, Felice responds, "Because the wind was blowing." This counterfactual statement, echoed by the teacher's question in turn 21, "Is there wind in the subway?" stirs a lot of talk among the students, all of whom are talking at the same time. Then in turn 22, Marion clarifies that the scarf's blowing is important because "they showed it twice." This is a very revealing response. These students have likely traveled on the subway. They know that unless a train is going by (which actually it is in the film at the point where you see the scarf blowing), there is no wind as such in a subway. Rather than responding to an obvious question posed by the teacher in turn 21, the student picks up on a device used by the director to bring attention, that is, she shows the scarf blowing twice. This device, as is the case with most cultural data sets, has an analogue in literary texts. When the author repeats a detail, that is usually an indicator that it's important, and if the other heuristics apply for rejecting a literal interpretation and defining the problem space as symbolic, the reader will read the text as symbolic.

I have mentioned before that one of the goals of modeling is for the teacher to provide a metalanguage to capture what students' responses signify. In turn 23, the teacher revoices and elaborates the student's prior observation in turn 22. Here the teacher describes some of the issues in defining the problem space. The details could simply be literal descriptions, that is, the scarf was blowing because there was wind in the subway; or there could be a meaning that goes beyond the literal, a meaning that could be symbolic. It became clear in small group discussions that followed that these students saw the flowers, the sign, the scarf with flowers blowing, and the train passing by, all as symbolic.

The point of relating these discussions from my English class has been to reveal the quality of literary reasoning in which these students engage from the beginning of instruction without any explicit teaching about the tropes they meet. The Cultural Modeling research groups analyzed the quality of literary reasoning in modeling discussions in contrast to the amount of teacher talk in these discussions. Figure 3.1 illustrates that the quality of reasoning was consistently high and that it was highest when the teacher did not dominate discussions (Lee & Majors, 2000).

The figure captures each of the first 10 days of instruction through modeling. It's findings are revealing. First, on the whole there is an inverse relationship between the quality of student reasoning and the level of talk by the teacher. In the first 2 days, students' reasoning is high and the teacher's involvement is high as well. It is expected that the teacher's direction would be high at the beginning, but generally we don't expect students to be as adept at the task being taught from the beginning of instruction. This level of reasoning from the beginning is testimony to their activation of very useful prior knowledge about the task, in this case interpreting cultural data sets from their everyday lives. The lower level of stu-

Figure 3.1. Quality of Reasoning in Modeling Discussions.

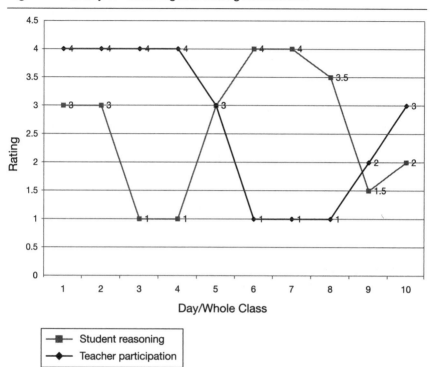

dent reasoning on days 3 and 4 occurred when the cultural data sets were an old R & B song, "People Make the World Go Round" (Stylistics, 1990), and an African American spiritual. This suggests to me that cultural data sets must be directly relevant to students' experiences. "People Make the World Go Round" is not a song they would have heard as it came out decades before they were born. I had assumed that since the genre was R & B that they would relate to it. That was not the case. They also did not respond to the spiritual as a source of symbolism, although later in the discussions of *Beloved*, their knowledge of the Bible was often invoked as a really powerful source of prior knowledge for interpreting tropes and actions in that novel. This suggests that careful attention must be paid to the cultural data sets selected. I have found it useful to involve students in the selection of such cultural data sets. Cultural data sets must have two crucial features. First, making sense of them must require problem-solving processes analogous to the school-based task to be taught. Second, the students must be very familiar with them already.

A second observation from Figure 3.1 is that learning has a curve. Students have good days and not-so-good days, but our interest is in the overall trend. This trend is a positive one. We did the same analysis of instruction with *Beloved* and found a similar pattern of high levels of reasoning as the consistent pattern and an inverse relationship between high levels of reasoning and dominance of talk by the teacher. These patterns in both the modeling phase and the canonical phase of the unit suggest that a culture of inquiry and engagement was established in these classrooms and that culture emerged from the very beginning of instruction. Figure 3.2 describes patterns of student reasoning and teacher participation during this canonical phase of instruction (Lee & Majors, 2000).

CONCLUSION

In Chapter 2, I argue that these students faced multiple developmental challenges: the normative challenges of adolescence in American society as well as the challenges that result from racism and poverty. I further argued that an important feature in designing learning environments was

Figure 3.2. Quality of Reasoning During Canonical Literature Phase of Instruction (*Beloved*).

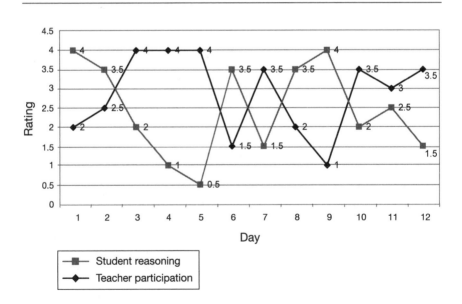

how to make such environments into spaces where students felt safe to take intellectual risks. Part of that willingness has to do with understanding the nature and rules of the game we ask students to play and with understanding how to play that game. Beginning instruction with cultural data sets and organizing the talk of instruction in such a way as to invite community-based discourses as a meaningful medium of communication together helped students to stretch intellectually, to make hypotheses when they were unclear, to engage in heated debate, and to clarify uncertainty by others. They were being asked to play a game about which they already knew something. The game was authentic because they valued it outside of school. The lively days of heated debate drew out a genie that in most of their other classrooms had been hidden from public view.

In this work I have tried to accomplish the following: debunk the long-held tradition of viewing the community-based experiences of low-income African American students and their primary language of communication —African American English—as deficits that schools must overcome; demonstrate what high expectations can yield when coupled with instruction that makes the inner workings of a discipline evident and public and connected to students' lives; and contribute to the well-established literature on culturally responsive pedagogy a framework that is both culturally responsive yet firmly rooted in the knowledge of academic disciplines. It is this connection with the discipline that helps teachers and curriculum designers think more critically about the nature of the subject matter we teach and through such understandings make more generative connections to students' lives.

When and Where I Enter: African American English as a Resource for Instructional Discourse

Celie speaks in the voice and uses the language of my step-grandmother, Rachel, an old Black woman I loved. Did she not exist; or in my memories of her, must I give her the proper English of, say, Nancy Reagan?

And I say, yes, she did exist, and I can prove it to you, using the only thing she, a poor woman, left me to remember her by—the sound of her voice. Her unique pattern of speech. Celie is created out of language. In The Color Purple, *you see Celie because you "see" her voice. To suppress her voice is to complete the murder of her. And this, to my mind, is an attack upon the ancestors, which is, in fact war against ourselves.*

—Alice Walker, 1983, pp. 63–64

Language has always been a source of contention in the United States (Ferguson & Heath, 1981). This country holds long-standing beliefs about correct and incorrect ways of speaking English (Wolfram & Schilling-Estes, 1998). Schools have long been the cauldron in which to wash away language that marks race, ethnicity, and working-class status deemed by the powerful to be wanting (Smitherman & Dijk, 1988; Wolfram, Adger, & Christian, 1999). Particular ways of using language have been presumed to characterize academic disciplines, and the default assumption is that those ways of using language deemed vernacular hold no hands with the demands of reasoning in the subject matters (Lee, 1997, 2005a). These assumptions have been very enduring in the field of English Language Arts, particularly as relates to classroom practice (Ball, 2002; Farr, 1991). Ironically, great writers of every tradition, and particularly in the tradition of African American literature, have taken great joy in sculpting the voices of the common people as medium through which to convey the deep secrets of the human experience. Alice Walker (1982) captures the sentiment of that authorial tradition as she describes above the voice of Celie, the protagonist of the Pulitzer Prize winning novel *The Color Purple*. I find it a fitting introduction to this chapter.

Gumperz has described the concept of "contextualization cues" (Gumperz & Hymes, 1972). These cues signal to participants what kind of activity this is, what people do here, how people talk. These cues may include the physical arrangement of space, the movement of people within a space, the physical and conceptual artifacts available and privileged for use in an activity, norms for who can speak and about what, as well as ways of using language, including gesture, intonation, and prosody. Each time we enter a new setting, our antennae go up to figure out what people do here and how we can behave here. If the goal is to participate, we will read very subtle features and map what we recognize of those features on to existing knowledge or cultural scripts (Schank & Abelson, 1977). The features that are relatively routine in a familiar setting are what help us to recognize it as such and to construct our own understanding of our relationship to that setting.

Research on classroom discourse has documented prototypical patterns of talk (Cazden, 2000; Cazden, John, & Hymes, 1972). Once students reach high school, they have been doing schooling for a very long time. They recognize the patterns of interactions that have characterized the classrooms in which they have studied. They attach to those patterns of interactions meanings about the purpose of schooling, including the purpose of schooling in this particular classroom. In the second edition of the classic text *Classroom Discourse* (2000), Courtney Cazden documents the traditional patterns of talk in classrooms, in particular the pervasive use of the IRE (Initiation-Response-Evaluation) pattern. In this pattern of talk in classrooms, teachers control the flow of participation. Teachers initiate questions, pick students who will respond, and then evaluate those responses, and the pattern continues. Turn taking is controlled by the teacher through the practice of having students raise their hands to be selected to speak. In this second edition, Cazden also goes on to describe new patterns of instructional discourse that are privileged by reform curricula, most notably illustrated through new standards in mathematics and science. In such reform classrooms, turn taking is not controlled solely by the teacher. Teachers devise innovative ways of turning more control over to students about getting the floor. In addition, these new forms of instructional discourse require that teachers and students learn to listen in new ways to ideas initiated by students. O'Connor and Michaels (1993) describe a pedagogical strategy called "revoicing" where teachers reformulate student initiated ideas, both to provide public recognition of those ideas (a perhaps more subtle version of teacher evaluation) and to recontextualize those ideas in ways that point the discussion toward a set of instructional goals. For example, O'Connor and Michaels describe a case of a teacher revoicing a scientific claim made by a student as a theory. Such routine recontextualization in a science classroom signals that the work in which these students are engaged is theorizing, similar to the work that professional scientists do. Cazden describes other strategies, such as "wait time" in which the teacher allows more time for students to respond, or use of "jigsaw" where different members of a small group take on different responsibilities for the completion of a larger project. I will describe in this chapter a different model of instructional discourse than is captured in the current literature.

AFRICAN AMERICAN ENGLISH AND INSTRUCTIONAL DISCOURSE

It has been widely noted that the most studied and demonized dialect of American English is African American English (Smitherman, 2000c). Research has documented the West African roots of this dialect, including features of its syntax, phonology, vocabulary, and prosody (Makoni, Smitherman, Ball, & Spears, 2003; Morgan, 1993; Mufwene, 1993; Mufwene, Rickford, Bailey, & Baugh, 1998). In the history of U.S. education, debates have abounded as to whether African American English is a resource or a detractor affecting the academic achievement of African American students (Delpit, 1986; Perry & Delpit, 1998). In the 1960s and 1970s, African American English was viewed by many as interfering with young Black children's ability to learn to read. Such assumptions lie beneath programs such as Distar and its current reformulations in Direct Instruction. Books such as *Teaching Disadvantaged Children in the Preschool* identified language deficits as major impediments for the Black child (Bereiter & Engelmann, 1966). In *Twice as Less* E. W. Orr (1987) argued that African American English interfered with Black children's ability to reason mathematically (for an insightful critique of Orr's argument, see J. Baugh, 1988).

Similarly, there has been an equally active counter argument, namely that African American English is a structured language variety and not a version of incorrect English (Labov, 1972). In 1979, 11 students from the Martin Luther King Elementary School sued the Ann Arbor school district for discrimination in *Martin Luther King Junior Elementary School Children v. Ann Arbor School District* which came to be known as *The Black English Case*. African American students at the school were routinely receiving unwarranted learning and speech pathology placements, seriously limiting their chances to learn. The case tested the applicability of the 1703(f) language provision of the 1974 Equal Educational Opportunity Act to speakers of Black English (Smitherman, 1981). While the case set an important legal precedent, the practical strategy approved by the courts for remediation was inadequate and underconceptualized. However, the fundamental argument made by the linguists who served as expert witnesses for the case consistently held that African American English is a legitimate and systematic language variety of English. This is the position adopted by most linguists and formally claimed in a public position by the Linguistics Society of America in 1997 in response to the decision by the Oakland School Board to focus attention on African American English as a resource and a stand taken by the College Composition and Communication Conference of the National Council of Teachers of English regarding the right of students to use their indigenous languages in 1974 (Smitherman, 1995, 1999, 2000b; Smitherman & Dijk, 1988). The Linguistics Society of America (1997) resolution states:

> 1. The variety known as "Ebonics," "African American Vernacular English" (AAVE), and "Vernacular Black English" and by other names is systematic and rule-governed like all natural speech varieties. . . .
> 3. As affirmed by the LSA Statement of Language Rights (June 1996), there are individual and group benefits to maintaining vernacular speech varieties and there are scientific and human advantages to linguistic diversity. (n.p.)

Linguists have documented the rhetorical features and speech genres of African American English (Baugh, 1983; Dillard, 1972; Morgan, 1998; Mufwene et al., 1998; Smitherman, 1977). Others have documented how its rhetorical features improve the quality of student writing (Ball, 1992; Lee, Rosenfeld et al., 2003; Smitherman, 1994, 2000a). Several programs in the 1970s documented how the incorporation of African American English features in texts—specifically using authentic texts that use African American English—in conjunction with classroom talk that included aspects of African American English resulted in improvements in reading comprehension (Rickford & Rickford, 1995; Simpkins, Holt, & Simpkins, 1977). Among the most recent controversies over the incorporation of African American English in instruction is the highly debated decision by the Oakland (California) Board of Education in 1996. The Oakland School Board passed the following resolution:

> RESOLVED that the Board of Education officially recognizes the existence, and the cultural and historic bases of West and Niger-Congo African Language Systems, and each language as the predominantly primary language of African-American students . . .

BE IT FURTHER RESOLVED that the Superintendent in conjunction with her staff shall immediately devise and implement the best possible academic program for imparting instruction to African-American students in their primary language for the combined purposes of maintaining the legitimacy and richness of such language . . . and to facilitate their acquisition and mastery of English language skills. (quoted in Smitherman, 2000b, p. 150)

Ironically, critics of the Oakland decision included African American political leaders, some of whom have developed a strong following precisely because of their creative uses of African American English rhetorical features in their public address. The Ebonics resolution of the Oakland School Board resulted in anti-Ebonics legislation being proposed in five states and passed in three, as well as a critical public statement by then Secretary of Education Richard Riley (Smitherman, 2000b).

I seek to enter this long-standing debate from a slightly different perspective. I continue to try and warrant my arguments about the deployment of cultural resources in instruction, specifically the uses of African American English linguistic resources, within the discipline of response to literature.

Induction into the playful world of response to literature involves learning how writers consciously craft language to entice the reader to enter an imaginary world. This induction also involves learning how to talk about what authors and readers, in sometimes complementary and sometimes conflicting ways, construct together as important ideas about both the world and the craft itself. We know that authors showcase and skillfully experiment with the vernacular. The early writers of England experimented with English viewed as a vernacular in contrast to Latin. Irish writers made great efforts to capture the language of the ordinary folk instead of what some considered the more polished English of the colonizing country of England. From Paul Laurence Dunbar to Zora Neale Hurston to Alice Walker, from Sterling Brown to the poets of the Black Arts Movement of the 1970s—Amiri Baraka, Sonia Sanchez, Haki Madhubuti—from Toni Morrison to August Wilson, African American writers have captured African American English as a medium of communication in works of poetry, fiction, and drama (For more information on these writers, see Gates, 1988; Gates & McKay, 2004; Jones, 1991; Jones & Neal, 1968; Morrison, 1984; Smethurst, 2005) . To understand the characters they create and to understand the tropes they employ, the reader must understand the language.

I have indicated that in understanding the language of the literary text, the reader must also grapple with the craft of the text, its structure, its devices, its themes. In Chapter 2, I argued that the work of literary analysis involves recognizing salient patterns that include character types, plot configurations, archetypal themes, and what I have called interpretive problems (symbolism, irony, satire, and point of view, including the many categories of each). Literary analysis requires not only recognition of such patterns, but also access to and invocation of strategies for making sense of these patterns in relation to the text at hand, the reader's interest and goals, other texts, and both the context of one's reading as well as the context of the text's production. Learning to reason in this way and to talk about one's reasoning is complex and difficult.

I have taken what for some will be a controversial position, namely that learning to engage in literary reasoning involving close textual analysis is the most important task for teaching in this domain. I believe this task is more important than only learning simplistic syntax and formulas for communicating ideas in Academic English. I believe learning to switch registers—for example, from African American English Vernacular to Academic English—is ultimately a choice that people make because they see the usefulness of doing so. I would almost prefer that we offer classes on speaking Academic English, including learning in explicit ways the many reasons why it's a useful variety of English. What speaking Academic English makes possible (but by no way guarantees) are options for which most youngsters want at least to vie. However, I believe that too much time is often taken away from instruction in the disciplines because of our preoccupation with being able to explain ideas in Academic English. Our preoccupation is primarily with the syntactical features of Academic English and less so with the ways of structuring arguments and reasoning about problem solving in the subject matters. I claim here that it is possible to reason and structure arguments according to disciplinary norms in a so-called vernacular variety of a national language. I also claim that learning to engage in this kind of reasoning and argumentation is far more difficult than learning Academic English syntax. Thus I have chosen in my work to place more emphasis on helping students to reason in a literary fashion than to "correct" how they speak. My "correction" is more in the form of revoicing their claims in ways that lead students to understand the significance of a claim in the larger picture of an evolving literary argument (O'Connor & Michaels, 1993).

I should add here that my thoughts about teaching composition are quite different. The primary job of teaching composition in school should be to help students learn the structure of written genres (primarily narrative and persuasion) and procedures for producing the features of those genres in ways that are unique and creative (Flower & Hayes, 1981a, 1981b; Hillocks, 1986, 1995; Smagorinsky & Smith, 1992). In the process of learning to edit, it is natural to look closely at spelling, diction, syntax, and so on. Writers write for audiences. If you're writing an editorial to send to the *New York Times*, as a writer you must be cognizant of the fact that certain diction and syntax will be deemed inappropriate and will likely lead to the editorial being rejected (Flower, 1994). In this sense, there is an authentic reason to pay close attention to particular aspects of syntax, diction, and spelling. At the same time, if you are composing a narrative and the characters you create speak in African American English, it is entirely appropriate and even necessary to create dialogue in African American English. Thus in creative writing there is a clear place for vernacular languages (Lee, Rosenfeld et al., 2003). It is also revealing to point out that academic writing can be done in African American English or other so-called nonstandard varieties of English. Geneva Smitherman, the noted linguist, has written academic publications in African American English and routinely includes elements of African American English in her academic writing in the form of aphorisms, titles, and personal commentary (Smitherman, 2000c). I, too, routinely try to include African American proverbs, sayings, and vocabulary, particularly in titles of works I have published. I think doing so makes an important statement about who I am and what I value.

All of this is not to say that I think African American students do not need to learn Academic English, or by extension other students who speak a so-called nonstandard variety of English or whose first language is a national language other than English. Rather, I think we need to put learning this variety of English in its place and understand that in the end it's always an option that we must help socialize students into wanting to make. In the United States we tend not to recognize the political and power dimensions of our attitudes toward language and how unclear the lines of demarcation are. Some years ago, Constance Weaver (1996) conducted an experiment. She sent out a letter to a number of businesses asking them to identify grammatical "errors" in the letter. She found that the errors most associated with African American English Vernacular were most likely to be noticed. Other "errors" that were not so racially or class marked were overlooked. Similarly, few people in the United States ever respond "It is I," although according to the standards of Academic English saying "It is me" would be considered incorrect. In addition, there is a huge range in variation among U.S. English dialects around pronounciation, prosody, and vocabulary (Labov, Ash, & Boberg, 2006). Bostonian English and Appalachian English have very different valence in the larger society (Wolfram, 1981; Wolfram & Christian, 1976). At the same time, we do not recognize how much and how often people code switch. All African American speakers of African American English Vernacular do not use all the features of this dialect. An Irish American man who grows up in a working-class community in Boston and goes on to Harvard will likely speak one way with his college or business peers and another way when he returns to the old neighborhood pub for a beer. I can remember very clearly many years ago visiting a Montessori preschool in a public housing project on the Chicago West Side. A 4-year-old African American girl was playing in the housekeeping area. In speaking with her friends, she clearly spoke African American English. While engaging in imaginary play in the housekeeping area, she picked up the play telephone and began speaking to an imaginary person on the phone like an upper-middle-class White girl from the affluent North Shore suburbs of Chicago, imitating a high nasal tone and elongation of vowel sounds that she had probably heard on television.

In documenting the instructional discourse of the Cultural Modeling classrooms, particularly those taught by me, I found patterns of talk that had not been planned for in the original conceptions of Cultural Modeling. Because of the modeling phase of instruction, described in Chapter 3, students learned from the beginning of instruction that they could be authoritative voices in the classrooms; they learned that in these classrooms we were playing a game about how language was used and that they already knew a lot about playing this game; they learned that deciding who could talk was not controlled solely by the teacher. This mix of instructional features seemed to be the catalyst for unscrewing the cap that had in previous classes (including other classes they were taking in the high school) bottled up a powerful energy. Once that cap had come off, an intellectual energy that I certainly had not anticipated took over. It didn't come out every day, but most days. It emerged when the students were most deeply engaged in playing this game of literary analysis.

Analysis by the research group indicated that the following features characterized such intense discussions:

- Use of African American rhetorical features
- High use of loud talk, rhythmic prosody, use of gestures, and figurative language
- Overlapping talk

Smitherman has coined the term *African American rhetorical features*. According to Smitherman (1977) African American discourse includes worldviews embodied through routine uses of language, including lexicon, stock phrases, and proverbs. She further describes the rhetorical qualities and modes of discourse as follows:

- Exaggerated language
- Use of proverbial and aphoristic phrasing
- Playing on words
- Use of indirection and tonal semantics
- Rhythmic, dramatic, evocative language
- Reference to color-race-ethnicity (i.e., when the topic does not call for it)

- Use of proverbs, aphorisms, Biblical verses
- Sermonic tone reminiscent of traditional Black church rhetoric, especially in vocabulary, imagery, metaphor
- Direct address–conversational tone
- Cultural references
- Ethnolinguistic idioms
- Verbal inventiveness, unique nomenclature
- Cultural values–community consciousness
- Field dependency; involvement with and immersion in events and situations; personalizing phenomena; lack of distance from topics and subjects (p. 86–87)

These rhetorical features exist along what Smitherman calls a sacred to secular continuum. Genres of talk such as playing the dozens, a specialized form of signifying (because the target of the insult is always someone's mother), represent the secular end. For example, "Your mama is so fat, she irons her clothes in the driveway" (Percelay et al., 1994, p. 41). Modes of argumentation that invoke religious argumentation using moral proverbs and Biblical citations as warrants, often couched in the form of narrative or storytelling, represent the sacred end of that continuum (Ball, 1992, 1995). Tonal semantics involves the manipulation of tonal qualities in oral speech to communicate meaning and point of view. It is interesting to note here that a number of African languages are tonal languages (Odden, 1995). Another important example of African American rhetorical features in oral talk is the use of *call-and-response*. Call-and-response is most often associated with the African American church where the minister in his or her sermon puts forth a moral proposition and the audience affirms out loud and collectively with the use of stock phrases, such as "Amen" or "That's right." As is evident from the analyses of instructional dialogues in Cultural Modeling classrooms, the use of call-and-response as well as the other features described are not limited to one context of use.

I argue here that one of the ways in which African American English served as an important resource in these literature classrooms is that many of its norms for use position the subject of discourse—in this case, literary texts—as objects of intense linguistic play; and position the interlocutors in discourse as needing to be attentive, engaged, playful, and intense. You can't sit in church and daydream without being totally outside the game. You can't be on the playground talking "He-said she-said" without being intense or you'll get *whupped* real quick. "He-said she-said" describes speech events documented by Marjorie Goodwin (1990) in which interlocutors (African American girls and boys between the ages of 9 and 14) engage in disputes and gossip. Both of these orientations (i.e., playful attitude toward language and intense engagement in responding creatively) are useful positionings in what I will call the "game of literary response." I have described the Cultural Modeling framework for instruction that combines modeling rules for identifying types of interpretive problems and problem-solving strategies through examinations of everyday texts from youth culture (in this case African American youth culture) and the popular media (especially hip-hop cultural artifacts). Such modeling is combined with the invitation to use a way of talking that signals to students that playing the game is fun. It further signals that engagement requires intense attention to how language is being used (both within the texts themselves as well as with one another). The dual affordances of such modeling represented a double inoculation against disengagement and boredom. This does not mean, of course, that students were never bored or disengaged. They certainly were. That is to be expected in terms of a learning curve for anybody. However, the modal response across classrooms was an amazing level of engagement and high levels of literary reasoning.

WHO IS THAT WOMAN? LITERARY REASONING IN AFRICAN AMERICAN ENGLISH

I will illustrate the quality of reasoning in which students engaged using the case of a literary argument students in my class constructed regarding a particular passage in Toni Morrison's *Beloved* (1987). I will further use this case to illustrate how students employed rhetorical features of AAEV to communicate their arguments.

Beloved is the story of Sethe, a formerly enslaved woman during the African Holocaust of Enslavement, who in a fit of utter fear kills her baby girl to keep her children from being taken back into enslavement. Morrison uses masterful tropes of understatement to place in stark relief the consequences of slavery. The story is fundamentally about the human and spiritual costs for the alive and the dead of having lived through this period of total and unabashed terror. The baby returns to haunt Sethe's house. Students have read Chapter 5 that opens with the following paragraph:

> A fully dressed woman walked out of the water. She barely gained the dry bank of the stream before she sat down and leaned against a mulberry tree. All day and all night she sat there, her head resting on the trunk in a position abandoned enough to crack the brim in her straw hat. Everything hurt but her lungs most of all. Sopping wet and breathing shallow she spent those hours trying to negotiate the weight of her eyelids. The day breeze blew her dress dry; the night wind wrinkled it. Nobody saw her emerge or came accidentally by. If they had, chances are they would have hesitated before approaching her. Not because she was wet, or dozing or had what sounded

like asthma, but because amid all that she was smiling. It took her the whole of the next morning to lift herself from the ground, make her way through the woods past a giant temple of boxwood to the field and then the yard of the slate-gray house. Exhausted again, she sat down on the first handy place—a stump not far from the steps of 124. By then keeping her eyes open was less of an effort. She could manage it for a full two minutes or more. Her neck, its circumference no wider than a parlor-service saucer, kept bending and her chin brushed the bit of lace edging her dress. . . .

The woman gulped water from a speckled tin cup and held it out for more. Four times Denver filled it, and four times the woman drank as though she had crossed a desert. When she was finished a little water was on her chin, but she did not wipe it away. Instead she gazed at Sethe with sleepy eyes. Poorly fed, thought Sethe, and younger than her clothes suggested— good lace at the throat, and a rich woman's hat. Her skin was flawless except for three vertical scratches on her forehead so fine and thin they seemed at first like hair, baby hair before it bloomed and roped into the masses of Black yarn under her hat. (pp. 50–51)

In typical Morrison mastery, the reader does not know who this woman is. However, a more expertlike reading not only raises the question of who she is, but turns our attention to particular salient details. The expert reader realizes that these details have been consciously crafted by Morrison, and knowing the tradition of her other novels, recognizes that each detail is likely to carry the weight of many meanings that are interwoven together as strands in a rope of tropes. Just as during the modeling phase of instruction students noticed unusual details in Julie Dash's short film "Sax Cantor Riff" and the Fugees' rap lyrics in "The Mask," (see Chapter 3 for a detailed analysis), students make parallel moves now in the service of interpreting a very complicated and subtle canonical literary text. In earlier work modeling literary problem-solving strategies using signifying, students made similar moves in noticing important details in stretches of signifying dialogues and in canonical works of literature (Lee, 1993).

In the transcript included below, a group of students argue about who they think the woman is, how they know who she is and is not, and why the author had the characters react in the way they did to this unknown woman. It is important to note that this discussion is neither about the plot per se, nor even about students' personal response to the texts in terms of their own lives. It is really a discussion about the function of how Morrison has constructed this passage in relation to earlier parts of the novel. The discussion is an outgrowth of the design of Cultural Modeling. Students have been given graphic organizers where they record what they notice and learn about particular characters. The observations about what is salient to them about the woman and about Sethe are not the result of teacher direction, just as what the students noticed about the details of "Sax Can-tor Riff" in the modeling phase of instruction was their thoughts, not the teacher's. The direction of the argument is driven by what the students notice and value about the text. In conjunction with other evidence that I will present in Chapter 5, I offer this as an exemplar of a quality of reason-ing and engagement that is not typical in high school literature classrooms, be they in historically underachieving high schools in low-income urban communities or historically high-achieving high schools in affluent sub-urban school districts. I also remind the reader again that these students had standardized reading scores largely in the bottom quartile. As seniors, few were going on to elite universities. The nagging question is what would have been the trajectory of achievement had these students experienced instruction from elementary school forward and across subject matter that was designed to scaffold their prior knowledge and community-based experiences in ways that mapped strategically on to the demands of aca-demic disciplines.

The students recognize that something unusual is happening because a grown woman suddenly walks out of the water fully dressed. They rec-ognize that the details of her dress map back on to other details about dress from a prior chapter. In this case, they argue that the details of this woman's dress differ in small but important ways from descriptions of how Baby Suggs dressed. The fact that the students have decided that the woman is either Beloved or Baby Suggs is interesting because both are dead. Baby Suggs is Sethe's deceased mother-in-law and Beloved is the infant that Sethe killed. Taquisha asserts that she cannot be Baby Suggs because Baby Suggs hated buttons on her dress. In these examples, students are using what Rabinowitz (1987) calls "rules of signification" and "rules of configuration." *Rules of signification* alert the reader that some details are more important than others. The knowledge base that readers use to impute meaning to the details they deem significant lies outside the text per se. Such exper-tise includes knowledge of how particular tropes or interpretive problems function; what may be relevant from knowledge about the world outside of the text, from other parts of the text, and from other texts by this author and others. *Rules of configuration* involve recognizing patterns among the textual details deemed significant and imputing some meaning to those patterns. The meaning imputed to those patterns may relate to archetypal themes, assumptions about human intentionality, or the meaning of everyday cultural scripts. It is important to note that the meanings we as readers im-pute to patterns we see in literary texts are cultural (Scholes, 1985).

The students' argument that this woman is the baby is compelling for several reasons. The rules of notice employed seem to be derived from world knowledge that this is an unusual event—that a woman fully dressed will suddenly walk out of the water. We are warned by Morrison that "Nobody saw her emerge or came accidentally by. If they had, chances are they would have hesitated before approaching her" (p. 50). The rules of configuration employed involved making connections across a set of observations about the woman that on the surface seem not only unusual but unrelated (acting here as rules of notice as well). These details include the following facts:

- Her lungs hurt.
- She breathes shallowly.
- She is very sleepy.
- At first she can barely lift herself.
- The circumference of her neck is no wider than a parlor-service saucer.
- She is very thirsty, gulping the water; and water drips from her chin when she finishes (she doesn't wipe her chin).
- Her skin is flawless.
- The scratches on her forehead seem at first like baby hair.

These are the specific observations that the students make on their own. Employing rules of configuration, the students use their knowledge of the behaviors of newborns to infer that although Morrison presents this character as a woman, as readers we know that she is really the baby, the ghost returned of the baby Sethe had killed. The details listed above cohere around the behaviors of young babies, particularly newborns, but there are other details that suggest this is Beloved, a particular baby ghost. After what is clearly a difficult ordeal, she emerges out of the water smiling and goes directly to Sethe's house, number 124. Whoever she is, she knows where she is going. Why would she go to Sethe's house unless she had a relationship with the people who lived there, now only Sethe and Denver.

Having inferred this to be the ghost of the dead baby, the students use rules of signification to assert that certain details are important not only to signify that this is Beloved, but also to connect this woman to Sethe in other important ways. They use rules of configuration to connect patterns of repeated images across different parts of the text. The following transcript begins with Victor, who was described in the Introduction as one of the young men who question Jan Derrick's entering the building, and whose brother had died the year before. Here Victor asserts that Beloved's sitting on the stump of a tree when she comes out of the water is important. When the teacher asks him to repeat what he has said, Victor automatically goes to the text and reads that portion that supports his claim that Beloved's sitting on the tree stump is important. David follows, again without any explicit request from the teacher, to warrant Victor's claim by asserting that the presence of the tree as an image is repeated in other parts of the text.[1]

(1) *Victor*: When she came out of the water she sat in on the tree all day and night resting her head on the trunk ((inaudible)).

(2) *Teacher*: Hee::y Ah::. ((the class says that at the same time.)) Wo:w ∧

(3) *S2*: WHAT DID HE SA:Y ∧?

(4) *David*: =He /talkin/ /bout/ the tree

(5) *S4*: The tree ∧

(6) *S5*: =The *tree*

(7) *S3*: =He put something under the tree.

(8) *S2*: =Beloved is a tree ↑

(9) *Victor*: Yes. ((Raises right fist)). Ye:: ↓s ((Emphatically shaking his head up and down))

(10) *Teacher*: Victor. ((Students are all talking at the same time.)) Hold up. ((Raises her hand up to quiet students.)) Victor please explain that. That's pow:erful. =((overlapping talk))

(11) *Victor*: Let me tell you exac:tly ((Victor opens his book))

(12) *Teacher*: Alright Victor. Tell us the page.

(13) *Victor*: ((Reading directly from the novel)) "Walk down to the water, lean against the mulberry tree all day and night, all day and all night she sat there with her head rested on the trunk in a position abandoned enough to crack the brim in her straw hat."

(14) *Teacher*: Hm. Hm. She's not only resting on a *tree* but she seemed to be *aban::doned* on this tree. Ooo::h >this is deep<

(15) *Joe*: =Deep

(16) *Others*: =Deep

(17) *Teacher*: = Now, so alright David, a little bit louder so everybody can hear you. Charles Johnson are you listening? David a little louder.

(18) *David*: Everything in this book is almost connected to trees like tree is sweet home. *Tree* >on her back<, >tree in her back yard<.

(19) *Teacher*: A::hhh.

(20) *David*: = >Tree on this, tree on that<
((overlapping talk by other students))

The argument these students make takes me, the teacher, by surprise as I had not paid any special attention to that detail about the woman sitting on the tree. Their comments about the structural use of the tree helps me as a reader to connect the woman's sitting on the tree to another detail that Victor reads, "her head resting on the trunk in a position abandoned enough to crack the brim in her straw hat." Morrison's use of the word *abandoned* there reverberates with the scene of the baby's killing. Sethe ironically refuses to abandon her infant daughter back into enslavement, but the baby girl in the afterlife does not understand her mother's intention, and feeling abandoned, returns to not only reconnect, but try to understand how a mother could kill her own child. This interchange between the students' thinking as a catalyst for my own thinking about the novel is the work of communities of shared practice. We are all now playing the game.

In addition to the compelling logic of Victor and David's argument, through transcription conventions I have attempted to capture something of the AAVE rhetorical features evident in their talk—their changing prosody typified by elongation of vowels and rising pitch index engagement. Such prosody has been documented in sociolinguistic accounts of African American English discourse in many settings, including the church and the playground, but not typically in classrooms (Erickson, 1984; Foster, 1995; Goodwin, 1990; Majors, 2003; Morgan, 1998; Moss, 1994). The multiple instances of overlapping talk and turn-taking with virtually no timed interval are another index of engagement. Victor and David both use physical gesture to emphasize points. In turns 5–6, 15–16 students employ call-and-response patterns.

After the instructional unit, a group of senior classes are invited to discuss their final thoughts on the novel and to engage in a public debate about Sethe's decision to kill her baby girl. One of the senior teachers, Mrs. Hayes, who is featured is Chapter 3, asks what final thoughts students have about *Beloved*.

> *T*: So, okay, what comes to your mind, and if I don't know your names, I'm pointing at you.
>
> *Belinda*: Beloved comes to my mind because, she was like, the book was based on her, and it was like a lot of transition because, from her coming back to life, and it's like a reincarnation thing.
>
> *T*: Okay, Beloved, transition, reincarnation. Tell me more. I'm trying to see if I'm thinking like you.
>
> *Belinda*: Right. When she came back from out of the water, and that was like being reborn. And remember Sethe had to pee real bad when she came from the carnival. It was like, felt like, her water you know, broke or something like that.
>
> *T*: So out of the whole novel, that's what sticks in your mind?
>
> *Belinda*: Yeah, it was like, it was kind of awkward how she came back, but I could understand it was like being reborn.

This final reflection on the novel was not part of any direct instruction. It was not a response to a prepared set of questions designed to help students reason through a problem. It was, rather, an open question. This student's response is revealing because it is neither a literal representation of the plot nor even a purely personal response (i.e., Reader Response). Rather, this student positions key details of the plot as instantiations of an archetypal theme, namely the symbolic significance of reincarnation, of rebirth.

Students taking on the actions that characterize reasoning in the discipline without being asked to do so by teachers is evidence of a shared culture within the classrooms. In this case, it is a culture that privileges attention to subtle details of the text, formulating goals to inquire about literary tropes and their function in the text, of using the text as evidence for claims, and for questioning the intentions of the author. The African American English rhetorical features of the talk provide evidence of this shared literary culture, as features of the discourse index engagement.

INSTRUCTIONAL TALK BASED ON AFRICAN AMERICAN ENGLISH NORMS AS IMPROVISATION

I have characterized stretches of interchanges involving multiparty overlapping talk, use of rhythmic prosody and intonation, body language and gesture, and call-and-response as instances of instructional improvisational talk (Lee, 2005b, 2006). It is improvisational because how it emerges and flows cannot be predicted in advance (Berliner, 1994). It operates very much like jazz where the band begins with a joint melody that follows a predetermined script, but then as intensity builds, each player drifts into a riff that is both responsive to what all the other players are doing, but is also unique; a kind of call-and-response conversation among musical interlocutors. An important question for the work I describe here is how teachers can "manage" such improvisations, or in fact, how teachers can orchestrate such improvisations. It is the teacher's job to manage such improvisations because the teacher as the representative of the domain knowledge into which students are being apprenticed must understand what students' statements signify about their emerging understanding; not just their understanding of the text or specific problem being discussed, but rather of how what they say about the text or problem reveals something about their more general knowledge of the discipline. Such instructional improvisations are essentially hybrid in nature (Gutiérrez et al., 1999) because they involve an interweaving, in this case of African American English Vernacular discourse patterns and canonical literary reasoning. The teacher then must understand where is the literary reasoning in the AAEV discourse and how is the AAEV discourse structured.

In my observations of Cultural Modeling classrooms as both a teacher and a researcher, I have found that the multiparty overlapping talk begins when students are deeply engaged and excited about the problem they are trying to solve. The multiparty overlapping talk can sound to an outsider like noise. However, careful observations reveal that students are actually talking to one another in small groups all at the same time. These small groups are not defined by the teacher, but usually involve one or two people who are sitting close to one another. Something is said to the group to which most people want to respond. In the multiclass debate over *Beloved* that is described in the next section of this chapter, around 50 students are engaged in the most raucous literary debate one is ever likely to see. I and several other teachers in the room get frustrated by the fact that so many students are all talking out aloud at the same time. I turn off the lights in the room for a second to get the students' attention and announce that they will have to speak one at a time to hear one another. One student then shouts out, "That's gonna take too long." It is clear from the debate that students do hear one another, and that the opportunity to enter the debate, even just with one or two students sitting next to you, is important to sustain engagement.

I learned as I was teaching to let the multiparty overlapping talk build up steam. I would walk around the room listening for the gist, gems, and misconceptions that emerged in the students' unplanned interchanges with one another. In the midst of what I have come to call "the performance floor" of the classroom, I learned very quickly to map what groups of students were saying onto my internal map of the domain in order to evaluate what in their statements needed to be elevated to public investigation. While I used the same approach in planned small group work, I had to learn to think on my feet very quickly when these improvisational interchanges bubbled up because if I tried in any way to constrain them too early, the range of innovative ideas would be squelched and many students who would have been quiet under other circumstances would shut down. A persistent challenge in any kind of verbal exchange is getting the floor. Typical scripts for getting the floor in classrooms are defined and controlled by the teacher. Scripts for getting the floor in many reform classrooms, across subject matters, involves students exerting more control over who gets the floor, but often in small group configurations that are organized by the teacher. In addition, little work has been done to document who is silenced in such groupings, particularly when such groups are diverse along racial/ethnic and language groups.

One interesting example of uptake from multiparty overlapping talk is in the discussion that precedes the one about the significance of the image of the tree in the description of the woman coming out of the water. Taquisha's assertion is both preceded and accompanied by multiparty overlapping talk.

> *Taquisha*: Now ↑ wouldn't you (wanna) know, >you know<, the questions hair *all* straight >like a baby<, >you know and stuff<, drinking *all* this water, okay, >you know<, she said she ran away and stuff, you got some bra:nd new shoes on yo feet, you *too* clean to run away, yo *feet* ain't swole you ain't gonna expect (nothing), you ain't gonna ask her *no* questions.
> *Prof. Lee*: Alright hold up this is—
> *Joe*: =It's a story.
> *Taquisha*: It *don:'t* matter.
> *Joe*: Did you write the story?
> *Prof. Lee*: Excuse me. (laughs from the students.) This is a very important point Taquisha has made. Who feels the way that Taquisha is saying somebody would feel? (students are talking, inaudible) Who feels that way? (All the students were talking at the same time.) Now hold up, hold up, excuse me. Alright, first Taquisha has raised a very important point. She's saying that common sense would suggest that somebody would react the way she's described. Now my question is, of the other people who were there, Charles Johnson, does anybody else react the way Taquisha says?
> *Taquisha*: Paul D.
> *Teacher*: Paul D.
> *Taquisha*: Paul D was asking her a question. How she (gonna) just pop up and stuff. Ask her where she from.

Taquisha clearly uses AAEV syntax in her assertion ("yo feet, you too clean to run away, yo feet ain't swole, you ain't gonna expect nothing, you ain't gonna ask her no questions"). This is an example where I took (and stand by) the position that for Taquisha in this moment, it is more important that she articulate what is an extraordinarily important observation in a way that captures the intensity of her concern about the problem than that I "correct" her English. I understand her claim to be an instance of a kind of literary problem that is extraordinarily important for expert readers to think about. She fundamentally questions authorial intent. Questioning authorial intent is a stance that is generative in the sense that it is the gateway for several kinds of important problem solving in the domain of response to literature.

Problems of irony and satire require that the reader question authorial intent because such problems presume that something is happening in the text with which the author expects the reader to understand that the author would not be aligned. So for example, in *A Modest Proposal* when Jonathan Swift (1729/1995) says to the reader that the famine in Ireland could be solved by the Irish eating their children, Swift expects that we understand that he does not agree with that position (and that presumably we as readers will also not agree with this position). Second, questioning authorial intent is in many ways the prelude to critiquing the text. The reader who invokes a feminist perspective to critique the historical-social codes of *The Scarlet Letter* is questioning the values the reader imputes to Hawthorne (1850/2000). So when Taquisha asks with great credulilty why Morrison would not have Sethe and Denver recognize that something was wrong with the picture of a woman coming out of the water, walking to their house, "her feet ain't swole," she is engaging in a very literary act. She is demonstrating a habit of mind, in this case questioning authorial intent, that will serve her well not only for reading *Beloved*, but for the other canonical texts that will follow. It is important then that I as teacher recognize this, make what she has done public so that she and the rest of the students can understand what she has done and why it's important and how it will be useful as we proceed in this game.

The response of other students to Taquisha's frustration with the author reflects a revealing dialogue that is fundamentally about literary epistemology. Joe says, "it's a story." Taquisha responds, "It don't matter." That is, fiction still must be anchored to social norms of the real world; characters must recognize danger when it appears and they are naive when they don't. Taquisha has referenced back to readings the class had done prior to *Beloved* about the experiences of people of African descent during their Holocaust of Enslavement. It was common in the Black community, certainly just outside Cincinnati where the story takes place, for Africans who had escaped from slavery to show up suddenly at someone's door in the Black community (Bennett, 1964; Harding, 1981). In fact, in an earlier chapter that describes Sethe's escape from enslavement, carrying Denver in her womb, giving birth to Denver under horrendous circumstances in the woods, we are explicitly told that unknown people were always showing up at someone's door step. With this as the historical/real-world backdrop, Taquisha cannot understand why Sethe and Denver would not be alerted to the danger at the doorstep.

My response in that moment is also revealing. I had to be able to make sense of Taquisha's assertion at that moment. This happened often in the course of instruction. Sometimes, as with the case of Victor's observation about Beloved coming out of the water and sitting on a tree stump, students raised issues about which I had not thought. I made the decision in the instant of this interchange to reconfigure the problem Taquisha raised in a way that would allow the students in the class to work through the problem themselves. This is a fundamental problem of teaching, especially teaching that purports to position students as problem solvers (Lampert, 2001). It is a complex and fundamental problem of teaching that cannot be learned except in the context of practice with feedback from experts, in the same way that a novice doctor learns to diagnose in the context of supervised hospital rounds.

I reconfigured the problem in terms of asking the students why the characters respond as they do. Taquisha recognizes that Paul D has responded to this new woman with the same credulity that Taquisha had as a reader. To wrestle with the question of why Sethe and Denver respond in one way and Paul D responds in another is to do two things. First, it involves taking on a powerful habit of mind in terms of literary response; that is, even if the details of a narrative appear to be unrelated or nonsensical, there is a rhyme and reason that as readers we can construct. Second, it is a way of taking Morrison's intentions seriously; that is, to assume that Morrison as the author has all her characters act as they do for a reason and that this reason is part of the puzzle that as readers we are slowly putting together, constructing as we read. This act of the teacher to reconfigure or revoice the students' move into an investigation of a kind of metarule is an important pedagogical strategy of Cultural Modeling, a crucial part of making problem-solving strategies and heuristics visible and explicit. In this case, the metarule is that it is possible that the intentions of the characters may be a window into the intentions of the author. It is a compelling example of wrestling with problems of point of view that Taquisha has initiated. This is a complex metarule because it is not always the case that a character's actions are a window into the author's point of view. For example, in satire the intentions of characters who are being satirized do not generally reflect the point of view of the author. Here, the line of inquiry is, why would Morrison have Paul D respond differently than Sethe and Denver?

In these examples, African American English is the medium of communication through which students make literary arguments about a rich and complex canonical text. The features of AAE are an index of point of view and engagement on the part of students. The evidence of engagement is revealed in turn taking, distribution of interlocutors—including multiparty overlapping talk—as well as in the intonation and prosody of the talk, in the form of particular tonal qualities characteristic of African American English Vernacular. This level of engagement naturally leads to propositions and questions that the teacher cannot predict in advance. As such, the teacher must learn to follow what is essentially improvisational talk. In so doing, she must recognize the utterances of students as instances of naive conceptions or misconceptions of concepts, strategies, habits of mind, and ways of reasoning that characterize the discipline in question. In the section that follows, I illustrate how one rhetorical feature of AAVE, the use of preacherly style and sermonic tone, functioned in the development of a distributed literary reasoning about *Beloved*.

PREACHERLY STYLE AND SERMONIC TONE

Bahktin (1981) argues that our talk is always dialogic in nature. We speak in dialogue with other voices, voices we have engaged directly, or voices that are part of the ongoing dialogues that surround us. According to Bahktin, we ventriloquate the voices of others. This ventriloquation may be communicated through direct speech or through reported speech. Goffman (1974) and Bateson (1972) both use the term *frame* to describe an "interpretive context providing guidelines for discriminating [how] a message" is to be interpreted (Bauman, 1977, pp. 9–10). Such frames may serve to cue performance, insinuation, joking, imitation, translation, or quotation. In any case, there are lexical and syntactic markers that cue our audience about the authorities we invoke as we speak. Bauman (1977) also makes the point that an ethnography of performance should empirically "determine the culture-specific constellations of communicative means that serve to key performance in particular communities . . . what are the specific conventionalized means that key performance in a particular community" (p. 32). Generic features that may key performance include rhyme and speech play, but Bauman argues these take on culturally specific nuances and features. Knowledge of these dimensions certainly distinguishes insiders from outsiders, novices from experts, discourse with a little *d* from Discourse with a capital D (Gee, 1990, 2000b).

One of the keys to African American verbal performance is the use of a preacherly style and sermonic tone (Moss, 1994; Smitherman, 1977; Smitherman, Daniel, & Jeremiah, 1987). Black preachers are known for their powerful rhetoric, epitomized in the public speaking of Dr. Martin Luther King, Jr. Even Black politicians invoke a preacherly style and sermonic tone in order to maintain the attention and allegiance of their constituencies. This preacherly style is characterized by the use of Biblical stories to warrant moral claims, interspersing narratives within what might otherwise be expository arguments, use of parallel structure, figurative language, especially metaphor and hyperbole, physical gesture, and emphatic, rhythmic prosody. The preacher and the rapper represent two ends of the sacred-secular spectrum that Smitherman (1977) attributes to African American English discourse.

I noted earlier that from our observations of Cultural Modeling classes, when there is a large, whole-group discussion, students who are more verbose and creative, using AAVE norms, tend to take and hold the conversational floor more than others. It seems as though other students, instead of competing for the conversational floor, elect to engage in cross-party talk with others physically close to them in order to gain access to the conversation (Lee, 2005b). This results in the multiparty overlapping talk that is characteristic of the times when the students are most engaged in instructional discourse.

After reading *Beloved* as the first major canonical text in the unit on symbolism, students from three different classrooms came together to take a position pro, con, or undecided as to whether Sethe was morally correct and courageous in killing her baby. One group of students take the position that Sethe is morally correct to take the life of her child. Selena is an especially adept speaker who blends the syntax of Academic English with the prosody, tonal semantics, and use of parallelism and figurative language that are characteristic of the preacherly style and sermonic tone of the Black preacher. Her rhythm is quick. Selena is supporting the position that Sethe is justified in the act of killing her baby. In fact, Selena's group came up with a conditional claim: that is, Sethe is morally courageous, but not correct. They refused to be bound by the claim inherent in the question as formulated by the teachers. They would not take the position that the killing of a child was in any absolute sense correct, but that the depth of the depravity of the conditions of enslavement made a credible case for Sethe's actions.

Another group argues that Sethe is morally incorrect. Both groups make conditional claims that are warranted by Biblical authority. Both groups use a form of narrative interspersion (Ball, 1992), illustrating with stories points they wish to make in an expository argument. It is important to note that the students in these two groups are not members of the same English classes. They share a common set of experiences preparing them to read canonical works like Toni Morrison's *Beloved* through the Cultural Modeling Project's curriculum enacted at the school. They also share common cultural experiences as members of the African American community, in particular as members of the African American English speech community. Their experiences over time with the Cultural Modeling curriculum socialized them to identify and tackle problems of interpretation using norms for literary reasoning. Their experiences as members of the African American cultural and language community provided them with mediational resources, including commonly shared indexical referents, that all members of the group could use as contextualization cues for the practice in which they were engaged.

Selena uses an analogy to support the claim that there were circumstances so harsh and inhumane as to justify Sethe's act as morally courageous. She tells the story of Abraham and Isaac from the Bible. Genesis, Chapter 22, verses 9–13, reads as follows:

> 9: And they came to the place which God had told him of; and Abraham built an altar there, and laid the wood in order, and bound Isaac his son, and laid him on the altar upon the wood.
> 10: And Abraham stretched forth his hand, and took the knife to slay his son.
> 11: And the angel of the LORD called unto him out of heaven, and said, Abraham, Abraham: and he said, Here *am* I.
> 12: And he said, Lay not thine hand upon the lad, neither do thou anything unto him: for now I know that thou fearest God, seeing thou hast not withheld thy son, thine only *son* from me.
> 13: And Abraham lifted up his eyes, and looked, and behold behind *him* a ram caught in a thicket by his horns: and Abraham went and took the ram, and offered him up for a burnt offering in the stead of his son.

The manner in which Selena ventriloquates (to use Bakhtin's terminology) this Biblical story resonates with not only the style but also the authoritative voice of the African American preacher. I will illustrate not only how she uses this story rhetorically to warrant her claim regarding Sethe, but also the ways she appropriates a preacherly delivery of her reporting and interpretation of the story of Abraham and Isaac. I argue that it is both the shared indexical referent of this Biblical story and the oral delivery of that story that serve as contextualization cues for participation by other members of the group. I hypothesize that the use of this story as a warrant triggers meaning within the network of associations that people steeped in readings of the Bible would likely make of the characters and language of the Biblical story; and that these meanings are sufficiently shared knowledge that intense debate over significance to competing claims can happen.

Perhaps because this Biblical narrative is a common point of reference for the group, once Selena offers it to support the claim that Sethe faced conditions that were so morally repugnant that she was courageous in killing her child, Tareta questions both Selena's interpretation of this scripture and its relevance to the argument. Selena and Tareta debate Biblical interpretation of the story of Abraham and his son Isaac. Tareta has argued that God had Abraham kill Isaac. Selena responds:

When God had asked Abraham to sacrifice Isaac unto him—he was like—but she had said that God had people killing him, but that was really just a test of Abraham's faith. He didn't actually have Abraham kill Isaac. On the third day, ON THE THIRD DAY.

Here Selena ventriloquates not only the gist of the story, but just as important, she appropriates the very language of Biblical text. I am referring specifically here to her use of the phrase "to sacrifice Isaac unto him." While there may certainly be differences in translations of the Bible, the King James version to which I referred in examining this text does not include the explicit phrase "to sacrifice Isaac unto him," but rather the exact wording of Genesis 22: 2 reads as follows:

And he said, Take now thy son, thine only *son* Isaac, whom thou lovest, and get thee into the land of Moriah; and offer him there for a burnt offering upon one of the mountains which I will tell thee of.

However, the phrasing "sacrifice _____ unto him" is reminiscent of the verses describing Jesus as God's sacrificial lamb for the sins of humankind. This archaic syntax is certainly not part of African American English nor the modern English of Wider Communication. Consistent with Bauman's (1977) description of the ways that performances are cued, this syntax places Selena as an authoritative voice and interpreter of Biblical scripture. At the end of this turn of talk, Selena again appropriates explicit scriptural language: "on the third day." In the transcript, I mark her second parallel invocation of "ON THE THIRD DAY" in capital letters to identify the loud and emphatic pitch she uses to repeat the phrase. It is clear that Selena does not finish the point she wishes to make about the significance of the third day, in part because she is interrupted with multiparty cross talk that drowns out anything she would then say. Twelve turns later, Selena insistently returns to tell the group what happened on the third day. Within these twelve turns are three turns of loud, multiparty cross talk. I point this out to note that Selena must hold in short term memory the point she wanted to make about the third day across many turns of talk before she is able to regain the floor. Twelve turns later Selena completes her thoughts:

On the third day the angel came and he told him "No. Stop Abraham. God was testing your faith" to see if he would do it. He didn't actually kill him.

Selena uses reported speech in this response, reporting in her own words what the angel said to Abraham. She elects not to use indirect speech—that is, "the angel said to Abraham that God is testing you." As in the case of the first group who argued that Sethe was incorrect in her decision the kill her child, Selena assumes a field-dependent position (Saracho & Spodek, 1984). She assumes the role of the angel and in the voice of the angel speaks directly to Abraham. Although intended to capture the perspective of another person's speech, Bakhtin (1981) states that reported speech always is double-voiced, reflecting as well the perspective of the one who articulates the reported speech of others. In this instance, Selena reflects her own perspective on the story of Abraham through her use of reported speech to capture what the angel says to Abraham. While one would not expect Selena to remember verbatim the words of this scripture from memory, her rewording does suggest possible associations she has made in the act of reconstructing the angel's words. The actual Biblical texts state that "Abraham found Moriah, the place that God had directed him toward on the third day" (Genesis 22:2 and 4). Genesis 22:11–12 tells us the angel said to Abraham " . . . Abraham, Abraham . . . Lay not thine hand upon the lad, neither do thou anything unto him: for now I know that thou fearest God, seeing thou hast not withheld thy son, thine only *son* from me." There are interesting intertextual links between references to the third day—Jesus rose from death following his crucifiction on the third day— and Selena's linking of the third day with the words of the angel to Abraham. While the Biblical text says that Abraham found the place Moriah on the third day, it does not directly say the angel spoke to Abraham on the third day. There are also intertextual links between the Biblical text's reference to Isaac as Abraham's only son and references to Jesus as God's only begotten son. According to one Bible Concordance ("Introduction to the Cyclopedia of Interesting Facts about key people, places, and things in the Holy Bible," 1969), "because of his noble character and deep religious faith, he came to be called father of the faithful and friend of God. Outside of the Bible, nothing is known of him." The association between Jesus and Abraham as "the father of the faithful and friend to God" is telling. While I cannot make definitive claims about whether Selena is conscious of the parallels, it is still worth noting that she imports particular lexical and syntactical features of the story in the Bible of Jesus' crucifixion into her rendering of the story about Abraham's faith.

I have spun a web of literary-like associations that might be better suited to the textual analysis of literary criticism. I suspect my roots in the humanities has propelled me in this direction, while my training in the social sciences leads me to view such webs with some skepticism. A way of out this dilemma is what I view as central premises in Cultural Historical Activity Theory. That is, through engagement with routine cultural practices across historical time we inherit tools with which to mediate our problem solving (Cole, 1996; Rogoff, 1990, 1995, 2003 ; Rogoff & Lave, 1984; Vygotsky, 1981, 1934/1987; Wertsch, 1991). Sometimes these tools are symbolic and carry a weight of meanings about which members of our community of practice share common understandings. I want to argue here not only that the students in this group shared a common reference point on the significance of the story of Abraham and Isaac (even though Selena and Tareta argue over the exact events in the story), but also that the students and Toni Morrison share a vision of the relationship between the world of spirit and the world of the living. This common ground on which these students and Morrison stand is sacred covenant between literary author and reader. It is the exploration of this common ground on which authorial readings are built.

In the novel, Morrison presents and re-presents the killing of Beloved, Sethe's baby girl, over and over. Each time the re-representation offers an insight into this terrible act from a different point of view. There is no definitive point of view of the morality of Sethe's action because, in a sense, Morrison gives equal weight to the horror of the experience of being enslaved, to the horror of a mother carrying out the unimaginable act of brutally slitting the throat of her baby girl, and to the horror of the consequences of living with that act for Sethe and for the baby Beloved. In this way Morrison invites the reader to have a space to ponder the meaning and complexity of Sethe's act, a space circumscribed by the symbols and imagery of horror that Morrison so vividly portrays, no matter from which point of view you look at the act. Morrison also fills the subjunctive world of the novel with images of spirits acting in the world of the living. When Paul D listens, overwhelmed, to Sethe telling him the story of what happened, he perceives that the dead grandmother, Baby Suggs, is somehow standing from the ceiling of the house looking down, peering into his mind. The character Beloved is the dead baby having returned in the flesh as a young woman to occupy in the fullest sense of the term the house 124, Sethe, and Beloved's sister Denver, and indeed, Paul D as well.

Morrison also invites, over and over, Biblical allusion, for the weight of the shared meanings such allusions invite. The narrator—whose perspective shifts from omniscient to a detached third person presence—says in the beginning of Sethe's telling of the events to Paul D, "When the four horsemen came. . . ." Morrison, the crafter of this real and imagined story, consciously created four men, rather than two or three, coming on horse, rather than walking, toward the house. I associate them with the four horsemen of the Apocalypse, the Apocalypse representing doomsday, the end of the world, hell come to Mother Earth. The point I am making here is that the common ground on which these students and Toni Morrison stand is like pliant dough, filled with the airy bubbles of symbolism, metaphor, and irony—of playfulness with language. This kind of analogical reasoning has been closely associated with literary reasoning (Culler, 1975; Fish, 1980; Lee, 1993; Rabinowitz, 1987). It is a playfulness with language that these students routinely employ in their use of language outside of school. Through Cultural Modeling, they have learned to invoke it as a resource in the pursuit of making sense of complex canonical works of literature. In this instance, the potential warrantable associations between Abraham and Sethe, between Isaac and Beloved, are enormous and far-reaching.

The teacher attempts to reposition the debate by asking "What does this story about Abraham have to do with what we're talking about?" Cross-party talk surfaces after the teacher's question, and one person shouts out, "Nothing." That response is a form of signifying on the argument articulated by Selena. Selena responds:

> Yeah it does, cuz if she was going to sacrifice her own child and so in the Bible Abraham was supposed to sacrifice his own child Isaac, only difference was that he [overlapping talk from the group] Sethe was sacrificing her child for slavery and Abraham was sacrificing his child for God.

Two students then invoke call-and-response:

> *Tovis*: He did.
> *Ari*: He did. That was like violent stuff, sending your child to death
> *Group*: [cross-party talk]

Selena's response to the teacher's question states explicitly how she sees the connection between the Biblical story of Abraham and the story of Sethe. The call-and-response uptake by Tovis and Ari indicate they have a shared understanding of the story of Abraham. Ari's elaboration, "That was like violent stuff, sending your child to death," suggests that he sees connections between what Abraham was prepared to do and what Sethe actually did. There are several interchanges of cross-multiparty talk between exchanges of individual students. These cross-party exchanges are not off-task meanderings.

The teacher asks again, "So what does that say about Sethe?" Another boy begins to respond to that question: "He was going to kill his own son because God [what he says here is drowned out by cross multiparty talk] Isaac was going to suffer" [what he says again is here drowned out by cross multiparty talk]. Both this young man's comment and the cross-party talk represent elaborations and extensions of Selena's claim and the Biblical warrants that undergird her claim.

The teacher again asks, "So what does this have to do with Sethe?" Selena then regains the floor and answers:

> because she was killing her child—like she said—because she thought her child was going to heaven to be with God. She said it was better for the child to go and be with God and not have to suffer all that harm and experience on earth, which is the same.

Here, Selena uses indirect discourse to represent Sethe's reasons. This indirect discourse, however, is also pregnant with Selena's perspective. Nowhere in the novel does Morrison have a narrator or character state that Sethe explicitly thought "her child was going to heaven to be with God." There is, however, no question that such a reading can be fully supported by the text. This explict explanation of the claim is later picked up when all the groups come back together to debate their different positions. It is clear that this claim is not held solely by Selena, although its evolution is clearly initiated and to a great extent sustained by her. A number of students in the whole group debate, restate, and elaborate this position, with the full force of their African American English rhetorical discourse as the medium of communication.

What I have presented as small excerpts from an extraordinary culminating event and transcripts of regular Cultural Modeling classrooms across units of instruction are representative of the pattern of talk and reasoning (Lee & Majors, 2000). Thus the stretches of dialogue are presented as cases of *culturally responsive instructional discourse*. Such discourse is a principled part of the design of the Cultural Modeling curriculum. I have tried in this chapter to illustrate the functions that African American Vernacular English and its rhetorical features can serve as a resource for communicating complex discipline specific reasoning. The talk is fundamentally improvisational in its unfolding, not because the medium is AAVE, but because such improvisation is characteristic of complex reasoning in situ. Learning to design for and facilitate such improvisational talk is one of the fundamental problems of teaching. In the next chapter, I examine the demands of learning to engage in such coordination as teacher.

CHAPTER 5

Cultural Modeling and the Demands of Teacher Knowledge

The impact of teacher quality on student learning has been well documented (Darling-Hammond, 1987, 1999b; Haycock, 1998a, 2000; Ingersoll, 2002). What is more contested is how we define teacher quality. Another way of thinking about this question is to ask, "What knowledge is required for effective teaching?" An important extension of that question is "How do teachers gain such knowledge over time?" I have attempted in this book to describe what is entailed in teaching in ways that are subject matter specific and draw on the prior knowledge and experiences of youth, particularly youth from groups that face persistent historical discrimination. In this chapter, I argue for an integrated quality of reasoning that is required to teach in the ways I have described. I will anchor this argument in the Cultural Modeling framework regarding the teaching of literature to adolescents. As with other examples used throughout this book, the broader principles apply across subject matters and age groups.

There are many excellent overviews of how the field has conceptualized teacher knowledge over the years (Clark & Peterson, 1986; P. L. Grossman, 1990; Hillocks, 1999; Munby, Russell, & Martin, 2001; Richardson, 2001). These conceptions have been highly influenced by the leading orientations in the field of cognition at the time. The behaviorist model assumed that learning was a response to external stimuli. Behaviorist research on teacher knowledge was largely through the lens of what were called "process-product models." In the process-product model, it was assumed that standardized test scores were good measures of student learning. Thus if one observed in classrooms in which test score data indicated that good learning was taking place, one could describe the actions of good teachers and by extension their knowledge base. This led to studies in which researchers counted particular actions and strategies used by effective teachers; catalogs of those actions and strategies were then assumed to be indicators of the kinds of knowledge good teachers needed (Brophy & Evertson, 1977; Calfee & Calfee, 1976; Rosenshine, 1970, 1971, 1976). This research paid little to no attention to issues of diversity in terms of either students or teachers. It assumed that learning is a unidirectional process whereby teachers create the input that results in student learning. This model of teaching did not provide a way to think about student input and response, that is, what students contribute to the process of learning. It also did not take into account virtually any contextual factors beyond the individual classroom or school building. However, during this same era research in child development emphasized deficit views of the home and community experiences of youth of color and those living in poverty (Bereiter & Engelmann, 1966; Bernstein, 1961; Deutsch & Brown, 1964; Hess & Shipman, 1965).

The next wave of research was—and to a large degree still is—influenced by the argument in cognition that human learning is the result of constructive processes by individuals (Bereiter & Scardamalia, 1992; Bransford, Brown, & Cocking, 1999; Bruer, 1993; Flavell, 1981). This led to an emphasis on inquiry and projects as core instructional activities. The challenge in this model was (and still is) to figure out what teachers need to know about how people construct new knowledge out of experience. While we are still very much in the throes of constructivism, more recent research has raised questions about the role of context in learning (Chaiklin & Lave, 1993; D'Andrade, 1990; Erickson & Shultz, 1977; Hutchins, 1995; Jacob, 1992; Lave, 1988; Salomon, 1993; Saxe, 1999). Context here includes not only how a local setting, such as a classroom, is organized to support learning, but also the influences of a person's participation in other settings (such as family life, church, peer social networks, and community organizations) (Brofenbrenner, 1979; Nasir & Saxe, 2003; Rogoff, 1995). There is renewed interest in learning in organizations. In addition, the exploration of context also includes the influences of different scales of time: the moment, a day of instruction, a year of instruction; a student's age cohort; whether the event is happening in 1865, 1965, or 2005; and what a community inherits, uses, and adapts from prior generations, such as ways of using language, particular rituals, particular artifacts, and so on. (Bloome, Carter, Christian, Otto, & Shuart-Faris, 2005; Cole, 1996; Elder, 1985; Gonzáles, Moll, & Amanti, 2005; Green & Dixon, 1993; Lemke, 2000; Rose, 2004; Saxe, 1991, 1999; Saxe & Esmonde, 2005). Each of these waves has significant overlap historically and conceptually. Each introduces new orders of complexity (Holland, 1995). Together they have serious implications for what one needs to know, value, and practice in order to teach well.

Probably the most influential work on thinking about teacher knowledge is Shulman's (1986) description of what he calls "pedagogical content knowledge." Shulman argued that *pedagogical content knowledge* includes "the ways of representing and formulating the subject that make it comprehensible to others" (p. 9). Shulman's argument is one of the most cogent and comprehensive descriptions of the kinds of knowledge that are entailed in teaching. Still, the devil is in the details. What does pedagogical content knowledge mean for different subject matters, for teaching students of different ages, from different backgrounds, and under different material circumstances (Lampert, 2001)? I intend to take a stab at these questions with examples from a particular subject matter (response to literature), a particular age group (adolescents), and a particular group of students (African American adolescents who are largely speakers of African American English and from low-income backgrounds). In this chapter I will describe elements of teacher knowledge and then illustrate how they work together as dynamic and adaptive knowledge structures in instruction. These elements include subject matter content, what is entailed in youth's or novices' understanding subject matter content, child and adolescent development, general principles of how people learn, and language socialization.

RELATIONSHIPS BETWEEN CONTENT KNOWLEDGE AND PEDAGOGICAL CONTENT KNOWLEDGE

There is substantive research in both mathematics and science education about relationships between content knowledge and pedagogical content knowledge, although the research in mathematics seems to me more extensive than that in science education (Ball & Rundquist, 1993; Lampert, 1990; Ma, 1999; Peterson, Fenemma, Carpenter & Loef, 1989; Schoenfeld, 1988). However, history and response to literature have not wrestled with these questions in the same ways (Ball, 2000; Grossman, 1990; Holt-Reynolds, 1999; Wineburg & Wilson, 1988, 1991). These differences are very much influenced by fundamental distinctions in the epistemologies that undergird these subject matters and the historical traditions that inform them (Wineburg & Grossman, 1998).

I will illustrate some of the challenges involved in conceptualizing this relationship between content knowledge and pedagogical content knowledge in the area of response to literature, in part through comparisons with mathematics education. The question is fundamental to how we think about what teachers need to know. While much public policy, including state standards for accreditation, has clear requirements for content knowledge, such efforts typically underspecify what teachers need to know regarding pedagogical content knowledge. This question is also crucial to how we think about what teachers need to know about culture in relation to teaching subject matters. As discussed in Chapter 2, most of the discussions about the role of culture in learning focus on issues of motivation, relevance, and classroom management, but rarely about the innards of subject matter learning. Cultural Modeling takes the position that one cannot imagine points of leverage between everyday experience and subject matter learning without understanding the structure of disciplines in terms of both breadth and depth.

Content knowledge involves knowledge of the structure of the discipline, the modes of argumentation privileged, as well as habits of mind or dispositions entailed in doing the work of the discipline. In some subjects, distinctions are made between the work of professionals in the discipline and what students do in school (Lampert, 1990; Wineburg, 1998). For example, it is not the case that students studying even the most sophisticated calculus in high school are doing the work that theoretical mathematicians do. On the other hand, it is possible that the mathematics that students do in a good high school physics class may approximate in some limited ways the mathematics that a practicing engineer employs.

In literary reasoning, however, the terrain between what I would consider ideal school work and the "real world" are much closer. The question here is who we consider the professionals in literary reasoning. Many people might think of literary critics and creative writers as the professionals, but in many instances the best professional creative writers are not university trained in literary studies. Ideally, I think that the real-world counterpart are those people who vociferously read canonical literature as well as contemporary literature that is unique and complex (in contrast to more predictable formulaic works of contemporary fiction, like popular romance, mystery, or science fiction). I define *canonical literature* here as literature that stands the test of time and includes works from a wide array of national literatures. Thus I accept what some may consider a slightly elitist attitude. Nevertheless, I believe the best writers have the gift of second sight, and see in the human experience nuances that most of us do not. I believe the best literature helps us wrestle with the conundrums of being human and, as is the case with life itself, offers no simple, easily predictable solutions. These are the reasons why I am convinced that the teaching of great literature serves an enlightening function and why those youth who often grapple with life's most difficult circumstances need the rigorous study of great literature as a resource for coping and learning to be resilient. From my perspective, the gulf between the study of literature in school and the close reading of literature in life is not wide at all, and is influenced more by developmental differences, such as what you can understand as a teenager and what you can understand as a mature adult.

The structure of a discipline includes both breadth and depth. Breadth includes a declarative knowledge of the range of topics, the range of strategies available for solving problems, and the range of debates in the discipline, as well as a knowledge of the history of the evolution of knowledge within the discipline. Regarding literary reasoning, high school English teachers who were English majors in college typically understand the range of debates in the discipline that are most likely captured in literary criticism and will have studied national literatures historically, at least American, British, and some Western European literatures (Applebee, 1996; Applebee et al., 2000; Holt-Reynolds, 1999). In fact, the prototypical sequence of high school literature courses includes chronologically organized courses on American literature, British literature, and world literature (which is typically defined as European literature, and even then from a small subsample of Western European countries rather than Eastern European countries). Knowledge of topics generally includes particular authors, particular works of literature, and literary movements. The question of strategies is rarely even on the table. It is this conception of content knowledge as knowledge about authors, a limited range of literary works, and literary movements that drives English teachers and the high school literature curriculum to see coverage of these topics and exposure to these topics as the primary aim of instruction (Applebee et al., 2000). On the other hand, except for Advanced Placement Exams (which youth from so-called minority communities usually do not take) and specialized SAT subject matter exams, large-scale, high-accountability assessments generally will not even assess such declarative knowledge of literature. However, it should be noted that a few states are attempting to design more rigorous exit exams that include more authentic texts than has typically been the case in most standardized achievement tests.[1]

This singular focus on authors, particular texts and literary movements in the 4 years of studying literature in high school has led to an ironic outcome. Students learn to hate the very literature that English teachers want them to value.

This dilemma suggests the importance of depth of knowledge about the structure of the discipline. One thing depth includes is understanding what concepts are most generative, meaning that if you know these concepts well, you can do a lot of work in the discipline. In mathematics education, focusing on generative concepts has led to an emphasis on teaching fewer big ideas. For instance, in the Third International Mathematics and Science Study (TIMSS), researchers found that those countries scoring highest on international assessments focused on a few big ideas repeatedly and developmentally over time, such as introducing algebraic concepts early in the elementary grades (Stevenson & Stigler, 1992). By contrast, U.S. textbooks spend years of the middle school curriculum focusing on algorithms of multidigit multiplication and division, with little attention to the conceptual underpinnings of these operations. In literary reasoning, however, determining what concepts are generative has not been well specified.

In addition, depth of knowledge includes understanding the following issues in a discipline:

- How are concepts related to one another (e.g., the inverse relationships between multiplication and division)?
- What are procedures for determining and acting on those relationships (e.g., using repeated addition for multiplication and repeated subtraction for division)?
- Under what conditions are such procedures useful (e.g., distinguishing when the situation requiring division asks how many equal parts versus how many in each part)?
- What are a range of acceptable ways to operate on and with these concepts (e.g., solving a problem through estimation or through explicit computation; when it is sufficient to solve part of the problem to arrive at a reasonable response versus when the entire problem must be solved)?
- How does one extrapolate from these relationships to unknowns or less explored problems?

The illustrations included from mathematics are fairly straightforward and amenable to many teachers of mathematics, although not all (Ma, 1999). However, if the most frequently used high school literature anthologies were reviewed, a reader would have a difficult time figuring out if there were any concepts to be taught. What is usually discovered are occasional references to elements such as rhyme, onomatopoeia, alliteration, couplet, sonnet, and haiku in relation to poetry; or plot, climax, denouement, and omniscient narrator in relation to short stories; and a sprinkling here and there of references to irony, symbols, and satire. However, these are approached more as definitions or descriptions of structures. Rarely is there anything to suggest that knowing a poem is a sonnet or that there are such literary elements as symbols can be used to solve unexpected problems in making sense of literary works. Further, there is virtually nothing in the structure of the curriculum to suggest that any of these ideas bear any particular relation to one another, except perhaps that the first set refers to poems and the second to stories. (But even these distinctions do not hold: For example, a narrative poem will have some of the same elements as a short story, such as climax or denouement.) This truncated conception of the discipline does not provide the teacher with any resources to help novice, struggling, or resistant readers to figure out what they should do with a Morrison novel or a Shakespearean play.

I have discussed briefly in Chapter 1 a different orientation to the idea of breadth and depth of knowledge of literary reasoning required for teaching, particularly at the high school level. I have argued that literary reasoning entails concepts that have explanatory power and which involve particular strategies and heuristics. For example, a conceptual understanding of satire leads the reader (or listener) to view a stretch of text as entailing a problem for which a literal interpretation is not merely insufficient, but incorrect. A conceptual understanding of symbolism, on the other hand, leads the reader (or listener) to view a stretch of text as entailing a problem for which a literal comprehension is insufficient, but not necessarily incorrect (Ortony, 1979; Winner, 1988). The reader (or listener) needs some rules of thumb by which to categorize the problem that a stretch of text presents as one of either symbolism or satire, for example. One can find cases where a stretch of text can be both symbolic and satiric, or symbolic and ironic. However, the interpretation of its being symbolic will answer a different question being posed than the interpretation of its being satiric. In conversation with Yolanda Majors of the University of Illinois at Chicago, we concluded that the rose in Tupac Shakur's "The Rose That Grew from Concrete" is both symbolic and ironic. The image of a rose growing up out of concrete is symbolic. The fact that a rose *could* grow up out of concrete is ironic. The distinction is in the question being asked—that is, what does the rose mean; what does the act signify?

Failure to detect the kind of problem being posed leads to either a wrong response (e.g., the reader thinks Jonathan Swift actually believes that an appropriate solution to the problem of hunger in Ireland is to eat babies) or an inadequate or unembellished response. The criterion for adequacy of response is shaped largely, although not totally, by differences in traditions of literary criticism, including reader response theories in which personal taste and disposition are a primary criteria. Once the reader recognizes the kind of problem potentially posed by a stretch of text, he or she must then figure out how to go about tackling such a problem in order to make some sense of it. This is where the question of strategies related to particular concepts comes into play.

The idea of types of problems and strategies or heuristics for tackling such problems is generally anathema in the humanities although it is precisely the stuff over which literary critics vociferously fight (Fish, 1980). Some would argue that teaching literary strategies somehow makes the enterprise mundane and uncreative; others, that since literary reasoning does not privilege single right answers, strategies are inappropriate. I think both of these views are shortsighted with respect to teaching novices. First, you can learn to engage in literary reasoning without explicit teaching. In addition, people engage in literary reasoning about narratives they encounter across many media (television, film, music, as well as print literature). It is precisely this observation that Cultural Modeling draws on in the design and selection of cultural data sets used to elicit students' prior knowledge. On the other hand, in regard to the print medium, the people who learn to engage in literary reasoning more or less on their own typically read literature a great deal outside of school from the time they are children and interact with others who participate in the same practice, engaging in rich discussions about their sense making. More often than not, English teachers are such people. However, youth are generally in high school because they are legally required to be there and because it's a good place to hang out with their friends. Depending on their life circumstances, their goals, and how they have been socialized over time to view the work of schooling, they are not likely going to learn to engage in literary reasoning with print medium in the absence of explicit instruction. What teachers think youth need to know about literature is informed, in large part, by the content knowledge they have about the discipline itself (Bernstein, 2006; Grossman, 2001; Grossman, Wilson, & Shulman, 1989; Holt-Reynolds, 1999; Spratley, 2005; Zancanella, 1991).

The prototypical orientation to the literature curriculum I have described not only does not adequately specify generative concepts, but almost never addresses the question of how concepts are related to one another. These relationships are important for pedagogical content knowledge in terms of implications for what and how concepts are introduced and sequenced within and across the curriculum. For example, irony, satire and unreliable narration are related to one another in the sense that each requires a rejection of the literal and the reconstruction of an intended meaning that stands in contrast to, in tension with, or possibly in contradiction to the literal. In addition, the same stretch of text can be both ironic and satiric; a text involving unreliable narration may be both ironic and satiric. Thus the problems of distinguishing among these constructs involve subtle nuances. It makes sense then to consider sequencing instruction around these three concepts together. In addition, each involves a number of subcategories. For example, there is dramatic irony and situational irony. The distinction here is important for recognizing the circumstances that may signal irony. Dramatic irony involves a character saying something about which you as the reader recognize the irony while the character does not. There are a number of subcategories of satire: pun, parody, burlesque, and invective.

I have identified these problem types, that is, concepts that novices need to understand, because they are generative: symbolism, irony, satire, and use of unreliable narration. For each of these concepts, it is possible to describe strategies or heuristics that may be useful for identifying them as

kinds of problems to be solved and for reconstructing warrantable interpretations of what they can mean. Several important caveats must be noted
here. First, I distinguish between strategies and heuristics. *Strategies* are
more typically plans of action for solving a problem. *Heuristics* are less well
specified and represent general rule-of-thumb attempts. Whether strategies or heuristics may be necessary depends on the interpretive problem
posed. All such problems in literature involve making inferences. However, in some texts these problems are particularly complex and the texts
themselves are especially dense. I think that heuristics, for example, may
involve knowing that one should draw on multiple sources of information
to tackle the problem. This heuristic of course is influenced by how one
construes the problem. These multiple sources of information will be different for various kinds of interpretive problems, but can certainly range
from knowledge of the text structure, the author, other works by the author or related to the text, literary traditions, and the syntax within sentences and across sentences, as well as knowledge of human intentionality
and event scripts. Knowing when and how these bodies of knowledge may
be useful to bring to bear in an act of literary interpretation is more in the
order of heuristics than strategies. Strategies, on the other hand, may be
more useful when the text poses an interpretive problem that is more
localized—constrained to a sentence, paragraph, or a few pages (Hillocks
& Ludlow, 1984).

   Michael Smith (Rabinowitz & Smith, 1998; Smith, 1989, 1991; Smith &
Hillocks, 1988) has conducted a compelling body of research that draws
on strategies identified by literary critic Wayne Booth (1974, 1983) for identifying and reconstructing new meanings for problems of irony and unreliable narration. Smith tested these strategies in instruction with 9th–11th
graders and found that whether the strategies were taught explicitly or
implicitly, students significantly improved in their ability to interpret irony
and unreliable narration. In Chapter 1, I described a strategy we developed
for interpreting symbolism and tested in high school classrooms with success. Thus we do have some empirical evidence that strategies for particular concepts in literary reasoning are available, are used by critics (as
evidenced in Booth's explications), and are teachable to youth as novice
readers. It is useful to note here that Holt-Reynolds (1999) conducted a
study of preservice teachers who were English majors. She discovered that
while these English majors were very adept at interpreting works of literature, they did not understand what students needed to know in order
to do what these teachers as readers did themselves.

   In mathematics education, the structure of the discipline is fairly well
specified. In some countries, such as China and Japan, teachers generally
have a more detailed conceptual understanding of the structure of the dis-

cipline than U.S. teachers. LiPing Ma (1999) gave a group of U.S. and Chinese middle school teachers a problem involving dividing two fractions with unlike denominators, for example, $1\frac{1}{5} \div \frac{1}{2}$. Forty-three percent of the U.S. teachers could use a procedure to get the correct answer; for example, "convert the mixed number into an improper fraction, invert the divisor and multiply it by the dividend, reduce the product, $14/4$, and change it to a proper fraction, $3\frac{1}{2}$" (p. 56). However, not one U.S. middle school teacher in the sample could provide a mathematical explanation as to why. Every Chinese middle school teacher could provide multiple mathematical explanations as to why. Ma refers to the knowledge of these Chinese teachers as a "profound understanding of fundamental mathematics." I have wrestled with the question of what would be the counterpart to such knowledge in literary reasoning. I believe that a *profound understanding of fundamentals of literary reasoning* must involve breadth and depth of knowledge of the structure of the discipline, as I have described. It must also include an understanding of modes of argumentation and habits of mind valued within the discipline (Applebee, 1996; Applebee et al., 2000). As an example, the variety of explanations offered by the Chinese teachers about the math problem above represented modes of argumentation in the mathematics discipline. Modes of argumentation include (Kuhn, 1991; Toulmin, Rieke, & Janik, 1984):

- What counts as an important question
- What strategies and resources are appropriate to explore the important question
- What counts as evidence to whom
- What modes of logic reasonably connect evidence to claims (i.e., warrants)
- How to situate one's mode of argumentation within competing debates in the field
- How to communicate with others in and outside the discipline

The habits of mind or dispositions required to engage in such argumentation are also a fundamental aspect of content knowledge of a discipline.

I will briefly illustrate several of these aspects of modes of argumentation in literary reasoning. In a recent edition of the McDougal Littel literature anthology for American literature, Faulkner's (1930/1997) short story "A Rose for Emily" is included. Questions are asked about how the reader feels about the actions of the townspeople who are small-minded and espouse public expectations about the kind of social life that a woman of the social status of Emily, the protagonist, should have. While I have no doubt that this is an interesting and useful question to ask, it is possible to answer the question without even reading the entire story. In fact, if you simply had a summary of the plot, you could figure out a reasonable response to that question. On the other hand, the question of why the story is called "A Rose for Emily," what the significance of the rose is, why pay attention to it, is a fundamental question of literary reasoning worth asking.

In a similar vein, the opening section, "Autumn," of Toni Morrison's (1970) novel *The Bluest Eye* starts off, "the nuns walked by quiet as lust." Students typically are socialized to pay attention to the who, what , when, and where of the story, thus paying attention almost solely to plot. With such an orientation, the novice reader may pause at the sentence but then look to find out more of what Morrison has to say about nuns. However, there are no other references to nuns in the novel. With the primary orientation to plot, the novice reader then most often will simply ignore this sentence and continue to read on to find out more about the major characters, their actions, and the logic behind those actions. As with the rose in the Faulkner story, close attention to details such as a single sentence that says "the nuns walked by quiet as lust" sparks the literary imagination like a magnet drawing the reader into figuring out how to make sense of this odd detail. Attending to and asking questions of these details are examples of understanding what counts as important problems in literary reasoning. The other issues that flow from such key questions, as referenced earlier, have to do with understanding how to tackle such ill-structured or open problems. Once one has claims to make about the problem—including claims as to why the problem is worth tackling—the issues of what counts as evidence and what logic connects evidence to claims become salient.

I believe that the problem of the rose in the Faulkner story is amenable to strategies as described in Chapter 1 for detecting that a stretch of text is likely symbolic rather than literal, and then for reconstructing a warrantable interpretation. "Rose" is marked as prominent because it is both in the title as well as at a pivotal transition point in the story; and Faulkner uses great detail to describe the rose on the bed where the dead Homer (Emily's fiancé) lies. Real-world associations with the rose (e.g., romance and beauty) when compared to how it is situated in the story lead to seeing a stark contrast between the two situations. Such contrasts with the literal are typically indicative of irony, satire, or unreliable narration. In fact, one could make a cogent argument that the rose is both ironic and satiric and that Emily as a narrator is unreliable. One could also make a different argument, namely that the rose does signify romance to Emily, but that this significance for Emily is indeed ironic. While in this example, arguing from the text and real-world associations would be good and sufficient sources of evidence, more elaborate arguments would also use evidence from other works by Faulkner, from works by other authors who write in the same or related tradition, as well as from the reader's own life experiences.

In terms of teacher content knowledge, the issues are whether the teacher knows (1) how to design instruction in ways that will facilitate students' grappling with such questions; (2) how to tap what students already know and value as a way of making public for them that posing such questions is important and useful; (3) how to hear with understanding the range of arguable responses that students might come up with and how to respond to that range, and why. I further argue that helping students see the relevance and importance of such questions requires much more than simply telling them they should tackle such a problem or simply adding the question to a worksheet.

The problem in Morrison's *The Bluest Eye* is more complex, in that local details are insufficient to construct a warrantable explanation of what may be meant or intended by "the nuns walked by quiet as lust." Similar to the rose in the Faulkner story, the sentence cries out for attention because it is such an anomaly, both in terms of the paragraph in which it is found and the larger novel itself. This complex question requires a heuristic described by Rabinowitz (1987) in what he calls "rules of configuration and coherence." Rabinowitz makes the case that much of what we use to make sense of literary texts are forms of knowledge of reading such narratives that actually precede our engagement with the text itself, a kind of literary toolkit that we bring to the enterprise; a toolkit that is constructed as a result of reading widely. *Rules of configuration* refer to the reader's attempts to construct meaning or impart some level of coherence onto details that we meet while we are reading. These attempts are always hypothetical, constantly being tested by the continued unfolding of the text. As we look back, from one section to another or after having read the text as a whole, details of the text take on new salience and new meanings that we could not have anticipated ahead of time. It is precisely the habit of mind to be so inclined to keep trying to connect details into patterns that makes rereadings of rich texts both a compelling and rewarding enterprise.

Knowledge of this aspect of the structure of the discipline—content knowledge—would lead teachers to create many opportunities for multiple readings of rich texts. Wolf (1995) suggests that in the high school literature curriculum, students should have multiple opportunities to reread a text within a semester, but also to revisit works read early in the high school career at later points, in part in order to reflect metacognitively on their growth as readers over time. In studies I have conducted in the Cultural Modeling Project, using talk-aloud protocols with students whose standardized reading scores would label them as struggling readers, having the opportunity to read a new story more than once has consistently yielded deeper insights with each new reading (Lee, Rivers, Hutchinson, Bernstein, & Dixon, 2000). While rereading a rich text is clearly part of the practice of literary reasoning in the real world, it is certainly not valued in typical forms of high-stakes assessments (Wolf et al., 1991). I have often wondered what test scores would look like if students simply were not timed.

PEDAGOGICAL CONTENT KNOWLEDGE

I hope it is clear that the level and quality of content knowledge required for the best teaching is indeed rigorous and complex. Yet if such knowledge in itself were sufficient, we should be able to take great undergraduate English majors or great literary critics or, for that matter, great writers and put them in urban high school English classes (or chemists in chemistry classes or physicists in physics classes). If the goal is to help young people learn to reason in the ways I have described, the pedagogical question is how do people learn how to engage in these thinking practices. Pedagogical content knowledge (PCK) involves understanding the following:

- Developmental progressions (e.g., children versus adolescents)
- The continuum between novice and expert practice
- Enduring misconceptions and naive theories held by youth and novices generally (Clement, 1982; Clement et al., 1989; DiSessa, 1982)
- Multiple routes to maximize opportunities to learn
- How to assess what learners understand and don't understand

These competencies are based on a deep understanding of cognition, of human development, and of language socialization, as well as understanding these in relation to the subject matter and the students one is teaching.

The research on the cognitive processes that undergird reading comprehension has consistently documented that reading is inherently a process of constructing mental representations (Garner, 1987; Kintsch, 1998; Pearson & Fielding, 1991). These processes involve interactions between the reader, the text, and the context. Reading involves knowledge in a number of areas: phonemic (sound-symbol relationships), syntactic (sentence structures), text structures (overall organizational patterns), vocabulary (words, roots, affixes, relations across words, such as synonyms and antonyms, or the functions of prepositions and conjunctions), content or topical knowledge regarding propositions in a text (e.g., knowledge about baseball), as well as domain-specific knowledge (e.g., knowledge of event scripts and human intentionality in works of literature).

Reading involves an interaction between bottom-up processes—e.g., understanding words and sentences—as well as top-down processes—e.g., using what you already know to make sense of what you see in the text (Kintsch, 1992, 1998). These top-down processes are very much influenced by cultural experiences in the world (Kintsch & Greene, 1978). For example, researchers working with Richard Anderson at what was the Center for the Study of Reading at the University of Illinois at Urbana documented how readers from different cultural groups would interpret the same texts in entirely different ways (Reynolds, Taylor, Steffensen, Shirey, & Anderson, 1982; Steffensen, Joag-Dev, & Anderson, 1979). Good readers are flexible, always monitoring understanding, and knowing what to do when comprehension breaks down (e.g., they get to a point where fluid processing is not occurring), always actively trying to make sense of the text in relation to their goals for reading.

There are important pedagogical implications for this conception of reading. The reader must be active in the process of trying to make sense of a text. This means the teacher must have knowledge of how to design learning environments in ways that maximize the likelihood that students will be actively engaged in trying to make sense of what they read. It also means the teacher must have a good way of figuring out what in a given text is likely to pose particular problems for specific readers. In the elementary grades, readability formulas are most often used to match texts with students. However, even at the lower grades when youth may still be struggling with sound-symbol relationships, research has documented the creative ways that even novice readers can compensate when they can't read a given word (Goodman, 1973; Goodman, 1989; Stahl & Miller, 1989). They may use context in terms of what they've understood so far from the sentence, paragraph, or overall text, as well as pictures to predict a reasonable substitution for words they cannot fluently recognize. At the secondary level, readability formulas are even less reliable. For example, a teacher could use a readability formula to ascertain the grade level of a Hemingway story. Readability formulas measure text length, sentence length, word syllables, and the frequency of words at particular levels of difficulty to ascertain a grade level for a text. I recently typed out the opening of Hemingway's (1938/1995) classic short story "The Snows of Kilimanjaro." The Flesch-Kinkaid grade level (Flesch, 1974) was 2.5. However, that does not mean second or third graders could understand the Hemingway story, even if they could say most of the words on the page. The more recent work in using lexiles (White & Clement, 2001) to assess readability levels is somewhat better, but still clearly insufficient for selecting the appropriateness of texts to be taught. Instead of using grade level equivalents, lexile scores assign a general developmental level, such as advanced high school. Thus in the teaching of literary reasoning, understanding developmental progressions from childhood to adolescents involves much more than issues of fluency.

Alexander (1998, 2003; Alexander, Kulikowich, & Jetton, 1994) has put forward a very interesting model for what she calls a lifespan developmental perspective on reading. She argues against simplistic notions of good readers, poor readers, and struggling readers. If reading is a straightforward singular developmental pathway, how do we explain the fact that most 17-year-olds leaving high school are not able to read specialized texts, even those who have scored well on earlier assessments (ACT, 2006)? Alexander (2003) describes five stages in reading development: acclimation, early reading, middle competence, later development, and proficiency or expertise. She argues that situational interest (interest of the moment) and surface processing strategies (e.g., developing fluency in recognizing words and developing speed in reading) are high in the early stages, while over time enduring individual interests, topic knowledge, domain knowledge, and deep processing strategies increase across the five stages. She makes several important observations: "Although the stages of reading development correspond, to some degree, to years of schooling, the three stages of development—acclimation, competence, and proficiency/expertise—are not specifically age or grade related. . . . Readers in acclimation exist at all ages and in all grades. . . . The longer it takes students to acquire the fundamental knowledge, seeds of interest, and strategic repertoire, the more problems they are likely to face in the future" (pp. 12–13). She describes four profiles of typical readers: highly competent readers, seriously challenged readers, effortful processors, knowledge-reliant readers, nonstrategic processors, and resistant readers. Alexander's model is intriguing. Particularly in regard to older students, such as adolescents in high school, recognizing these profiles is part of understanding several aspects of pedagogical content knowledge: (1) developmental progressions, (2) continuum between novice and expert, and (3) enduring misconceptions. The pedagogical challenge is not simply to recognize these profiles, but also to understand the fourth aspect of pedagogical content knowledge: the ability to design multiple routes to maximize opportunities to learn, and to design learning environments that allow learners to draw with supports on multiple resources (i.e., multiple languages, peers, experts, tools, and so on. (Gutiérrez et al., 1999).

From the perspective of Cultural Modeling, conceptualizing resources that students already bring with them from their experiences outside of school is a fundamental element in the teachers' PCK toolkit. We have consistently found in Cultural Modeling classrooms that students who would be designated as seriously challenged readers, effortful processors, knowledge reliant readers, nonstrategic processors, and resistant readers show astounding progress in engaging in literary reasoning with very complex texts. This is the case for several reasons. First, in preparation for disciplinary learning, work with cultural data sets makes domain-specific reading strategies public. Second, use of cultural data sets also demonstrates the relevance of the cognitive work entailed in literary reasoning in the everyday lives of youth. Third, sequencing texts in ways that build on knowledge of event scripts, character types, and human intentionality makes the new use of existing strategies—the form-function shift that Saxe (1991) speaks of—a safer enterprise because students' existing prior knowledge is privileged. Finally, as described in Chapter 3, the design of instruction in ways that privilege contextualization cues regarding language use that students already value provides incentives to be effortful and actively participate. This ability to recontextualize instruction in ways that draw on what students already know and value has leverage power for all the types of readers Alexander has described.

Understanding reading, especially learning to read in domain-specific ways, is a form of language acquisition and socialization (Gee, 1990). The literature on first- and second-language acquisition documents what novices learn through patterned errors, that is, using a rule in a context that does not apply, such as applying the rule of adding *s* for plural to pluralize *child* by saying *childs* (Gee, 1994). Experts—be they parents, preschool teachers, or bilingual teachers—come to understand these "errors" as evidence of knowledge of a pattern, and therefore as useful, generative knowledge, implying that instruction at this point is about helping youth learn the circumstances under which the generic rule does not apply. In Cultural Modeling, the act of drawing on students' knowledge, dispositions, and competencies outside of school does not imply a simple one-to-one correspondence between the everyday and the academic. Indeed, Cultural Modeling is to a large degree about helping students understand how their everyday knowledge is related and different from the academic. The literature on language socialization documents that learning a new language, language variety, or social register entails understanding the epistemological assumptions behind genres, the rules for participating (e.g., how to get and hold the floor), the rules for what counts as good questions, good claims, and good evidence; in other words, learning how to engage the world through language in new ways (Ballenger, 1997; Bauman & Briggs, 1990; Cook-Gumperz, 1986; Gee, 2000a; Gumperz & Hymes, 1972; Heath, 1983; Morgan, 1998; Smitherman, 1977). Certainly learning to read disciplinary texts, be they in literature or physics, is about learning new ways of understanding and producing language.

IDENTITY AND DEVELOPMENT AS LINKS BETWEEN CONTENT KNOWLEDGE AND PEDAGOGICAL CONTENT KNOWLEDGE

In Chapter 1, I discussed the importance of issues of identity in academic work in terms of its role in motivation. Motivation includes peoples' "beliefs about their competence and efficacy, their expectations for success or failure, and their sense of control over outcomes" (Eccles et al., 1998, p. 1022), as well as the value people attribute to tasks (Eccles-Parsons et al., 1983). While motivational research typically focuses on the individual, a cultural orientation considers how beliefs about competence and efficacy as well as the value attributed to tasks may be shaped both by community-level factors as well as the organizational features of settings .

My focus in Cultural Modeling and in this book is on youth from communities that face persistent intergenerational discrimination and limited access to resources (e.g., housing, health care, jobs, quality schooling). All people face challenges in figuring out how to move from one setting to another. However, youth from these communities face qualitatively different kinds of challenges in terms of managing what may be conflicting demands for participation in different settings (Graham & Taylor, 2002; Spencer, 1999, 2000; Steele, 1998). How one identifies with a particular practice has strong implications for how one participates and what effort, if any, one uses. Nasir (2000; Nasir & Saxe, 2003) talks about how a track coach positioned a young female novice track runner as a hurdler. He gave her explicit instructions about why she knocked over the hurdle and fell, while at the same time telling her she is a hurdler. Simply telling people they can accomplish a task without providing them with explicit support for doing the work the task requires is shallow and is not likely to inspire someone who sees herself as failing to put forth the extraordinary effort that will be required to change these circumstances. Many of the youth with whom Cultural Modeling is concerned have faced many years of schooling where they have not only experienced failure, but have been explicitly labeled in ways that position them as incapable.

In addition, at each developmental transition across the life course, there are special challenges involved in negotiating that transition (Bowman, 1989; Spencer, 1999, 2000). In adolescence, these include physiological changes in which issues of sexuality become very important, maturational changes involving renegotiations over one's role in the family structure, sociological changes in which multiple kinds of relationships with peers take on great prominence, and academic changes in which the nature of schooling is reorganized in fundamental ways. High schools are typically larger and more impersonal institutions than elementary or middle schools, although there is a significant movement toward creating smaller learning communities in high schools (Ancess, 2003). High school teachers are more likely to see themselves as teachers of subject matter, and the task for these teachers of getting to know students personally is harder because they may have 150–200 students a day. Learning how to navigate what can be anywhere from five to seven different adult personalities a day is a developmental challenge for students. The subject matter in high school typically becomes more abstract and more divorced from everyday life; so figuring out why you need to study British literature, chemistry, or algebra and trigonometry can certainly be halting. Even though there are many new curricula—especially in the sciences and mathematics—that attempt to make connections with the everyday world, they rarely are designed flexibly enough to accommodate what may be very different everyday experiences for youth who live in an affluent suburb, youth who live in public housing in a large urban area, and youth who live in a poor rural community such as the Mississippi Delta.

In addition to these developmental challenges, these youth must also learn to navigate challenges in their neighborhoods concerning high levels of violence, limited resources for extracurricular activities, and limited availability of resources—such as particular kinds of social networks —that provide access to opportunities outside their neighborhoods (Jencks & Mayer, 1990). William Julius Wilson (1987) points out that during the era of legal segregation, African American neighborhoods had residents from upper-, middle- and working-class positions living together. While there is no question that there was elitism in these communities, youth from working-class and low-income backgrounds could see people working in professions, owning businesses, and going to college (Irvine & Irvine, 1983).

The issue of violence in low-income urban neighborhoods poses many problems, some of which are gender related. Spencer (2000; Spencer et al., 2006; Spencer, Swanson, & Cunningham, 1991) has documented the developmental trajectory of identification with bravado and machismo behavior as an indicator of manhood among African American adolescents. She notes that the identification with bravado is highest in the early stages of adolescence, a time when young men often identify risk taking as an index of their evolving sense of manhood. She documents that this identification levels off as the young men approach young adulthood, in part because many have seen the real consequences of risky, violent behavior. Spencer argues, quite cogently, that how youth learn how to respond to these various sources of risk depends not simply on the objective reality of the risk (net vulnerability level), but rather on how they perceive the risks and what they imagine are possible responses to it. Their perception of risk is what she calls "net stress engagement level." The coping responses they learn emerge from the balance between the actual sources of risks and the protective factors that help youth learn how to respond. These protective factors may include institutional supports, personal relationships, and belief systems. Over time, Spencer argues, these coping responses become part of the emergent identity of a youth and over time part of that person's stable identity. Figure 5.1 captures the elements of Spencer's Phenomenological Variant of Ecological Systems Theory (PVEST) model (Spencer, 1999).

Spencer's model is particularly useful in conceptualizing teachers' pedagogical content knowledge. It certainly can be used by teachers as a

Figure 5.1. Phenomenological Variant of Ecological Systems Theory (PVEST).

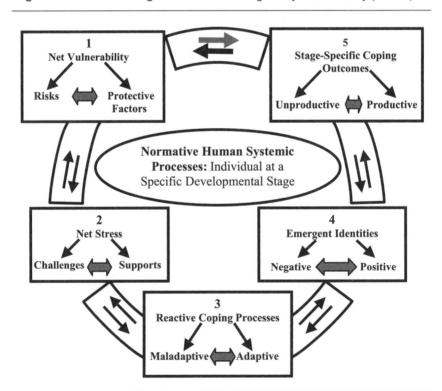

Source: Spencer (1995, 2006). Reprinted with permission of Margaret Beale Spencer.

general model for understanding what may be antisocial and other forms of resistance by students. It also has implications for subject matter learning. This is, in part, because problems of classroom management, for example, do not happen in isolation. They typically occur in the midst of instruction. Some of the sources of risk that students face in school are not so much from tensions arising from their lives outside of school, but through their history of schooling in tandem with the microlevel face-to-face interactions inside classrooms. There is a whole field devoted to understanding how people "read" the social world, identified as either social cognition or social psychology (Bandura, 1986; Bruner & Tagiuri, 1954; Kunda, 1999). The signals that position students as incompetent can be very subtle, and when they are persistent and consistent with other such signals students have seen in their histories of schooling, the students typically have coping responses that have served them well, at least in their eyes. These often maladaptive coping responses, to use Spencer's term, may include not doing either class work or homework, skipping class, coming to class late, being disruptive in class, or simply spacing out and not paying attention at all.

Learning to "read" a social world that is racialized is also a significant developmental challenge (Bowman, 1989; Graham & Taylor, 2002; Mills, 1997; Nobles, 1985; Spencer, 1987, 2000). Stories from the era of legal segregation abound about African American elders telling young people that in order to succeed they had to be better than Whites, based on the realistic and life-learned assumption that simple merit alone would not be sufficient. The kinds of racial socialization that empowered even young children to serve as the front guard in desegregating schools represent a phenomenal apprenticeship into coping strategies and resilience that is sorely needed today (Bell, 1992). Even though legal segregation has ended, discrimination based on race is alive and well. For example, statistics show that college-educated Blacks and Whites do not have the same earning power, just as there are both gender and gender by race differentials in earning power, with White males continuing to have the greatest earning power (Urban League, 1999, 2005). L. Scott Miller (1995), as well as other researchers, has documented the implications of these tremendous inequalities in terms of wealth for opportunities to learn, by which I mean not only money earned across a lifetime, but more so inherited wealth in the form of stocks and bonds, real estate, businesses, as well as social networks that enhance access to wealth.

These persistent inequalities clearly affect the level of resources, including the quality of schooling available to African American, American Indian, Latino, Pacific Islanders, some Asian Americans, and all groups who live in persistent intergenerational poverty. For example, dropout rates for African American, American Indian, and Latino youth are consistently higher than for Whites (Fry, 2005; Kaufman et al., 2004). This problem of inequitable access to resources is not only a problem for those who are racialized, but is also a problem of class, as is evident in the devastating dropout rates for low-income Appalachian Whites (Hicks, 2002). This racialized world (and this class-based world) is one that African American, American Indian, Latino, Pacific Islanders, and Asian Americans must learn how to "read" and resist in ways that promote progress for both individuals and communities. Vanessa Siddle-Walker (1993) and James Anderson (1988), among others, have documented how during the era of legalized segregation (the Jim Crow period) and even during the African Holocaust of Enslavement, the traditional public schools in African American communities served both educational as well as socialization and community empowerment functions.

What then are the implications of these sets of issues for teacher's pedagogical content knowledge? Primarily, these issues are related to what I and others consider the ethical and moral dimensions of teaching (Noddings, 1984). In recent work studying preparation for an array of professions, a separate category emerged called the caring professions (Hansen, 2001a, 2001b; Shulman, 2004, 2005; Sullivan, 2005). These include medicine, the ministry, fire fighting, and even the military. These are occupations in which professional training explicitly addresses the ethical dimensions of the work. For example, doctors take the Hypocratic Oath to do no harm, and other professions take similar oaths. When our oldest son, Bomani, graduated in civil engineering from Northwestern University, he joined the professional society of engineers, and as part of his induction, he had to take an oath to do no harm: The preface to the oath described how the public expects the bridges and buildings designed by engineers to be sound and not crumble on top of us.

During the horrific moments of September 11, 2001, the public saw many instances of heroism that were rooted in fundamental assumptions that caring and doing good for others were essential to being a priest, a fire fighter, a police officer, and a teacher. We think of the priest who reentered the burning towers to give last rites when he knew he was risking his life to do so; the fire fighters and police officers who risked their lives to save others; the teachers who made sure that the children in the preschool in one of the towers escaped from the burning building.

I believe that teaching is a caring profession, that most people enter teaching because they want to do good for youth. I further believe that as a teacher, I must see the growth and development of each student I teach as a life opportunity entrusted to my hands, as a investment, if you will, in the future of myself, that youth, my children, and society at large. This fundamental moral and ethical commitment is what allows a teacher to wrestle with her own demons, prejudices, and limitations, rather than to take the easy way out and blame the student, his family, his neighborhood, or the board of education.

This kind of ethical commitment has distinct implications for subject matter learning. First, it means the teacher must come to know each student and the life circumstances that student brings with him when he enters a classroom. Some will certainly argue that, especially for high school teachers, this is very difficult, if for no other reason than they teach many students for short periods of time during the day. I respond, however, by pointing out that all students do not require the same level of monitoring or understanding; even in the most difficult schools, a majority of students are usually at least willing to try, to behave in class, to do schoolwork and homework, and to show up. In addition, part of the toolkit of teaching involves understanding an array of typical developmental patterns that one is likely to meet. This means, for example, understanding the challenges of navigating into manhood, trying to figure out the functions and functionality of machismo or bravado behavior, understanding that such machismo behavior is a typical pattern for most males, and an especially typical pattern for adolescent males from certain communities (Spencer et al., 2006). A teacher need not necessarily know the precise details of every teenage boy in her classroom, but she certainly should be able to read bravado behavior as an instance of a particular kind of vulnerability and adaptation. This is the reason that it is imperative for teachers to have detailed training in child and adolescent development, with a special emphasis for the diversity of pathways to development that may occur in different historically defined cultural communities (Greenfield & Cocking, 1994; Rogoff, 2003). Unfortunately, this is not the case for most preservice teacher training.

Second, it is important to recognize what may be sources of vulnerability for students. For example, Alexander's (2003) typology of profiles of readers across the life course is a useful resource for anticipating the kinds of resources and challenges that successful and struggling readers bring. Specifically in reading, any of the following may be sources of vulnerability that inhibit students' competence as readers and that may influence maladaptive coping responses to their own sense of vulnerability when instruction is not designed in ways to help them learn how to overcome these difficulties in ways that are developmentally appropriate:

- Comprehension problems due to vocabulary, syntax, text structure
- Lack of prior knowledge of domain concepts, such as in literary reasoning, plot configurations, character types, event schemas & scripts, archetypal themes

- Lack of metacognitive awareness and fix-it strategies for times when comprehension breaks down
- Competing interests and needs
- Not understanding rules for participation—appropriate uses of language, how to get and maintain the floor
- Interpersonal conflicts with other students, with the teacher
- Disabilities

A teacher of reading must understand these potential sources of vulnerability, how to diagnose them, and how to mediate them. Part of the mediation process involves conceptualizing the array of resources that are in fact available to the student to leverage learning. This may include any of the following: (1) ways of using language, such as work documenting the metalinguistic skills of bilingual youth translators (Orellana, Reynolds, Dorner, & Meza, 2003; Valdés, 2002), or my own work documenting signifying as a language practice that entails comprehension and production of an array of figurative language; (2) experiences in everyday practice with ideas or artifacts related to the discipline, such as knowledge about estimation among youth who engage in buying and selling or among youth who routinely play basketball (Nasir, 2000; Nasir & Saxe, 2003); (3) experiences in everyday practice on which instruction in the discipline can be anchored, such as the use of the urban transit system as an anchor for understanding and operating with integers in The Algebra Project (Moses & Cobb, 2001); (4) habits of mind or dispositions that are socialized in everyday practice, such as a disposition to appreciate and respond to language play as an aesthetically pleasing end in itself, among speakers of African American English, or a disposition to engage intently in forms of argumentation through *bay odyans* among Haitian Creole speakers (Conant et al., 2001; Rosebery et al., 2005).

Sometimes such resources may include social networks in the lives of youth. For example, when I was working at Fairgate High School as part of the Cultural Modeling Project, I learned that if certain young men missed my class, I need only find one of the security guards in the building. These men, some older and some young, typically had closer relationships with young men in the school than any of the teaching staff. I needed only tell Marcus that Montell missed class and Montell would be sure to show up the next day. We know that relationships are important in all schools, but especially in high schools; students who are typically failing many classes will still show up in the building to see their friends, and will selectively decide which classes they will attend.

How to "read" what students say and do, both in terms of general classroom management issues as well as what they say and do inside instruction, is foundational to teachers' pedagogical content knowledge. Developing a toolkit of such skills is not easy to learn. I do not believe teachers can learn such pedagogical content knowledge in methods classes (although I do think they can learn the foundational principles in such classes). Typically their experiences in student teaching are not long enough to develop such skills. In addition, many preservice teachers end up teaching in schools that are very different from those in which they interned. This pedagogical toolkit consists of knowledge-in-practice, a kind of flexible and adaptive knowing that requires integration across many domains —cognition, content knowledge, pedagogical content knowledge, child and adolescent development, and language socialization, to name the most fundamental. Such knowledge must operate as a flexible, dynamic, and interdisciplinary whole. It must be flexible and dynamic because part of what makes teaching interesting is that you can never fully specify in advance how students will respond to what you plan and design. In addition, the problems in each of these domains rarely present themselves in isolation. Any act and set of acts in which a teacher must respond almost always involve student thinking, subject matter, pedagogy, developmental issues such as identity and motivation, as well as ways of using and making sense of language. I think all human interactions involve most of these domains, perhaps not subject matter issues but some content related to what is entailed in carrying out a particular task. As humans we are fundamentally sense-making organisms, always wrestling with making sense of the complex ecologies in which we live and act in the world. Teaching is just a microcosm of that fundamental human challenge.

CHAPTER 6

Understanding Teacher Knowledge and Commitment in Practice

As part of the work at Fairgate High School, I collected videotapes, assessments, and student work over the course of 3 years. From other teachers in the project, I collected all quarterly assessments and videotaped at least 4 times a year. In my own class I videotaped every day. I have found these videos to be invaluable resources for helping me as a teacher to think about what is entailed in teaching. Every time I view one of these tapes, I learn something new about my own knowledge and about my students. It is fascinating for me to look at a single moment in time and try to reconstruct the sources of knowledge on which I drew to make in-the-moment pedagogical decisions. It is in part because of these reflections over the last 10 years that I now argue that these multiple sources of knowledge operate in tandem, coordinated to respond to one's perceptions of particular moments, influencing over the long term how a teacher conceptualizes the design of learning environments. In this chapter, I will illustrate what these knowledge packets and ethical commitments can look like in practice, and specifically how issues of culture came into play for me.

In the 1997–98 school year, I was teaching a class of seniors. As was the case historically with many students at Fairgate High School, most students had reading scores in the bottom two quartiles. The initial unit of instruction focused on symbolism. Cultural data sets were used to elicit strategies that students used in everyday contexts for detecting problems of symbolism and for reconstructing warrantable interpretations. We used rap lyrics, rap videos, African American spirituals, film clips, and television programming that required the interpretation of symbols to understand them. One of these cultural data sets included a short film called "Sax Cantor Riff," from the HBO series *Subway Stories*. As described in Chapter 3, "Sax Cantor Riff" was directed by Julie Dash (1997), famed African American independent filmmaker who made the acclaimed *Daughters of the Dust*. Typical of Dash's other work, this short film is rife with symbols.

132

We selected it as a cultural data set for several reasons. First, we assumed that the students did watch the television series; many in fact did, but had not seen this particular episode. Second, it was full of nuanced symbols and also allowed for discussions of authorial intent (see Chapter 3 for a summary of the film's story).

This class of seniors did not have prior experience with the Cultural Modeling curriculum, as we had phased in the intervention over a 3-year period. This third year of the intervention was the first year for seniors in the project. The students knew that these cultural data sets were intended to prepare them for reading Toni Morrison's novel *Beloved* (1987). It should be noted that the movie *Beloved* had not been produced and none of the students had ever read anything by Toni Morrison before. In fact, prior to the Cultural Modeling Project, only students in the single honors class per grade level typically read novels in class. After viewing "Sax Cantor Riff" and fielding reactions and questions from students, I notice that Taquisha is reading a newspaper. The following exchange occurs at the point that I try to address the fact that Taquisha is reading a newspaper when she is supposed to be taking part in instruction.

(1) *T*: Other questions. Other questions. Taquisha you have a question inside that paper there?

(2) *Taquisha*: Yup.

(3) *T*: What's your question?

(4) *Taquisha*: I put what does the [film have to do with anything we're studying?]

(What Taquisha says is inaudible on the tape. Carol Lee has reconstructed the statements in brackets from her memory and the context of her response to Taquisha's statement.)

(5) *T*: Well that might be a question for me.

(6) *Taquisha*: Well what does the book have to do with the girl and the man singing?

(7) *T*: Say that again. That's a good question.

(8) *Taquisha*: What does the——(Inaudible) ? (Students were all talking at the same time.)

(9) *T*: What does the girl have to do with what?

(10) *Taquisha*: What does the girl have to do with the girl and the man singing? (The teacher is writing the questions down on the board.)

(11) *T*: What is the girl singing is her question have to do with the man singing? That is a beautiful and sound question. Found it in the *Sun-Times* too, didn't you?

(12) *Taquisha*: Yup.

This interchange takes place over a matter of minutes. In that moment, as the teacher, I had to make an instinctual response to a behavior that is clearly a public form of resistance. Taquisha is actually reading the newspaper while I am conducting the lesson. My reasoning here was certainly not the result of a conscious process at the time. However, in retrospect, I believe that I drew on multiple sources of teacher knowledge and that these domains of knowledge were accessed as a holistic packet. These sources of teacher knowledge included the following: how people learn, adolescent development, content knowledge, pedagogical content knowledge, community-based discourse norms, and language socialization.

The design of the lesson in terms of showing the 5-minute film (i.e., use of cultural data sets) was based on the learning principle that merely telling students about a set of strategies would not be sufficient for them to actively represent the propositions in long-term memory for future use. The cultural data set serves as an anchor for inquiry, with the assumption that these particular students have the appropriate prior knowledge to recognize salient patterns. One of the goals of instruction is to help students name these patterns and to articulate the details that signal these patterns for them. A second goal is to help them develop a metalanguage by which to categorize the strategies in ways that are usable across different contexts beyond the one they are currently investigating. The principle behind the use of cultural data sets in Cultural Modeling is that the process of actively observing and looking for patterns in details observed will lead students to search their existing knowledge base, to attend to connections between their existing knowledge base and the target problem, and to be metacognitive by describing their own reasoning processes. The persistence of this routine over time serves an apprenticing role, socializing students into expectations for participation in class.

My knowledge of adolescent development comes into play because it provides me with a framework for interpreting Taquisha's resistance and that of other students (Finders, 1998; Goodenow, 1993). In Western societies, adolescence is typically a time when young people begin to define their emerging identities as young adults in terms of resistance to adult authorities (Paikoff & Brooks-Gunn, 1991; Steinberg & Silverberg, 1986) . It is important to note that this is not the case in all societies (Rogoff, 2003), nor uniformly the case within Western societies, in part because of the ethnic diversity now found in so many Western societies, particularly in the United States (Cross, 1991; Jones, 1998; Spencer, 2000). With this recognition, I do not take Taquisha's resistance as a personal affront. Understanding such resistance is often a challenge for new teachers, especially teachers of older youth. This also leads me to establish a goal in that moment of bringing Taquisha back into the learning activity without alienating her. I could have embarrassed her, punished her with additional work, lowered her grade, or sent her to the office. However, such reactions would have achieved exactly the opposite of what I wanted and precisely what Taquisha wanted at that moment, to be removed from any responsibility for active participation.

I am also using my knowledge of Taquisha as an individual, the personal identity that she has made available to me within the class over time. Taquisha is a very strong-willed young lady. Anyone who has worked in an all African American high school has certainly met Taquisha. She is the sort of person with whom you do not pick a fight unless you're willing to go to the mat and be ready to strike with definitive force to win. I was certainly not afraid of such a confrontation with Taquisha, but in the end it would have accomplished nothing of significance. I am convinced that a major challenge for teachers is to understand the myriad forms of resistance that students present, particularly in schools in low-income urban neighborhoods with histories of low academic achievement. It is the adult's response to these forms of resistance that teach young people how to cope and often determine whether they will be resilient in the face of daily experiences that are risky or threatening. To ignore the resistance teaches the youth that their actions are acceptable. Simply to punish—depending on the punishment—often reinforces for them that the world is a harsh and dangerous place that requires one to be constantly on the warpath although there are certainly punishments that can teach. I decided in that moment not to feed directly Taquisha's sense of anger, but rather to entice her by providing another route for a different quality of resistance.

I used my knowledge of African American discourse practices to reconfigure the situation by initiating a form of "signifying" with Taquisha. As I have said before, signifying is a form of discourse in African American English that involves ritual insult. It is fundamentally a game of word play in that the insults cannot be real and the retorts must conform to rigorous rules of uptake (Mitchell-Kernan, 1981). In turn 1, when I ask Taquisha, "you have a question inside that paper there?" I initiate a game of insult in which Taquisha can respond in a playful manner. Her response in turn 2—an emphatic "Yup"—indicates that she has taken the gauntlet. I liken this small but powerful move to a kind of Tai Chi move in which I deflect her motion toward me by simply getting out of the way. There can be no fight if I don't hit back. At the same time, I am not willing to let Taquisha off the hook, so I ask her in turn 3, "What's your question?" This could have been a risky move in that had Taquisha simply not been paying any attention to the film, she would have had no questions.

However, I had observed her during the film, as I had the other students, and no one was reading the newspaper during the showing of the film. I think this is in part because such media are inherently enticing to young people for whom television, film, music, music videos, and video games represent major time investments. Taquisha's response in turn 4, "I put what does the film [have to do with anything we're studying]" places her back on the attack again. Essentially Taquisha is publicly assaulting the design of my lesson. She is fundamentally asking, "so if we're supposed to be reading books in this English class, why the devil do you have us looking at movies?" Continuing in my Tai Chi mode, I again deflect Taquisha's punch by responding in turn 5, "Well that might be a question for me." This kind of response became a typical orientation for me because I knew this form of instruction was very different from what the students had been used to; and after all, these were seniors. It was important that they saw the big picture and made sense of what they were being asked to do. After all, I know that personally I do not put forth my best effort when the activity seems meaningless to me.

This consistent pattern of putting the ball back in Taquisha's court led her through turns 6, 8 and 10 to begin a process of honing what were actually two real and very important questions for her. In turn 4, Taquisha is questioning the lesson. In turn 6, Taquisha reformulates the question to ask about the relationships between the book, namely *Beloved*, which we are preparing to read, and two actions in the film, namely the girl who is the protagonist and the man, the cantor, singing. By turn 10, Taquisha has further refined the question to ask how are the actions of the girl and the cantor, both singing, related. I think one of the reasons that Taquisha now focuses her attention on refining her question is my response in turn 7, "Say that again. That's a good question." There is no longer any resistance on Taquisha's part and I have positioned her as a meaningful participant in the ongoing activity.

It is both my content knowledge and my pedagogical content knowledge, working in tandem, that allow me to understand Taquisha's emerging question as an instance of a proposition within the discipline that is important and generative. I recognize her question as an instance of a habit of mind or disposition that will prove particularly useful when we meet the very difficult and dense text in *Beloved*. Taquisha has noted two actions that on the surface appear to bear no relation to one another. The "author"—in this case the director, Julie Dash—places the onus on the "reader" to infer coherence. In many respects, this problem that Taquisha has identified is akin to the example I used in Chapter 5, where in Toni Morrison's *The Bluest Eye*, she begins the second chapter with "The nuns walked by quiet as lust." My content knowledge allows me to recognize that Taquisha's question is an instance of recognizing an apparent anomaly and assuming that one's job as a reader is to impose some form of coherence. As a sidebar, even if one were assuming the point of view of the literary theory of deconstructionism (Bloom et al., 1987), one still assumes a coherence across anomalies, namely the coherence is not stable and has many degrees of freedom.

My pedagogical content knowledge allows me to recognize that a novice reader is not likely to pose the problem as an instance of a larger principle, but rather as a local observation. If this were an advanced class in literary criticism at the college level, I would expect Taquisha to pose the question as an instance of a literary principle. My pedagogical content knowledge also leads me to recognize that I must make public to Taquisha and the rest of the class what she is doing, how this move by Taquisha represents a generative principle that can be used in other instances where in narrative an apparent anomaly is presented. My knowledge of language socialization allows me to use signifying as an invitation to participate, recognizing that this is a game that Taquisha knows well and values, while at the same time allows me to recognize that as the teacher I must begin to translate local explanations into propositions in order for the students to have a language with which to problem solve as they meet new literary narratives over time.

My final response in this episode, in turn 11, serves as a kind of coda, marking the close of an episode of signifying. The signifying has taken on a form-function shift (Lee, 1993; Saxe, 1991), from a tool for ritual insult on the street, to a pedagogical move to invite participation in the classroom: "That is a beautiful and sound question. Found it in the *Sun-Times* too, didn't you." Clearly she did not find that inventive and compelling question in the *Sun-Times* [a Chicago newspaper]. I am playing with Taquisha. Taquisha completes the signifying move with a resounding "Yup!"

This discussion takes place early in October of 1997. After the work with cultural data sets over 10 double class periods, the students initially read the chapter "Damballah" by John Edgar Wideman (1998) from his novel of the same name, and then move on to *Beloved*. The interchange below comes from a discussion of Chapter 5 from *Beloved*. I offer it as an example of Taquisha's movement over time. I do not intend by this example to suggest that Taquisha's movement was a simple set of linear moves always going forward. That is definitely not the case. There were days when Taquisha was distant and I had to reentice her. But it represents an example of Taquisha taking a stance that she already had evidenced in response to the "Sax Cantor Riff" film. I discussed this example in Chapter 4 (where I included two paragraphs of the *Beloved* text) to illustrate how AAVE rhetorical features (prosody, intonation, syntax, and turn taking) served as a medium of communication for complex literary reasoning. I reinvite the reader to think about this example from a slightly different point of view here. I offer it as evidence of Taquisha's change over time as a reader, noting both the facilitation of the emergence of Taquisha's literary stance in the example of her reading the newspaper while the class discussed "Sax Cantor Riff" and the expansion of that same stance over time with a canonical text.

The exchange below is completely different from the discussion in October. Taquisha has initiated the exchange. In the videotape of the class, one can see that she is highly animated and her tone of voice throughout is one of a different kind of anger. She has recognized that the young woman coming out of the water is the baby Beloved. In the novel, the protagonist Sethe killed her baby girl in order to save the child from being taken back into enslavement. The novel is in large part about the consequences of living with this terrible act for Sethe, her children, and for Paul D, the man who shows up at her door 18 years after they were both enslaved human beings on a plantation ironically called Sweet Home.

> (1) *Taquisha*: Now wouldn't you want to know? You know. The questions—hair all straight like a baby, you know and stuff, drinking all this water? Okay! You know she said she ran away and stuff. You got some brand new shoes on yo' feet. You too clean to run away. Yo feet ain't swole. You ain't gonna expect nothing ? You ain't gonna ask her no questions?
>
> (2) *Teacher*: Alright hold up this is—
>
> (3) *Joe*: It's a story.
>
> (4) *Taquisha*: It don't matter!
>
> (5) *Joe*: Did you write the story?
>
> (6) *Teacher*: Excuse me. (laughs from the students.) This is a very important point Taquisha has made. Who feels the way that Taquisha is saying somebody would feel? (students are talking, inaudible) Who feels that way? (All the students are talking at the same time.) Now hold up, hold up excuse me. Alright, first Taquisha has raised a very important point. She is saying that common sense would suggest that somebody would react the way she's described. Now my question is, of the other people

who were there, Charles Johnson, does anybody else react the way Taquisha says?

(7) *Taquisha*: Paul D.

(8) *Teacher*: Paul D.

(9) *Taquisha*: Paul D was asking her a question? How she gonna just pop up and stuff? Ask her where she from.

My analysis of these comments in Chapter 4 focused on Taquisha's attention to issues of authorial intent. Here I want to focus on Taquisha's relationship to the text. Taquisha's relationship to the text and the task has completely changed in contrast to her resistance in October. She is totally invested in her reaction to the text. Her fundamental assertion goes as follows: "I can recognize that this person is the baby. We know that the baby has shown she is dangerous. Why can't the characters in the story see this?" In prior chapters of the novel, the ghost of the baby has been haunting the protagonist Sethe's home, knocking over furniture, making noises, and otherwise venting her anger over the fact that her mother murdered her. I take Taquisha's question, in part, as an instance of questioning authorial intent, as I discussed in Chapter 4. In our examination of "Sax Cantor Riff" we were constantly raising questions about why the "author" Julie Dash decided to have a sign that said Church Avenue, have the cantor and the sax player on different tracks in the subway, have the girl carrying flowers and having images of flowers on her scarf. I would initially raise such questions and then the students would initiate their own questions.

Taquisha's perspective taking is evident across several turns. In turn 1, she asks "Now wouldn't you want to know? You know." The "you" is directed to me and the other students in the class. Her consistent use of the referent "you" to refer to us places the other students not only as readers, but as participants in the subjunctive world of the text. She says, "You got some brand new shoes on yo feet. You too clean to run away. Yo feet ain't swole," as though we were the woman coming out of the water. Then "you ain't gonna expect nothing? You ain't gonna ask her no questions?" as though we were one of the characters observing this strange young woman coming toward Sethe's house. Samuel Taylor Coleridge (1816/2000) noted long ago that immersion into the narrative requires a suspension of disbelief: "That willing suspension of disbelief for the moment . . . constitutes poetic faith." Taquisha's positioning is complex in that she actually enters the narrative world and positions the rest of us as participants in that imaginary world, but then takes a position of disbelief as a character herself inside that world. This is precisely the kind of habit of mind or disposition that is crucial to engagement with rich literary texts.

In terms of literary reasoning, one of the points of leverage that Cultural Modeling as a framework draws on is that all cultures have a rich narrative history. Every day people watch television, films, hear oral stories, and listen to narrative lyrics in which they enter a subjunctive imaginary world, interpret tropes, and construct coherent representations of the significance of these stories. Taquisha has initiated a very controversial proposition that ignites a flurry of sidebar responses in terms of multiparty talk. This was a very common event in these classrooms, as described in Chapter 4. The participation structure of the classroom allowed, even privileged, such displays of engagement. It allowed more people to participate, although it certainly placed strenuous demands on me as the teacher to follow the flow of the conversation. Taquisha has clearly paid very careful attention to the details of the plot unfolding because when I ask in turn 5, "does anybody else react the way Taquisha says," she responds "Paul D. was asking her a question? How she gonna just pop up and stuff? Ask her were she from."

As noted in Chapter 4, it is also important to note that Taquisha speaks in African American English Vernacular: *yo* for *you*; *ain't* for *is not*; use of double negatives—"You *ain't* gonna ask her *no* questions"; lack of copula— "How she gonna just pop up and stuff" instead of 'How is she going to just pop up and stuff." Her intonation is rhythmic and her prosody is clearly AAEV. It is crucial that I understand the essential propositions she is raising and am able to situate those propositions within a map of the domain of literary reasoning. Asking Taquisha to translate her heartfelt response into academic English would most likely shut her down. I do not belittle the problem of helping youth learn to communicate orally and in writing using Academic English. However, I do disentangle enticing and apprenticing them into learning to reason within the norms of the discipline and teaching them to communicate that propositional knowledge in terms of language and genres accepted in the academy. I will discuss this challenge in further detail in the next chapter.

I have tried to make the case in this chapter for the complex nature of teacher knowledge required to teach in ways that put at the forefront both cultural experiences and forms of knowledge that youth construct from their lives outside of school and also norms for reasoning within subject matters. In these discussions, I have maintained that one of our goals is to make the norms for reasoning and for participation in academic tasks explicit. This question of being explicit has been taken by some to mean scripted lessons and direct instruction. Public policy initiatives in many districts and states now require that teachers use scripted lessons and curriculum packages that posit themselves as direct instruction. In the San Francisco Bay Area, a group of high school English teachers protested outside their high school, reading from *Farenheit 451* to make a case against California public policy requiring scripted literacy instruction in which high school English teachers must use a literature series only, instead of teaching whole novels. I'd like to explain in more detail and illustrate what I mean by being explicit in instruction.

ON BEING EXPLICIT IN TEACHING COMPLEX REASONING

The kinds of scripts one typically finds in what is termed *direct instruction* involve routines for teachers to use to elicit prescribed responses from students. The underlying assumption is that through repetition of such scripts students will learn to engage in a set of practices that support learning. If the object of learning is to remember facts or rules or even types of questions or scripted ways of responding, then direct instruction has proven to be very effective (Adams & Engelmann, 1996; Gersten & Keating, 1987b). However, complex subject matter learning involves more than memorization of propositional knowledge. If memorizing a "rule" were sufficient, we could have skipped all those weeks of working with cultural data sets and simply given the students a list of rules that defined and provided strategies for recognizing symbols.

The problem with such an approach is that the array of circumstances under which one will meet this quality of problem are so varied that a simple rule will not work across cases. Further to take literary reasoning as a case, the kinds of knowledge that one needs to bring to bear to pose and consider literary problems is sizeable and quite varied: plot types, character types, archetypal themes, knowledge of authors, of literary traditions; scripts from everyday life, knowledge of human intentionality, what makes people tick; and more local knowledge of vocabulary and syntax. The process of learning how to draw flexibly on this array of sources of knowledge in relation to how one construes the problem one is trying to solve is simply not amenable to memorization or scripts. I think it is a form of knowing that one learns through guided practice, that is, through engaging in wrestling with complex narratives that are sequenced in ways that give one repeated exposure. The guidance through this process of authentic engagement comes from someone who has sufficiently detailed, coherent, and flexible knowledge of such problem solving to be able to make public and explicit what is useful in a students' reasoning, and to guide them through the process of trying to figure things out. It is the problem of being explicit about these things that is at the heart of Cultural Modeling.

When we began the design of the Cultural Modeling curriculum for Fairgate High School, I did not understand this problem of being explicit in the way I do today. I learned the nuances of being explicit by being engaged in the act of teaching and studying it as a sense-making practice. My examination of the corpus of videotapes of my instruction and those of other teachers in the project led me to identify the following principles for teaching in ways that make complex subject matter–specific reasoning explicit:

1. Using guided questions
2. Creating participation structures in which students know how to take part and value taking part; that require attention by all in ways that invite effort and position students as competent
3. Revoicing student utterances as instances of larger propositions and norms within the subject matter, including helping them understand what is generative in the utterance and what is missing from the utterance
4. Making the structure of debates around questions public and objects of joint inquiry
5. Separating out problems of oral communication and problems of discipline-based representations, but recognizing the need to attend to both
6. Creating routines that socialize the kinds of practices required for complex problem solving in the discipline

I will illustrate these six principles under three broad categories: (1) maximizing participation, (2) culturally responsive–subject-matter-specific guided participation, and (3) distinguishing problems of representation. They represent goals for teaching within the framework of Cultural Modeling and embody the kinds of integrated knowledge-in-action required for effective teaching.

MAXIMIZING PARTICIPATION

I do not want in any way to imply that the exemplars of student-initiated complex literary reasoning somehow just emerged because students were examining familiar texts such as rap lyrics and TV programs. It took some time to establish a culture in the classroom where it was clear that everyone was expected to participate. In the first several months I was constantly saying things like, "Are you listening, Carey?" "What did

Taquisha say, Jason?" "If you're not completing assignments, you're just digging a deeper and deeper hole for yourself." "Jason, is this what you're going to do with your drill sergeant in basic camp? If you continue this way, it will become a habit that will be hard to break." "Is your book open? Do you see where we are." I designed the physical space in ways to maximize the likelihood that students would have the materials they needed to work each day. I kept paperback dictionaries in the classroom for use while reading. I created a storage system in which each student had a cubby to hold his or her in-class journal and ongoing assignments. I had each student keep a log of all work assigned with a record of whether the assignment was turned in and what the grade was. For the first few months, I played soothing music at the beginning of each class to create a calm and serene environment in the room. As students entered class from the roar of the hallway, they were typically very anxious and talkative. I would often remind students when they complained about the amount of reading they had to do that Black people had died for their right to read and they had a responsibility to those on whose shoulders they stood. I always kept extra copies of the novels in class for students who would forget to bring their books to class. As I walked around the class while students worked either individually or in small groups, I would put my hand on a shoulder and give encouragement, "I know you can do this, Jelani." This was a class of seniors. In an ideal world, I should not have had to work so hard to enlist their engagement and persistence. But I knew that my personal future depended on their success. It was these young people on whom I would count in my old age. These were my children.

At the end of the unit on symbolism, we hosted a debate that included students from three different classes. I described this debate in Chapter 4. The session began with a typical IRE (Initiation-Response-Evaluation) pattern where Mrs. Hayes asked the group if they had any enduring questions about the novel. They came up with an interesting and compelling set of questions. Shetunda, one of the young ladies in my class with whom I had to work very hard to pull in and keep motivated, sat with her head on the desk during this part of the discussion. Shetunda is a student with whom I had to work with on penmanship so that her writing would be legible. I knew, however, that when heated debates arose, Shetunda would most likely weigh in. This was the case that day. The students had self-selected into different groups based on their position on the question: Was Sethe morally correct in killing her baby? Shetunda selected the group who took the position that Sethe was morally incorrect in her act. The debate abounded in raucous multiparty overlapping talk. Students would finish one another's sentences. Getting the floor required rhetorical agility and often emphatic physical gesturing to gain attention. The fundamental argument that Shetunda's group had been making was that Sethe was not warranted in killing her baby because even at that time there could have been other alternatives and no one can truly predict the future (i.e., don't kill your child because you think you know definitively what is in store). Shetunda gestures to get the floor in the midst of ongoing multiparty talk:

> Okay I got something to say. [holds both hands up in the air to signal her desire to take the floor] Like I said before, don't nobody know the future. [moves hands across her body in an emphatic gesture and leans toward her audience] How y'all know? You don't know what tomorrow may bring [leans forward toward her audience, moves hands outward to further emphasize her point]. You do not know. Don't nobody know. Don't nobody know.

It is entirely possible that a participation structure that includes unsolicited multiparty overlapping talk and that is loud, prosodic, and rhythmic could serve as more of a detractor for many people. However, inevitably across these classes, this participation structure that was always largely initiated and driven by students provided opportunities for more students to take part. I think this is because it is a participation structure often found in African American speech genres and is assumed when people are talking about something about which they care deeply. It is a participation structure that I have attempted to capture in Chapter 4, but one that is not at all well represented in the research literature on classroom talk. However, it allowed these students to assume quite productive roles in argumentation involving claims, evidence, and warrants, including nested arguments. Nested arguments are quite complex and involve the use of subordinate claim-evidence-warrant sequences to support larger claims (Toulmin et al., 1984). While this participation structure was rooted in African American English Vernacular norms, there are other participation structures rooted in everyday practices of other speech communities, including the use of multiple national languages, that often go untapped in schools (Gutierrez et al., 1999; Orellana et al., 2003; Phillips, 1983; Rosebery, Warren, & Conant, 1992; Valdés, 1996, 2002; Warren et al., 2001).

Overall, our attempts to maximize participation involved creating roles and supports that affirmed students' competence, providing material supports and routines that created multiple resources to serve as artifacts to mediate learning (i.e., dictionaries, spaces to keep ongoing work, work in small groups, guided questions that support routine metacognition, and working in individual journals before any group talk to force an effort to make sense of the task for one's self first).

CULTURALLY RESPONSIVE, SUBJECT MATTER–SPECIFIC GUIDED PARTICIPATION

Rogoff (1995) uses the term *guided participation* to describe how social interactions are organized in ways to support the learning of novices. In this case, the process of making literary reasoning explicit here involved the following:

- Using guided questions to structure modes of reasoning
- Creating public representations of the evolution of arguments as artifacts to spur metacognitive reflections about the logic of the reasoning
- Providing ongoing in-time feedback on student responses in terms of how they add to or constrain the evolving argument

These routines provided a predictable structure for problem solving that required students to pay close attention to the details of a text, to look for patterns across details, to use agreed upon—in fact, mutually constructed—strategies for determining what details would be most salient, to hypothesize generalizations that could explain the pattern of details to which students attended, all in service of making sense of whatever interpretive problem was the focus of the unit of instruction (e.g., symbolism, irony, and so on).

These routines were *culturally responsive* in two ways. First, the use of cultural data sets provided a way for students to link their experimentation with these routines to existing prior knowledge. However, I want again to emphasize that the reasoning with cultural data sets does not represent an everyday activity for students in the same way as what they do with these cultural data sets in class. The process of reasoning about interpretive problems posed by these cultural data sets is within what Vygotsky (1978) calls their "zone of proximal development" because they have sufficient prior knowledge about the topics and problems posed by the data sets, and yet what they are doing in class with these everyday texts is beyond what they would normatively do on their own without assistance (Lee, 1993). Second, the participation structures in the classrooms are also culturally responsive in that they reflect ways of participating in intense debate that students already know and value. While I will discuss this point in more detail in the next section of this chapter, the everyday rhetorical moves by students using vernacular everyday language certainly differs in significant ways from the genres and syntactic forms of Academic English into which we certainly want to apprentice students. On the other hand, these everyday rhetorical moves also share really important features with the fundamental logic of disciplinary argumentation into which we also want to apprentice students (Rosebery, Warren, Ballenger, & Ogonowski, 2005; Rosebery, Warren, & Conant, 1992; B. Warren et al., 2001) .

I will illustrate this process of culturally responsive, subject matter–specific guided participation with an example from the modeling phase of instruction. The following interchange takes place early in the discussions of the cultural data set "Sax Cantor Riff," the 5-minute film by Julie Dash. Students have been debating why the girl in the film is singing, "Soon I will be done with the troubles of the world." The question involves weighing competing explanations as to whether the statement is literal or figurative, and if figurative, what it might signify or symbolize. Several students have hypothesized that the girl wants to kill herself because she is distraught over her mother's condition and likely impending death, a literal interpretation.

Others have countered that she's just singing the song to comfort her mother because it's her mother's favorite song, a competing or perhaps complementary, but still literal, explanation. One thing that is important about this discussion is that the students have determined that this detail of the plot and the imagery surrounding it are important to pay attention to and require an explanation. Attention to such details is part of the discipline specific reasoning into which the modeling is attempting to apprentice students. They have gone through a similar process with the rap song "The Mask" by the Fugees wherein they identify details that require their attention as "readers" because the author has provided signals that these details are important—perhaps because they are in a salient place, such as a title, or are repeated a lot through some portion of the text. Guided participation here involves routines, not simply a single introductory advance organizer (Ausubel, 1960). Students gain repeated experience with the same kinds of practices using cultural data sets before they move to the canonical texts. They have employed a similar reasoning for rejecting a purely literal interpretation and are therefore exploring the possibility that the act of singing could be symbolic. The routine tool—i.e., artifact for guided participation—for such explorations was the development of a table with a column for the image or action in question, real-world associations with that image or action, and some generalizations about how one's real-world associations and the actual text are related to one another (see Figure 2.6 for an illustration.) The students have on their own identified a list of images and actions that they think are important to consider and about which they have genuine questions: the sign Church Avenue, the girl's singing, the flowers, the cantor, and the sax player. The teacher is filling in the table on the board of what details the students think are important and their real-world associations with these details. This table is a public representation of their evolving argument, collectively constructed, with targeted questions being posed by both the teacher and other students.

(1) *Teacher*: We can at least add, let's put it this way, we can at least add up here that this idea of the troubles of the world will be over when you are in heaven with God or whatever, and we've got two interpretations which we have not resolved over whether the girl is saying this to herself which I think is Joe's position. She is telling herself this is what she wants for herself and the other position is . . .

(2) *David*: But it's her mother's favorite song. She's singing it for her mother, know what I'm saying, not for herself.

(3) *Taquisha*: I think it's both of em.

(4) *Teacher*: Taquisha.

(5) *Taquisha*: I think it's both of em cuz if she worried about her mother and she cryin' she in trouble too.

(6) (intervening cross-party talk)

(7) *Teacher*: So let's go down to that next image that you talked about, the image of Church Avenue. What were your associations with church?

(8) *Students*: Something religious. Something spiritual.

(9) *Joe*: A street.

(10) *Teacher*: Well we know it's a street, but . . .

(11) *David*: Sanctity.

(12) *Teacher*: Meaning?

(13) *David*: Sacred.

(14) *Janae*: Holy.

(15) *Aretha*: Where people express different feelings in different ways.

(16) *Teacher*: (writing on board) Where people express different feelings in different ways. Okay, what else do you associate with the church?

(17) *David*: It's universal.

(18) *Teacher*: Ah, ha! A church is something that's universal. Everybody has some kind of church. Good.

(19) *David*: It's all different kinds of ethnic groups in there.

(20) *Teacher*: Okay. Over here. Keep this in mind now. Because we're trying to put these tables together the same way we did with "The Mask." So if we're looking for examples that have something to do with these associations in the poem (drawing the second column of the table on the board while students duplicate in their journals). One of them, rather in the video, if I'm understanding correctly, David is saying is the different ethnic peoples (writing in the table). What are some of the different ethnic groups that you see in the video?

(21) *Different students respond*: Blacks. Latino. Jewish. White. Polish.

(22) *Ari*: What?

(23) *Lauren*: Where you see Polish at?

(24) *Ari*: Ain't no Polish people up in that room?

(25) *Sarah*: Hispanic.

(26) *Hank*: Turkey.

(27) *T*: Okay. Alright. (drawing a line to begin a new row in the table)

(28) (Intervening talk)

(29) *T*: Now we have the cantor. (turns around and looks directly at students, pointing her finger at the students) Remember I'm going to give you all an essay topic. All of this stuff will be very useful. So if I were you I would be keeping up with all these ideas and examples.

In turn 1 the teacher is writing on the board, filling in a table the claims being made by students. This act of creating a public representation of the rival positions on the floor invites public critique of the positions. Before the teacher can finish summarizing what she is writing in the table around the significance of the girl singing, David and Taquisha in turns 2–5 offer a critique of Joe's claim and a synthesis of both Joe's and David's claims. These conflicting positions lead to a scurry of cross-party talk where students further debate the questions among themselves, with students who sit in close proximity. In turn 7 the teacher moves the discussion to the next image, the sign Church Avenue and again begins to fill in on the blackboard their associations with the word *church*. The question the students had raised earlier is why was the stop called Church Avenue, really a brilliant and very literary question. Joe had a tendency to always be excruciatingly literal, I think at times to frustrate the rest of us. The teacher's response in turn 10 to Joe's literal statement that it's a street provides a value judgment on his literal response, implying not that his answer is wrong, but likely insufficient.

This in-time feedback leads to a series of responses in turns 11–17 where students offer abstractions for the significance of the name Church: sanctity, sacred, holy, where people express different feelings in different ways. Although I cannot make any definitive claim, I suspect that David's response in turn 17, "It's universal," is at least in part a reaction to Aretha's statement about people expressing different feelings in different ways. In turn 18 the teacher again makes an in-time evaluation, "Ah, ha! A church is something that's universal. Everybody has some kind of church. Good." I think that both the affirmation of the value of this contribution and the act of revoicing a synthesis of both David and Aretha's comments gave David the time to extrapolate to another claim that was not directly about the significance of the name of the street. In turn 19 David says, "It's all different kinds of ethnic groups in there."

The evolution of this discussion marks several important points. First, it is this routine of asking guiding questions that over time becomes part of the way of participating, that socializes routines for reasoning: What do you notice or have questions about? What patterns do you see? Why did you pay attention to these details? As the routine develops over time, the guiding questions are posed by both the teacher and students. For example, when students rebut one another's claims, they are inherently asking, "How do you know?" These are not scripted procedures because it is difficult to anticipate what students' responses will be. In this instance—as was the case with "The Mask—it is a problem of both determining what may be the significance of each key image or action, but then extrapolating across these images and actions to infer something about the general meaning or theme of the work as a whole.

Throughout all of the instruction, I was continuously learning from the students. I actually had not paid attention to the sign Church Avenue before the students pointed it out. I was very much thinking on my feet as students made comments about the different ethnic groups represented in the film, trying to anticipate what themes could possibly be extrapolated from these details. The attention to the different ethnic groups was initiated by David. The responses in turns 21–26 are interesting and provocative. Since our routines for participation always included active debate, students question one another about whether the claim that there are Polish people in the film is accurate. This in-time feedback comes from students, not the teacher. In virtually every instance where you see students responding to one another, the teacher is not selecting who has the floor.

Finally, in turn 29 the teacher is also making explicit why the students are going through all this. While it might be idealistic to tell the students they are doing this so they will become better readers of literature, such a goal would not be particularly enticing. Rather, the teacher articulates a practical and short-term goal, namely, they are going to have to write an essay about the symbolism and themes in the video. Grades meant something to seniors because they have a one-shot opportunity to graduate on time and not have to go to summer school. This practical goal setting is also a part of being explicit.

DISTINGUISHING PROBLEMS OF REPRESENTATION

As part of our efforts to make instruction explicit, we elected to make a distinction between phases of representations of student understanding or comprehension. In the study of algebra, one can distinguish among explanations students give in everyday language, explanations through drawings, explanations through algorithms, and explanations that include appeals to mathematical laws. Each of these forms of explanations can be considered a public representation that captures some elements of a student's understanding. In teaching literary reasoning at the secondary level, I am distinguishing between explanations in everyday language that include often implicit articulation of claims, evidence, and warrants, and formal explanations that include appeals to literary principles and constructs as a backing for claims, evidence, and warrants. Both kinds of explanations, the everyday and the formal, may be either oral or written. However, I argue that novices, especially resistant novices, must first learn to provide everyday explanations—be they oral or written—as a bridge to the development of more formal explanations. I learned in this work that there are at least two levels of scaffolding that are needed. First, it requires creating everyday explanations orally and then being able to translate those everyday explanations into a form that people not immediately present can understand. This includes appropriate use of Academic English syntax, vocabulary, and text structure. Second, it requires being able to articulate formal literary explanations and appropriate written versions of them. It has taken me some years to come to this conclusion.

While teaching, it was always evident that helping the students move from what were always very vibrant and intense oral explanations into written explanations was a very tedious process. I noticed that students often initially would write as though they were writing to themselves, leaving out the kinds of details that someone not in the immediate room would need to understand the argument. This is not at all uncommon in the teaching of composition. In addition, we had to go through mini–grammar lessons to teach particulars of capitalization, spelling, and appropriate punctuation. We found that having the students compose using a word processor had several effects. First, they wrote more and were more fluid. Second, the process of revising was much easier than physically rewriting. We used a composition support program that allowed students to review and comment on each other's work. And finally, there was something about the physical neatness of a computer-printed document that seemed to be particularly helpful, especially to struggling students.

More recently, however, in reviewing the corpus of data collected across the project, I have thought about the qualitative differences between the oral explanations students gave and what I knew would be expected, for example, on an Advanced Placement exam. In Table 6.1, I contrast Taquisha's explanation about why the characters should have suspected that the woman coming out of the water was the baby Beloved and dangerous and the kind of explanation that I think the AP exam might expect.

Taquisha's everyday explanation and the more formal explanation are similar and different in important ways. First, there are obvious differences in terms of the register of language used and the length and levels of explicitness of the explanations. It is actually more likely that one would see this more formal explanation in written form than verbal, but it is certainly possible to hear oral explanations of this sort. The claims made are the same. However, in some instances Taquisha simply implies a claim that is made explicit in the formal explanation. The formal explanation says, "If she has been haunting the house for years, her appearance now suggests possible danger for Sethe and those around her." This is a subclaim in support of a larger claim made explicit in the formal explanation: "Since the house was haunted and Sethe had killed her baby, it is reasonable to assume (1) that the house was haunted by the baby, and (2) this woman is the baby."

Both the superordinate claim and the subclaim are implied in Taquisha's explanation. No other assumptions explain why Taquisha would be bothered by the fact that this woman is the baby Beloved returned. If Taquisha did not assume that the woman was dangerous, and especially if she thinks the woman is the ghost of the baby, Taquisha herself would be happy to see the baby come back to life. Taquisha does provide warrants for her claims. For example, she says "Okay! You know she said she ran away and stuff." However, this warrant is truncated and does not make explicit Taquisha's knowledge of how enslaved Africans would come across the Ohio river and knock on someone's door in the town where Sethe lived. We know Taquisha knows these facts because they are in the novel and because the class did a significant historical review of the circumstances of the African Holocaust of Enslavement, reading from Lerone Bennett's *Before the Mayflower* (1964) and viewing the film *Sankofa* by independent film maker Haile Gerima (1993). One conclusion is that the ability to be

Table 6.1. Contrast of Novice and Expert Explanations of Complex Characterization, Authorial Intent, Irony, and Unreliable Narration

	Novice Explanation	Expert Explanation
Speaker/Writer	Taquisha	Advanced Placement Student
Type of Explanation	Everyday—Within Zone of Proximal Development	Formal
Content	Now wouldn't you want to know? You know! The questions—hair all straight like a baby, you know and stuff, drinking all this water? Okay! You know she said she ran away and stuff. You got some brand new shoes on yo' feet. You too clean to run away. Yo feet ain't swole. You ain't gonna expect nothing? You ain't gonna ask her *no* questions?	I am questioning authorial intent in terms of how Toni Morrison as author has crafted the reactions of the characters to the woman. The woman appears out of nowhere, hair straight like a baby, drinking a lot of water. These characteristics give the woman the attributes of a baby. Since the house was haunted and Sethe had killed her baby, it is reasonable to assume (1) that the house was being haunted by the baby, and (2) this woman is the baby. If she has been haunting the house for years, her appearance now suggests possible danger for Sethe and those around her. In addition, the woman appears and I see that her feet are not swollen; she has on brand-new shoes; she has on clean clothing. We know that historically Africans escaping from enslavement would suddenly appear at someone's door, especially in this town just across the river. This woman does not look like she just escaped from enslavement. Thus it is not reasonable to assume that she is an escapee. Therefore, I have serious questions about who she might be, and about whether she may be dangerous. If I can see this, why can't the characters see it. I see this as a critique of how Toni Morrison has crafted the characters in this scene.

explicit about claims, evidence, and warrants and articulating the formal logic among them is one distinction between the everyday and the formal explanations.

A second distinction is the appeal in the formal argument to literary principles and theory as in, "I am questioning authorial intent in terms of how Toni Morrison as author has crafted the reactions of characters to the woman." Taquisha is not able to articulate a basis in literary theory for her claims; although we did allude to the problem of authorial intent in our discussions of the decisions made by the film director Julie Dash. I think this is one reason that Taquisha is intuitively questioning authorial intent.

Overall, I am claiming that Taquisha's explanation lies in Vygotsky's "zone of proximal development." The connections made between cultural data sets such as the film "Sax Cantor Riff" and rap lyrics such as "The Mask" created a space in which students such as Taquisha could engage in literary reasoning in ways they would not have done on their own even with such popular texts. Taquisha's explanation here is what I would call an intermediary representation, not yet at the level of the formal, but capturing the rudimentary elements of the formal logic. It is this new level of participation that provides a bridge for the next level in what should be a spiraling of zones of proximal development. Unfortunately for Taquisha and the other students in this class, this would be their last such opportunity in high school. One can only imagine Taquisha's potential had such connections between her everyday knowledge and the formal knowledge in the disciplines made explicit over the course of her K–12 education.

CONCLUSIONS

Overall, I have tried to describe what is entailed in doing culturally responsive, subject matter–specific instruction in schools like Fairgate. It requires a deep knowledge of subject matter, of how students learn, of language and language socialization, and of child and adolescent development, minimally. Such knowledge must be deeply interwined and flexible to the array of unexpected circumstances that inevitably arise on the performance floors of classrooms. Creating such a climate of explicit instruction of complex reasoning in literary response involves creating the kinds of routines captured in Table 6.2.

Classrooms are communities where cultural norms are established and identities as learners are socialized. The evidence is overwhelmingly clear that we in the United States do not take seriously the demands of meeting the educational needs of all of our youth. I hope in this book to make a case for how we can accomplish these goals. One important prerequisite is to

Table 6.2. Generative Routines to Establish Classroom Culture

Creating community	Building new norms for reading	Valuing complex problems	Modeling strategies	Building intertextual links	Artifacts
Expect all to read the text	Value multiple readings	Symbolism, irony, satire, unreliable narration	Strategies extrapolated from cultural data sets	Common problems across cultural data sets	Reflective journals
Speak so others can hear you	Multiple points of view	Problems of point of view	Close reading	Canonical texts close to students' experiences	Tables to analyze symbols, irony, satire, and unreliable narration
Praise the disengaged	Invoke textual evidence	Complex inferences	Attention to details		
Link to prior experience			Hypothesizing		
Take responsibility	Attend to unusual details		Weighing evidence	Canonical texts removed from students' experiences	Close reading questions
	Link to life experiences				Graphic organizers
	Close reading of the text				Using context vocabulary sheets

From Lee C. D., *Is October Brown Chinese: A cultural modeling activity system for underachieving students, American Educational Research Journal 38*(1) pp. 97–142, © 2001 by American Educational Research Association.

understand and appreciate the complexity of the knowledge base required to teach all students in ways that are true to the demands of disciplines and responsive to the array of cognitive, linguistic, and socioemotional resources that students inevitably bring to classrooms from their experiences in the world.

CHAPTER 7

Documenting Student Learning: Challenges and Opportunities

We are continuously swamped with data documenting the grossness of the achievement gap based on race, ethnicity, and SES (Education Trust, 2004). Federal and state governments, along with districts across the country, have responded to this consistent lag with greater demands for accountability (Elmore & McLaughlin, 1989; Roderick, Byrk, Jacob, Easton, & Allensworth, 1999; Roderick & Camburn, 1999; Spillane, 2006). On the surface, these efforts are indeed laudatory. For too many years, it didn't seem to matter that the high school dropout rates, for example, for African American, American Indian, Latino, and some Asian American groups and for poor Whites, was substantively below that of middle-class Whites. I am heartened that there is at least public outcry for accountability. However, the dominant focus of these accountability efforts has been to prescribe scripted forms of instruction and increased use of basic skills multiple-choice timed exams. In many states and districts we do see some increases in achievement for ethnic minority students and students from low-income communities (Education Trust, 2005a, 2005c; Langer, 2001). However, it is rare to see evidence that these youth are learning to engage in highly complex reasoning and problem solving across subject matters. Typically, we see evidence of students moving from the bottom quartile of the distribution to the third quartile, with the hope of getting most students at the 50th percentile.

This slow level of progress is attributable to several important factors. First, districts and schools typically design back-to-basics, scripted curriculum designs. Second, insufficient attention is paid to the multiple dimensions that drive learning, including developmental challenges, identity work, making the demands of complex problem solving public and visible. Third, in very few districts are there policies that support teacher learning in ways that provide conditions under which teachers can grapple realistically with the challenges of conceptual change. Fourth, we have insufficient measures of complex learning, especially at the secondary level,

155

in terms of deep reading and writing within subject matters. This problem of testing is further complicated by the various functions that such assessments can serve: diagnostic testing that is sufficiently detailed to inform instruction and summative evaluation for purposes of accountability. The Opportunity to Learn Group organized with support from the Spencer Foundation has developed a series of papers to address the many aspects of this problem, including the psychometric issues (Moss, in press).

In the Cultural Modeling Project's intervention at Fairgate High School, we faced a problem finding adequate measures of student growth over time in literary reasoning. The district used the Test of Academic Proficiency (TAP) at the high school level to be consistent with the Iowa Test of Basic Skills used at the elementary school levels. The TAP was a timed test and included short selections, often contrived for the purposes of the test, in both expository and narrative genres, followed by a series of multiple-choice questions testing the typical array of literal, inferential, and vocabulary item types. It was clear from the inception of the project that this test would not capture what we wanted to know about these youth as readers, and, in fact, that the timed nature of the assessment was antithetical both to authentic reading of rich literature and to the aims of our project. The assessment closest to our needs that we could find to consider in the first year was the open-response test that Riverside Publishing had developed to go along with the Iowa Test of Basic Skills; and the most advanced version of that test was normed for the latter part of the eighth grade. However, the test included only one reading that was not a literary narrative. During the second year of the project, we began looking at the New Standards Projects and the early assessments that were emerging from it. While the spirit of the standards and the exemplars of the kinds of student thinking that were being valued were clearly consistent with our aims, the assessment available was a historical text. We decided to take a more innovative approach to document changes in students' literary reasoning over time.

We developed three kinds of assessments. Each quarter, students were given a full short story they had not read before that posed interpretive problems comparable to those with which they had been wrestling in the instructional unit. Questions were constructed to match objectives for skills in comprehending fiction developed by Hillocks and Ludlow (1984). These skills move from the most basic to the most complex: basic stated information, key detail, stated relationship, simple implied relationship, complex implied relationship, author's generalization, and structural generalization. In testing this taxonomy, Hillocks and Ludlow demonstrated through rigorous statistical analyses that these question types represent a hierarchy in scale of difficulty.

In a prior study (Lee, 1993), I devised assessments of literary reading using this same scale, employing Rasch analysis to document that each question type did indeed represent a unique level of difficulty and that these question types moved hierarchically in levels of difficulty. Unfortunately, we did not have sufficient resources to conduct such a rigorous analysis in the large scale intervention at Fairgate High School. However, we did field test the questions to determine that responses to these question types did constitute a hierachical pattern; that is, typically respondents would get the easier questions right and would get those questions presumed more difficult right less often. We devised two formats for each story: one multiple-choice test and one essay response. We did not time the tests. Students could take as long as they needed to complete either format.

In addition to these assessments, we also selected each year a cohort of students whom we asked to read short stories that posed interpretive problems similar to those in the instructional unit. Three times during the school year—the beginning, middle, and end—students would engage in talk-aloud protocols (Pressley & Afflerbach, 1995). The stories were typed in such a way that students would read one meaningful chunk of paragraphs at a time and then talk aloud about what they were thinking while reading and what sense they were making of the texts. As much as possible, we used the same interviewers with each student across the year. Protocols were developed for probing students when they were not responsive or when an analysis they offered seemed either wrong or unusual. In each story we selected one portion of the story that was particularly dense and asked the students to read that section one sentence at a time. We also left room for students to read the stories twice whenever time permitted.

In this chapter I will first discuss the findings from two of these assessments. I will then discuss the implications of the use of the findings from these assessments for the broader problems of documenting subject matter reading comprehension, especially in settings where a majority of students are struggling readers.

HOW WELL CAN THESE KIDS READ?

We collected a wealth of data on the Cultural Modeling Project at Fairgate High School. It is complicated to make an empirical argument for how these students progressed as readers in large part because of the challenges I have discussed so far in regard to authentic assessments. However, I will attempt here to illustrate what we tried to accomplish and what we learned by using the last two unit exams given to students in the senior class, using data from four classes taught by two of the other teachers in the project.

The final unit exam was based on a short story called "The Wolf" by Giovanni Verga (2000). A very complex story of rustic Sicilian life, it is the tale of a middle-aged woman who lusts after her son-in-law. Symbolism is central to understanding the story. The middle-aged female antagonist, described in terms of attributes of a wolf, is herself symbolic.

To illustrate the nature of the skills being tested, I provide examples of a simple implied relationship and a complex implied relationship question. Figure 7.1 includes an example of one of the simple implied relationship questions and the relevant local text needed to appropriately answer the question.

Hillocks (Hillocks & Ludlow, 1984) defines a *simple implied relationship* (SIR) as follows:

> Questions of this type are similar to those of stated relationship with the important difference that relationships and causes must be inferred. To make these inferences, readers must deal with denotative and connotative clues in the text, relate them to their own personal experience and knowledge, and

Figure 7.1. Example of Simple Implied Relationship Question and Relevant Text

---

Why was she called the wolf?
  a. She lived with other wolves in a pack.
  b. She was never satisfied and hunts men just like a wolf.
  c. She is a coward just like a wolf.
  d. She is a nurturing mother just like a mother wolf.

Text Which Contains Target Information

She was tall and slim, and though no longer young, had the strong firm breasts of the dark-haired woman. She was pale, as if she suffered permanently from malaria, and out of that pallor her cool red lips and her huge eyes devoured you.

In the village they called her "The Wolf" because she could never be sated. The women would cross themselves when they saw her passing with the cautiously ambling pace of a hungry wolf, alone like an ill-tempered bitch. She could deprive them of their sons and husbands in the twinkling of an eye, with those red lips of hers, and one look from her devilish eyes could make them run after her skirts, from the altar of Saint Agrippina herself. It was a good thing the Wolf never came to church, even at Easter or Christmas, either for mass or for confession. Father Angiolino of the Church of Saint Mary of Jesus, a true servant of the Lord, had lost his soul on her account.

---

then infer the cued relationship. To make the inference, the reader need only refer to very limited portions of the text—two or three pieces of information which are often closely juxtaposed. (p. 10)

A good reader eliminates the first answer by rejecting a literal interpretation, namely that the "she" is actually a real wolf. A careful reader will be able to identify the specific sentence that identities the reason she is called the wolf: "In the village they called her 'The Wolf' because she could never be sated." However, that sentence requires substantive inferencing. The reader must either know what the word *sated* means or be able to infer its meaning from the context. Even if the reader knows what the word *sated* means, the reader must still figure out why she could never be sated in order to choose Answer B as the correct answer. In either case, the reader must pay attention to several classes of details in these two paragraphs. First, there are the details in both paragraphs that attribute wolflike qualities to her: "huge eyes that devoured you"; "passing with the cautiously ambling pace of a hungry wolf, alone like an ill-tempered bitch" (understanding the double entendre of bitch as female canine and bitch as a bad tempered female); "one look from her devilish eyes." Second, and more directly necessary to infer why she is called the wolf, the reader must use syntactic and semantic knowledge to infer that while a causal reason is given in the first sentence of the second paragraph, the sentences that follow are intended to enumerate the actual causes. In expository texts, colons can serve the same signaling function. The sentence which most explicitly answers the question is "She could deprive them of their sons and husbands in the twinkling of an eye, with those red lips of hers, and one look from her devilish eyes could make them run after her skirts, from the altar of Saint Agrippina herself." A combination of semantic knowledge and real-world knowledge should lead the reader to infer that running after her skirts means she could attract the men to her either sexually or romantically or both.

There is no evidence to suggest the wolf is a coward (Answer C); but it is possible that a poor reader who is not attending to the rhetorically marked details of Mother Nina's wolflike qualities could misread her intentions and read the fact that the wolf marries her daughter off—in another part of the story—as a sign of her being a nurturing mother (Answer D).

A second category of inferences are what Hillocks (Hillocks & Ludlow, 1984) calls *complex implied relationships* (CIR), defined as follows:

Questions of this type require inferences based on many pieces of information. Their complexity arises from the fact that they involve a large number of details which must be dealt with together. Questions about the causes of character change, for example, relating details of personality before and after a change and inferring the causes of the change from the same details and from interceding events. (p. 11)

The question in Figure 7.2 represents a complex implied relationship question from the exam on "The Wolf." This question is a CIR because it requires drawing on details from across the text. The proposition that Nanni cheated on his wife Maricchia must be inferred as there are no direct descriptions of any elicit affair, but rather rich descriptions of internal states of Mother Piña (Maricchia's mother) and Nanni. The answers include information on Nanni's feelings, being sorry, and repenting his sins. There is an implication of someone being killed at the end of the story, but it is never explicitly stated. However, the implication is that Nanni kills Mother

---

Figure 7.2. Complex Implied Question on "The Wolf"

Nanni was all of the following EXCEPT
   a. A man who cheated on his wife and was sorry for it.
   b. A soldier who had an affair with his mother-in-law.
   c. A field hand who repented his sins.
   d. A husband who killed his wife.

Text Which Contains Target Information

But she came back to the threshing stead, time and again, and Nanni did not object. And if she was late in coming, in those hours between midday sun and afternoon's heat, he would go with sweat on his brow to the top of the deserted White path to await her; and each time afterwards he would bury his hands in his hair and repeat, "Go away, go away! Don't come to the threshing ground again!"

Maricchia wept day and night, and every time she saw her mother coming back pale and silent from the fields, she pierced her eyes that burned with tears and jealousy, herself like a wolf cub.

"Wicked creature!" she spat. "You wicked mother!"

"Hold your tongue!"

"Thief! Thief!"

"Hold your tongue!"

"I'll go to the police, I will!"

"All right, go!"

And Maricchia did go, carrying her children, dry-eyed and fearless, like a madwoman, because now she loved the husband they had forced on her, greasy and grimy with oil and half-fermented olives.

The police sergeant sent for Nanni; he threatened him with jail and gallows. Nanni sobbed and tore his hair, but he denied nothing and made no excuses.

"It's temptation!" he said. "It's the temptation of hell!"

He threw himself at the sergeant's feet and begged to be sent to prison.

Piña. The entire story is one of innuendos and this question requires the reader to follows those innuendos across the entire text.

In Figure 7.3, we collapsed Hillocks's basic stated information, key detail, and stated relationship into a single category of literal questions. Figure 7.3 shows the percentage of students who scored correctly on each of the three categories of questions for four of the senior classes. While I acknowledge that the exam is not without flaws, it is equally clear that this is not an easy story and that the questions are reasonable approximations of an important set of reading skills. What is interesting is that the percentage of students who scored correctly across the three categories does not reflect how students scored on the Test of Academic Proficiency. I suspect there are at least two reasons. First, TAP includes a wider range of kinds of texts, but I strongly suspect that if we were to disentangle responses to the texts of fiction from expository texts, we would not find a substantive difference in levels of achievement. I think the combination of the timed nature of the text and the fact that it bore no authentic relationship to instruction led students both to be anxious about it and to not invest deeply

Figure 7.3. Percentage of Correct Scores—Results from Exam on Symbolism in "The Wolf"

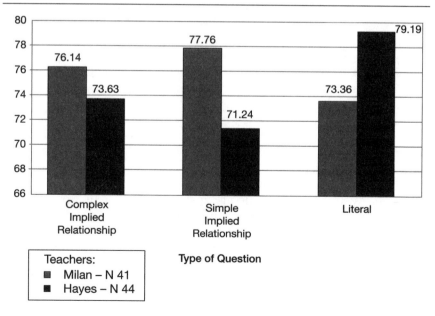

in it. Over the course of the intervention, several accountability moves were instituted by the district. The year before I came to Fairgate High School, the English Department met to figure out ways to get the students to come to school on the day the TAP was given. That was perhaps the most telling signal that the students did not take the exam seriously. During the height of the accountability moves of the Chicago Public Schools (CPS), high-stakes assessments were used to determine whether students moved forward based on scores at Grades 3, 6, and 8. Studies by the Chicago Consortium on School Reform document that the policy of holding students back did not result in academic improvement and eventually caused students to drop out of school at earlier years (Roderick et al., 1999; Roderick & Camburn, 1999). A second accountability move was the development by the central office of what were called the Chicago Academic Standards Exam (CASE). Results from CASE exams constituted 10% of students' grades in core courses. For English Language Arts, CASE dictated a set of required readings for all students. The impact on our intervention was negative: It led teachers to feel the necessity to replace some of the longer and more complex works in our curriculum with the shorter and simpler works on the CPS required reading list. The CASE exams are no longer required in CPS schools. However, the CASE exams were, in part, a response to the dearth of subject matter–specific assessments in reading at the secondary level that schools and districts could use to measure student learning over time in ways that reflect authentic and rigorous norms of discipline-based reading. This is as much of a challenge today as it was in 1995 when the Cultural Modeling Project began at Fairgate High School.

In addition to multiple-choice exams given each quarter for each grade level, we also gave essay exams. Essay questions typically focused on some combination of complex implied relationships, structural generalizations, and author's generalizations. We developed detailed rubrics for evaluating the essay exams. This corpus of exams were part of an effort to structure routines in which the teachers in the department could begin to analyze student learning by generating data themselves that directly reflected instructional objectives. As part of these efforts, the chair of the department had a reduced teaching load in order to provide some in-school resources for the management of this testing system and data analysis. My graduate research assistants ended up doing most of the grading and preparation of data tables for review by the faculty. This was in large part because the time required for such data production was far beyond what was reasonable to expect of the faculty. The school administration identified a room to be used by the English Department as an office. It was the only department to have such a space. Overall, the efforts to support the English faculty in looking at assessment data was a useful enterprise. However, it was very taxing primarily because teachers simply did not have the time to invest in these kinds of analyses. Most taught five classes with one preparation period. These kinds of working conditions stand in stark contrast to countries like China and Japan (Lewis, Perry, & Hurd, 2004; Lewis & Tsuchida, 1998), where ongoing professional development and reflection on practice is built into the working day of teachers. Time is a major structural barrier to the kind of professional development for teachers required to transform seriously underperforming schools. However, even though time is a necessary prerequisite, it is not a sufficient condition. The quality of assessments and of teacher knowledge for analyzing results of such assessments are as important as time for professional development.

ENGAGEMENT IN LITERARY REASONING

In addition to the schoolwide assessment system, we also identified a group of students in my class to serve as cases to follow across the year. We had these students read short stories that had not been assigned in class and talk-aloud about what they understood as they read and what they were doing to make sense of the stories. We also carefully examined their participation in class activity at three different points across the school year. (These analyses are reported in detail in Lee, Rivers, et al., 2000.)

The case study students are David, Victor, Joe, Raquel, Michelle, and Jonetha. You have heard the voices of David, Victor, Jonetha, and Joe in other transcripts throughout this book. Raquel is soft-spoken and doesn't talk a lot in class, but is an excellent student both in terms of the quality of her class work and her completion of assignments. You met her in the opening chapter, learning of her trials dealing with an unexpected pregnancy. Michelle and Jonetha participate more in classroom discussions. Although the quality of their work is good, they are less consistent in their completion of assignments. Michelle is very sociable and is occasionally off task in her social pursuits over against her academic press in class. Joe does little class work. His thinking as expressed in classroom talk is often frustratingly literal. He seems to take pleasure in challenging ideas on the floor, but his challenge is often based on very literal interpretations of the text. David and Victor are both active class participants. While both are often late in completing assignments, they seem to be genuinely interested in doing well and eventually turn in enough work for average grades. Their classroom comments are genuinely insightful and carefully reasoned.

In analyzing the talk-aloud protocols, we looked at student understanding of the core propositions or story grammar, ability to understand inferences, their attention to and understanding of figurative language in the stories, the quality of the arguments they made about what they under-stood, how they used prior knowledge to guide comprehension, and finally differences between the quality of first and second readings. I will focus here on two areas of that analysis.

The first area of analysis I discuss here is the examination of case study students' attention to and comprehension of the figurative language in the stories. I am not attempting in any way to extrapolate from these case study students to students at large. I think the patterns of their development over time illustrate the significance of individual variation. These patterns also reveal interesting relationships between analyses that focus on the indi-vidual and those that focus on group processes. The basic reason for the attention on the case study students was to document how individual de-velopment over time could be understood in relationship to group prac-tices within Cultural Modeling classrooms.

The analysis discussed here is based on two short stories. "Red-Headed Baby" by Langston Hughes (1934/1962) was read in October 1997 at the beginning of instruction. Results from this analysis are intended to cap-ture the point where students were early on in the school year. "If Beale Street Could Talk," part of a chapter from the novel of the same name by James Baldwin (1974/2006) and read in April 1998, was intended to cap-ture the point where students were near the end of instruction. In each story there are foundational symbols as well as complex relationships to be in-ferred among characters and events. Two expert readers read each story and generated a list of possible inferences that could be made that were based on figurative language in the story. Transcripts of each student read-ing and talking out loud were examined, for this particular analysis, to identify any propositions made that were based on figurative language in each story. We then calculated what percentage of the total possible figurative-based inferences generated by the expert readers were also identified by the students. We acknowledge some of the limitations of this approach. As is the case with any talk-aloud protocols, you can never definitively claim that what a student does not say he or she does not know. Also, our expert readers generated these figurative-based inferences by painstaking analysis. There is no reason to believe that they would have identified all of these possible inferences in a talk-aloud protocol. How-ever, the analysis does provide us with some sense of what the students on their own pay attention to, as they were not asked to do anything other than talk out loud about what they were thinking while reading each story. In the tables that follow, you will see that Raquel did not read "Red-Headed Baby" and Michelle did not read "If Beale Street Could Talk." Another student, Tamara, is included in the analysis of the second story, "If Beale Street Could Talk": Although Tamara was not one of the case study students, she was available the day we did the April protocol. We decided to include her because as a student she had been disengaged and had lots of problems as a reader; so we thought her analysis would be interesting. She was barely passing the class in large part because she would not turn in homework.

Figures 7.4 and 7.5 display the percentage of attempts at interpreting figurative language in each story. These percentages compare each case study student with the range of possible inferences based on figurative language generated by the two experts. Of the four case study students who completed both protocols, David, Joe, and Jonetha make more attempts— that is, they would appear to pay more attention to the figurative language of the story—in April than in October. Jonetha makes more attempts, but the difference is not significant. David and Joe pay significantly more attention to the figurative language later in the year. Based on the quality and amount of participation in class, I would have expected David to have made a significant shift. However, Joe is interesting because his comments in class were almost always over the board literal. This suggests several hypotheses. First, the dramatic nature of Joe's participation in class often

Figure 7.4. Percentage of Total Figurative Language Interpreted— "Red-Headed Baby," Oct. 1997

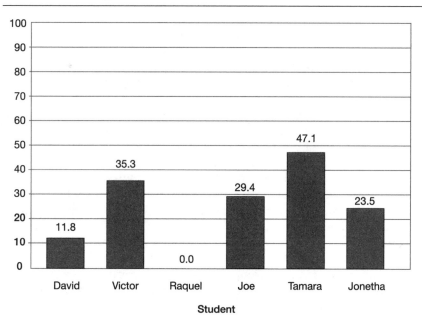

Figure 7.5. Percentage of Total Figurative Language Interpreted—
"If Beale Street Could Talk," April 1998

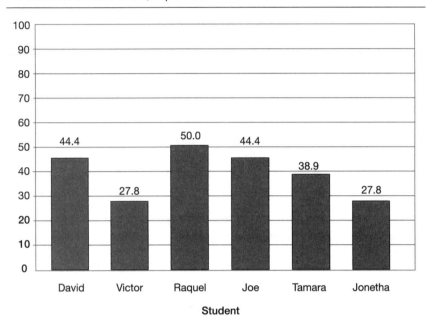

led me to believe that he was as much posturing as he was thinking. But it also suggests that it is not a simple matter for a teacher to make inferences about what a student is able to do. Much depends on what range of opportunities to assess a student are available, but equally on the goals of the student in demonstrating both his effort and his ability.

In other parts of this book, I have discussed a range of developmental issues that I think are foundational to teaching. Understanding how a student perceives his or her task in relation to others present is difficult to ascertain, but a teacher's understanding of students' phenomenology is as much a part of teaching as the cognitive work we tend to emphasize. Victor made some of the most revealing comments of all the students in the class. As a consequence, I would have expected Victor to have paid more attention to the figurative language of the text in April. The quality of his reasoning in class certainly would have predicted such growth. On the other hand, Victor was a very complex young man. He very much lived in two worlds: one close to a male-oriented gang-like culture, the other an intense intellectual realm that valued subtlety and nuance. There is certainly no reason to believe that these two world orientations are mutually exclusive in any way. In fact, there is reason to believe they are highly correlated. It is also interesting in this regard to compare the attempts at making sense of figurative language by Tamara and Victor as well as Jonetha. Again, in terms of classroom participation and quality of written work, Victor and Jonetha far out distanced Tamara. However, by the end of the school year, Tamara was more likely to take a chance, to step out on an intellectual limb and engage. That she paid so much attention to the figurative language of the text is impressive. In many publications and presentations I have used the African American proverb, "Every shut eye ain't sleep." I love the proverb because it proposes that just because someone doesn't seem to know or doesn't appear to be paying attention, doesn't in fact mean he or she does not know. People often take in more than we think, know more than we believe. This admittedly limited set of data on students' attempts to address problems of figuration in these studies confirms what I've always believed and what is a core premise of Cultural Modeling—"every shut eye indeed ain't sleep."

A second area of analysis of literary reasoning by case study students involved looking at the structure of arguments they made regarding objects of figuration. This analysis of argument structure was our attempt to capture something about students' abilities to construct literary arguments. Again, we acknowledge the limitations of this analysis. We know that students' abilities to construct oral arguments and written arguments were not at the same level. However, what is of interest in this part of the analysis is that we are looking at the kinds of problems that students themselves pose and the kinds of arguments they construct in pursuit of their hypotheses regarding these problems. We think this is a qualitatively different kind of assessment than one in which we posed particular questions to the students.

In the analysis of the structure of arguments, we again (as in Chapter 5) used Toulmin's (Toulmin et al., 1984) taxonomy including claims, evidence, and warrants. We did not address what he calls "backing," inferring that backing is inherent in the nature of warrants. We divided our coding into arguments involving only claims, those involving claims and evidence, and finally those including claims, evidence, and warrants. Consistent with Toulmin, we identify arguments with all three elements as being inherently more complex and sophisticated. In this examination, we did not analyze the quality of evidence or warrants. However, as a matter of some quality control, we only included propositions made by students that we felt could be reasonably supported by the texts. Attending to problems of figuration, supporting claims with evidence, and drawing on both textual as well as real-world knowledge to warrant evidence or claims were the routine practices of the Cultural Modeling instruction. We consistently saw students engaging in these practices within the social processes of small-group and whole-group interactions. However, we wanted to find out to what extent individual students had taken up these practices as part of how they read as individuals, absent the uptake and retort of their peers. Figures 7.6 and 7.7 display the percentages for each story for each case study student. Of the total sets of claims made by students, we calculated what percentage were simple claims, what percentage of claims were accompanied by evidence, and finally what percentage were accompanied by both evidence and warrants. Across the supported categories—claims with evidence and claims with evidence plus warrants—four of the five students showed gains from the first to the second story. In the category of claims with evidence plus warrants, two of the four students who read both stories showed gains: David from 0% to 63% and Joe from 20% to 38%. Jonetha remained relatively the same in this category, from 25% to 20%. Victor made

Figure 7.6. Depth of Figurative Language Inferences—"If Beale Street Could Talk," Argument Structure in October

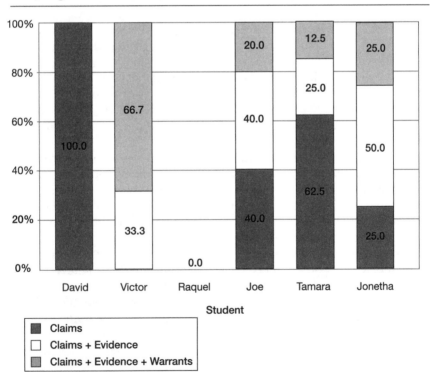

Figure 7.7. Depth of Figurative Language—"If Beale Street Could Talk" Inferences

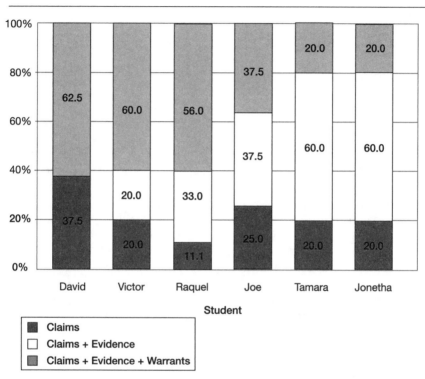

a greater percentage of both categories in his reading of the first story. He apparently paid less attention to figurative language details in the second story, as his overall figurative language inferences went down from 35.3% to 27.8% (see Figure 7.7). On the whole, the gains from story one to story two in terms of percentages of the total and within those percentages the proportion of increases in claims with evidence and claims with evidence plus warrants, represent evidence of meaningful changes over time.

WHAT A DIFFERENCE A SECOND READING MAKES!

I have discussed in some detail in this book how modeling explicit strategies by having students analyze their own everyday reasoning provided meaningful opportunities for students with long histories of low academic achievement to tackle complex literary problems and to construct very compelling literary arguments. I have illustrated how in many instances I learned from my students. The results from quarterly assessments along with our results from the talk-aloud protocols of case study students provide what we consider reasonable evidence that these students did in fact learn. In the analysis of the talk-aloud protocols I was also struck by the difference that having an opportunity to read the story a second time made in what students were able to understand. I decided to discuss the impact of a second reading in the talk-aloud protocol analyses in this chapter for several reasons. First, I have continued to argue throughout this chapter that the dearth of rigorous and authentic assessments in disciplinary reading at the secondary level is one of the field's most glaring limitations. Educators make very consequential decisions about students on the basis on what is generally pretty poor evidence. Educators take the findings from these assessments as unquestionable.

One of the limitations of existing assessments is the use of timed tests that encourage a quick single reading of a text. However, as one engages in consequential reading in the real world—whether reading to learn how to do something of consequence in our everyday life or work or reading for deep pleasure—there is rarely any reason to read quickly and only once. Thus I offer these analyses of differences in what students attended to and understood from a first to a second reading as a small piece of evidence for the importance of creating such opportunities both in instruction and in assessment. Rereading of text was a routine practice in the Cultural Modeling classrooms and often served as the basis for very close textual analysis.

I will illustrate differences from a first to a second reading with data from analyses of "If Beale Street Could Talk." We created a general construct that we called *depth of inferencing*. Here we were interested in capturing the confidence with which students made assertions about the story as well as capturing the structure of arguments as described earlier. We added to the Toulmin-inspired codes a code for the posing of questions. We saw the act of posing questions as a kind of hypothesis-building activity in which students identified a problem of interest, even if they did not yet articulate a tentative answer to that question. This interest in question posing was also captured in additional analyses we did regarding metacognitive moves by students. The act of posing questions while reading is an index of active reading and self-monitoring. It is one of the characteristics that distinguishes good readers from poor readers (Garner, 1987; Palinscar & Brown, 1984). Figures 7.8 and 7.9 below capture the distribution of these moves by each case study student in their first and then second readings of "If Beale Street Could Talk."

Figure 7.8. Depth of Inference—"If Beale Street Could Talk," April 1998

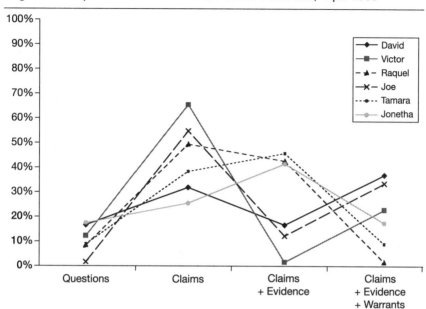

In both the first and second reading, the distribution of question posing is relatively the same. However, there is a dramatic shift in the use of claims plus evidence and of claims, plus evidence and warrants. Interestingly, the most dramatic shift is for Tamara, who I have described as the student whose class work would indicate was the weakest of all the case study students.

I will illustrate these qualitative differences with an example from Raquel's reading of "If Beale Street Could Talk." Most of the students interpreted events in the story more literally in the first reading, and made more detailed, and astute inferential comments in the second reading. The second readings demonstrated deeper understanding of character relationships, internal states, and events in the story. The scene that appears on page two of the protocol describes a meeting between Fonny and his pregnant girlfriend, Trish, who is visiting Fonny in jail:

> "We got to get some meat on your bones," I said. "Lord, have mercy."
> "Speak up. He can't hear you." But he said it with a smile.
> "We almost got the money to bail you out."
> "I figured you would."
> We sat, and we just looked at each other. We were making love to each other through all that glass and stone and steel.

Figure 7.9. Depth of Inference—"If Beale Street Could Talk," April 1998, Second Reading Comments

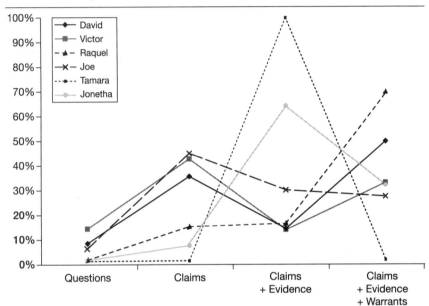

"Listen, I'll soon be out. I'm coming home because I'm glad I came, can you dig that?"

I watched his eyes.

"Yes," I said.

"Now. I'm an artisan," he said. "Like a cat who makes—tables. I don't like the word artist. Maybe I never did. I sure the . . . don't know what it means. I'm a cat who works from his balls, with his hand. I know what it's about now. I think I really do. Even if I go under. But I don't think I will. Now."

He is very far from me. He is with me, but he is very far away. And now he always will be.

"Where you lead me," I said, "I'll follow."

He laughed. "Baby. Baby. Baby. I love you. And I'm going to *build* us a table and a whole lot a folks going to be eating off it for a long, *long* time to come." (Baldwin, 1974/2006, p. 193)

After her first reading of page 2 Raquel stated,

OK, I suppose . . . what he said that um . . . when he come out, he gon' take care of her and the baby and they gon' be together for a long time. That's basically what they was talkin' about. Their plans after he gets out of jail. And that he'll be out soon.

Her interpretation of this page was a clear and concise description of events that can be inferred from the text. She makes a claim, but offers no evidence. Her claim is a relatively straightforward inference from the last paragraph, that is, Fonny is going to get out of jail and he plans to take care of them when he gets out. However, on her second reading Raquel goes further in interpreting the figurative language of the text. Her comments after the second reading demonstrated a very intuitive understanding of character relationships:

The author makes a comment that says Fon—Fonny is very far from her. He's with her, but he's very far away. And now, he will always —he always will be. What I think that means is that since he's been in jail, I guess he has a new perspective on life now. Not that she— she doesn't really agree with him, but he looks at it deeper than what she would. And so now he's on a whole 'nother level than she is. And she'll never be on that level, cuz she's never experienced what he experienced.

Raquel clearly went beyond what is written by saying that Fonny is on another level than his girlfriend because of his experiences. This interpretation of the notion of distance has a nonliteral meaning, and Raquel interpreted this distance in the figurative manner in which it was likely intended. She justified her position with text and gives a logical explanation of her reasoning. Here Raquel provides both a claim and evidence. On her own, she decides to focus on a problem of symbolism, the idea of distance. She attends to a qualitatively different problem in the second reading of this same passage.

CONCLUSION

I am attempting in this book to show how complex it is to know what students understand and are capable of at aggregate levels. Students like those at Fairgate High School are represented to the public as incapable. Assessments that bear little relationship to how reasoning in the disciplines is practiced are used to label them and to punish them. What they know and value outside of school is viewed as either irrelevant or detrimental to their academic learning. We have shown students who demonstrate very rigorous literary reasoning in classrooms where instruction is structured to help them see the links between everyday and academic reasoning, in which the norms for participation are both made explicit and also organized in ways that provide them with meaningful and accessible competent roles to play. We have shown that on one set of assessments they do not do well, but on others that are certainly rigorous, these same students do quite well.

Learning is not a simple linear process. Designing tools that adequately capture what students are able to do under specific conditions is difficult and always involves levels of inferencing. The variety of kinds of data that we have collected on the Cultural Modeling Project at Fairgate High School demonstrates that displays of competence depend a lot on how competence is both defined and assessed. It also demonstrates that trajectories of growth are difficult to predict and that sometimes what a student is internalizing from his participation in instruction may not always be what we think. We privilege particular kinds of displays as evidence of processes of internalization —active talking and writing—but some students learn while being quiet, on the surface distant from the action, yet inwardly attentive in ways that are difficult to assess (Rogoff et al., 2003).

CHAPTER 8

Blooming in the Midst of the Whirlwind

I opened this book with vignettes showing some of the kinds of life challenges with which the youth at Fairgate High School wrestled. Their life stories are not unique. Their challenges are faced by many adolescents who live in persistent intergenerational poverty, who are members of ethnic groups that face persistent historical forms of discrimination, and who, as a consequence, live in a web of institutional low expectations and assumptions of White privilege. But I have also offered examples that demonstrate what can be accomplished when instruction is organized in ways that leverage their rich world knowledge, position them as competent, create access by making explicit and public the rules for participation in complex subject-matter-specific norms for reasoning, and foster relationships that maximize a reason to persist and put forth effort. I have tried to make the case that these youngsters are more complex than teachers, policy makers, and the general public imagine.

In the Cultural Modeling Project we attempted each year to find ways to expand the network of resources available to these youth. This included in 1998 taking a group of students to visit the Northwestern campus. On the morning we were to leave the school, we only had responses from five students; by the time we left, we had to turn students away. During the 3 years of the project, I lived professionally in two worlds. I was always struck by the fact that I would pass the Fairgate library and see very few students there. Unless a teacher arranged to bring a class there, it was virtually empty. Then I would leave Fairgate and go to the Northwestern campus where the library was open until midnight. As part of the visit to Northwestern, we took the students to the Barnes and Noble store in Evanston and gave each student $12.00 to buy a book of his or her choice. It was an interesting experience for many reasons and revealed much about the reading interests of the students, which we did not tap in the curriculum and of which we and most of the teachers were unaware. There are virtually no bookstores, large or small, corporate or independent, in most low-income African American communities, and certainly not in the neighborhood that surrounded Fairgate High School. This means that in order to get books, students either had to travel away from their neighborhood or use public library facilities or the school library. Our project's Jan Derrick and student Allan have the following conversation during the visit to Barnes and Noble. Allan chose a book of romantic poetry. He was having a hard time making a decision between the poetry and Machiavelli's *The Prince*. The transcript is from Jan Derrick's rich field notes.

"M-m-m-m . . . interesting choice, Allan."

"I can't decide, Miss Derrick. I want the love poetry because it helps me write my own poetry and my own rap songs, and the women love to hear it."

"Did Taquisha [his girlfriend from last year] like it?"

Shyly, "Yes, Miss Derrick. She liked it. But I've always wanted to read *The Prince*."

"Why?"

"I saw it on the shelf in a library. I read a few pages and it seemed interesting."

"Why didn't you take it out of the library then?"

"I would have, but I didn't have a card, and even if I did, the library is in an area where I can't go alone—wrong gang area."

"Oh, tell you what. I have several copies of *The Prince* at home. You can have one. Then you can buy your book of poems."

"Thank you Miss Derrick."

I don't personally know Allan, and I can't say his choice is somehow representative of anything. However, I do know Taquisha, Tamara, and David. You've met both Taquisha and David in earlier chapters. Tamara looks for a Stephen King mystery. David looks for a book on the history of stadiums and when he can't find one decides to buy a book for his younger brother. Taquisha looks for *Jubilee* by Margaret Walker. For weeks after the visit to the Evanston Barnes & Noble, students stopped me in the hall to talk about what they were reading and how much they enjoyed the visit to the bookstore and the Northwestern campus.

Jan Derrick would take over my class when I was absent, and she developed a strong rapport with many of the students. The project had developed an independent reading list for students, but most of the books on our list were not in the school's library, and some students refused to go to the local public library because it was located in gang territory. Jan and the school librarian took it upon themselves to develop another annotated reading list of books that were available in the school library. On the days when Jan took the class, they would often go to the library and look for books. On this day, Tamara and Jan read excerpts from *For Colored Girls* (Shange, 1997):

> *Tamara*: I know people who act like this.
> *Jan*: You do?
> *Tamara*: Yeah. In fact, most women I know act like this.
> *Jan*: How is that?
> *Tamara*: They live from day to day.

Later, Tamara approaches Jan:

> *Tamara*: Miss Derrick, what about *Medea?* She sounds interesting.
>   The words aren't easy, but I get the meaning.
> *Jan*: If you're interested, we'll dig in.

As part of our research, we asked case study students across different classrooms to read new short stories and talk-aloud about what they understood and what they were doing to make sense of what they read. During that week of talk-aloud protocols, Tamara told Jan she wanted to read the full novel of James Baldwin's *If Beale Street Could Talk.* (1974/2006) We had selected part of a chapter from the novel to use for one of the talk-aloud protocols. Jan bought her a copy. Tamara later told Jan that she read the entire book and loved it.

All the statistics surrounding this school—achievement scores, dropout rate, poverty rate, gang concentration—would lead few to expect to find students who would look for Machiavelli's *The Prince*, Margaret Walker's *Jubilee* or Euripedes' *Medea* as independent reading. These students were not from Mrs. West's honors class.

The overall point here is that the lives of these students are richer and more complex than many people think, including educational researchers and policy makers. What is often missing from our analyses and prescriptions are the inside perspectives of the youth themselves. In the same neighborhoods where public schools fail dismally, community-based organizations in the arts and other areas create learning environments in which youth thrive (Fisher, 2003, 2004; Heath & McLaughlin, 1994; McLaughlin, 1993; McLaughlin, Irby, & Langman, 1994). These out-of-school learning environments typically create roles and opportunities that build upon the life experiences of these young people.

So the question with which we as a society—the general public, policy makers, educational practitioners, and educational researchers—grapple is how to design learning environments in which these young people thrive in terms of intellectual and psychological well-being. Historically, this fundamental question has been ignored or responses to it have been based on presumptions of innate deficits (Nasir et al., 2006). These deficit assumptions have pervaded not only the world of practice, but the very foundations of educational psychology as a field. Wade Nobles recounts positions taken by G. Stanley Hall who received the first doctorate in psychology in 1878 at Harvard University and went on to train Arnold Gesell, Lewis Terman, four future presidents of the American Psychological Association, and John Dewey, among others. Nobles and Adeleke (2005) illustrate Hall's thinking:

> "Among tribes of Dahomey, . . . and in the Fan, Felup Wolop, Kru, and other strips . . . sometimes resort to cannibalism, use anagglutinative speech, believe profoundly in witchcraft, are lazy, improvident, imitative, fitful, passionate, affectionate, faithful, are devoted to music and rhythm and have always practiced slavery amongst themselves." He goes on to state as fact that "polygamy is universal, fecundity is high, and mortality great. Strong sex instincts are necessary to preserve the race. As soon as the child can go it alone, it begins to shift for itself. Stealing is universal and is a game and falsehoods are clever accomplishments." This the most influential maker of American psychologists goes on to say, "Our slaves came from the long narrow belt, not many miles from the sea. . . . It is surprising to see how few of his aboriginal traits the Negro has lost, although many of them are modified." (1905, p. 350)

We try to find comfort in arguments that such positions are artifacts of the past. Yet in 1969 Arthur Jensen argues that we cannot boost IQ or academic achievement because of innate differences in the races. In 1994, Hernstein and Murray resurrect the question of innate racial differences in capacity to learn. And most recently, Sarich and Miele (2004) claim again scientific evidence for racial differences in capacity. Current views of cognition, in part influenced by emergent studies of the physiology of the brain, portray the brain as inherently plastic (Quartz & Sejnowski, 2002). We have good reason to believe that the brain has sensitive periods or windows in which particular domains of learning are more easily learned—such as the universal capacity of infants and very young children to learn natural language (Kuhl, 2004; Kuhl, Williams, Lacerda, Stevens, & Lindblom, 1992).

We also have good reason to believe that neural connections within the brain develop at different rates within different points across the life course, such as differences between childhood and adolescence versus elderhood (Gopnik, Meltzoff, & Kuhl, 1999). Yet within these broad windows, the brain remains plastic, capable of rewiring itself in response to experience and physiological states (Greenough, Black, & Wallace, 1987). What is most interesting in these studies are the implications for learning in the real world: understanding what is entailed in fundamental reorganization of neural connections; understanding what is entailed in forms of cognitive reorganization that involve making and adjusting connections between existing knowledge and new knowledge (Bransford et al., 1999; Poldrack, 2000). Because the human body is such a complex and dynamic organism, we have much to learn about how humans' relationships with their environments operate to shape individual functioning. We know that patterned ways of viewing experience in the world—that is, perceptions—trigger chemical responses in the body that influence what we pay attention to and how we attend to problems (Ochsner & Lieberman, 2001). Some of these perceptions and chemical responses are tied to hard-wired mechanisms such as immediate fight or flight responses to perceptions of threat. However, because the physical and social ecologies in which human beings live across the earth vary so greatly, it is reasonable to assume that how these fundamental processes of learning and development operate will vary greatly across humankind (Super & Harness, 1986; Weisner, 2002); while at the same time we can expect there will be broad parameters within which such variation will develop because we belong to the same species (Rogoff, 2003). I raise these hypotheses as fundamental questions for the science of human learning and development. I further assert that the question in the United States of how to design learning environments that powerfully support the development of what Edmund Gordon (Gordon & Bridglall, in press; Lee, in press-b) calls "intellective competence" of African Americans, Latinos, American Indians, Asian American groups who are not achieving adequately, and those youth across ethnic communities who live in persistent intergenerational poverty is intimately linked to the fundamental scientific questions I have raised. The field's inability to understand the intellective work of everyday experience of these young people and their families blinds researchers into detours that at best are often naive and at worst contribute to enduring assumptions of differences as deficits (Lee, Spencer, & Harpalani, 2003).

We researchers in education, cognition, and human development are expected to contribute knowledge that ultimately is translatable into what Ellen Lagemann (Lagemann & Shulman, 1999) calls "usable knowledge" in ways that at least approximate how medical knowledge developed in laboratory and epidemiological studies are taken up in medical practice. However, the general public and public policy makers often view our fields as irrelevant to practice, while policy makers in particular will use partisan politics to selectively appropriate areas of educational research that are aligned with their own agendas (Allington & Woodside-Jiron, 1999; Cohen & Barnes, 1993; Darling-Hammond, 1999a; Elmore & McLaughlin, 1989; McLoyd, 1998). In either case, neither educational researchers nor the policy-making community has responded to the crisis reflected in the achievement gap in ways that are acceptable. The problems of translating theory into practice and of transforming schools are huge. The many macrolevel issues involved have been addressed by others and while really important are not the purview of this book. However, it is clear that the assumptions of deficit embedded in popular folk theories and often curiously hidden in scientific explanations fuel the mechanisms that inform macrolevel policies.

Asa Hilliard (2001) raises this as a question of will. He says, "Our children's manifest problems in public education virtually all have to do with *opportunity to learn*" (p. 10). Opportunity to learn is constrained in devastating ways by a pervasive culture of low expectations (Hilliard, 1991). In a *Chicago Sun-Times* (Rossi, 2004) article on a proposed change in the criteria for schools to be placed on academic probation, an official of the North Lawndale Local School Council Federation is quoted as saying, "We're being asked to do the impossible by the ungrateful" (p. 9). I suspect that this official was referring to the fact that the Chicago Board of Education was proposing that probation schools be required to raise test score results so that 40% of students meet state standards and national reading norms in an environment in which the board would restrict how schools could use discretionary funds (including selecting from mandated programs identified by the board) without providing any additional sources of funding.

This is part of the shell game that policy makers and school officials play. There is no question that money matters and that differences in per-pupil funding between affluent, predominantly White districts and districts serving predominantly students from low-income neighborhoods with concentrations of African American, Latino, American Indian, and Asian American communities are gross beyond belief (Carey, 2004; Education Trust, 2005a; Hill & Roza, 2004). We have documentation of schools in districts serving students from low-income communities that are often overcrowded, with unsafe facilities and inadequate resources in terms of technology, science labs, and libraries. There is also no question that low-performing schools often spend discretionary funds in ways that do not contribute to student learning. We know there are also huge differences in salary scales between teachers working in underachieving urban districts and their more affluent suburban districts.

Liberal reformers will decry the heavy hand of central administrations in limiting the decision-making powers of teachers in local schools and the imposition of accountability measures in the form of standardized tests as the crux of the problem. Conservative reformers will insist that prescriptions from what they call "scientific research" must be imposed to assure equity. Ironically, there are elements of truth in all these positions. However, none of these arguments explains the persistent and unacceptable gaps in achievement that is predicted by race and SES. Because this book has focused on learning in high schools and because our Cultural Modeling Project took place in Chicago, I will share findings on the Chicago Public Schools (CPS) Design for High Schools that began during the 2nd year of our project. G. Alfred Hess and Solomon Cytrynbaum (1999) of the Center for Urban School Policy at Northwestern conducted an extensive study of the 2nd year of the reform during the 1998–1999 academic term. Their findings are chilling.

Hess and Cytrynbaum (1999) observed and collected data in high schools that had been placed on academic probation and in schools whose extremely low levels of performance resulted in reconstitution where the faculty and administration were replaced by the central administration. They also included high-performing schools and small schools. The probation and reconstituted high schools are the ones that most African American and Latino students in the Chicago Public Schools attend. Hess and Cytrynbaum found the following:

1. By 1999, reading scores for the system improved over the last decade with 32.5% of students in CPS high schools reading at or above national norms. However, the increases from 1997 on are attributable to gains made in the elementary schools, with little to no contribution being made by students' work in the high schools.
2. Classroom observations reveal that instruction is consistently at intellectually low levels as measured by the quality of questions posed by teachers and the nature of uptake by students.
3. Teachers continued to have low expectations of student abilities despite the fact that students were entering ninth grade with higher test scores.
4. The probation schools that exceeded citywide gains in reading had teachers who held higher expectations for student abilities and who demonstrated higher levels of intellectual challenge for their students.

The systemwide gains in reading are laudatory (moving from 20.5% at or above national norms in 1996 to 32.5% in 1999). In 2005, 43.7% of students in Grades 3 through 8 are at or above national norms on the Iowa Test of Basic Skills. Still, 32.5% at or above national norms means that two thirds of the students are below national norms; 43.7% means that close to 60% of students are below national norms. I can say categorically that the tests are not adequate measures of students' reading abilities. But even so, they test basic skills and thus should not pose the huge achievement problems they do. Hess and Cytrynbaum (1999) collapse the top two quartiles to capture a broad category of achieving at or above national norms, but this masks the small number of students who score in the top quartile. Hess and Cytrynbaum conclude:

> On the basis of more than 400 classroom observations, it is the conviction of the CUSP [Center for Urban School Policy] staff that teacher change is an important component for improving Chicago's most poorly performing high schools. For some teachers, significant improvement in their skills is needed. For many teachers, a fundamental change in their expectations of what their students can accomplish is critical. For some, a better knowledge of the subject matter is required. But even if all of those improvements occurred, it is still true that nobody really *knows* how to be successful with low-income, minority, urban youth." (p. 16)

Although I understand their genuine skepticism, I do *know* how to be successful with low-income, minority, urban youth. We have three charter schools and one independent preschool in Chicago with proven histories of achievement. These schools are based on a 32-year history of building educational institutions through the Institute of Positive Education in Chicago (Lee, 1992). The hundreds of schools on the Education Trust's Web site that are successful with such youth also know (Education Trust, 2005b, 2005c; Haycock, 1998b). The schools cited in Judith Langer's (2001) research on successful schools serving such youth know. Barbara A. Sizemore (1985, 1987, 1988, 1995, 2007) knew, as evidenced by her many decades of turning around low performing schools in Pittsburgh and Chicago. Asa Hilliard (2000) captures this dance we in the educational community orchestrate to obfuscate why this dilemma persists:

> Currently the heaviest emphasis in the education research community in general is on children, how "intelligent" they are, which "intelligences" they have, how "motivated" they are, and on "special methods," etc. I think that the emphases are misplaced. By now it should be clear that, for the most part, our children are geniuses with capacities to go far beyond any school requirements. They respond very well to quite a variety of *well-executed methods and techniques*. There is no mystery about how to teach any of them. The priority that needs more emphasis is the deep study of the *quality of services* that we offer to students, the unequal distribution of those services and the structures of inequity, such as tracking and inappropriate special education, still existing in the school. Why do our children fail to get access to the many educators who are not puzzled about how to teach them? (p. 9)

I am a cofounder of an African-centered school that is more than 30 years old. Over these decades, our school has produced young people who have achieved great academic success, who are emotionally healthy, who understand the responsibilities they have inherited from those on whose shoulders they stand, and who have healthy views of the world and the contributions they are poised to contribute (Lee, 1992; Rattaray & Shujaa, 1987). Over these many years, we have been able to do this work with extremely limited economic resources.

What allows schools such as this to succeed on academic terms? Why do small schools nationally achieve in terms of GPA, high school graduation rates, and lower rates of discipline problems, but not show significant differences in academic achievement in terms of test scores, in an environment in which they are being inundated with economic and other forms of support (Wasley et al., 2000)? Why is it that affluent suburban districts maintain significant gaps in achievement (in terms of GPA, enrollment in honors and Advanced Placement courses, and test scores) between so-called minority and so-called majority students, even with the laudatory efforts of national organizations such as the Minority Student Achievement Network (Ferguson, 2002a, 2002b)? I have no intention here to make a simplistic argument that kids of color are simply geniuses that schools don't recognize; nor that there are no factors from within African American, Latino, and American Indian communities and low-income communities generally that contribute to the achievement gap (Bell, 2004; Madhubuti, 1990, 2002; Wilson, 1987). However, I do strongly believe that the institutional forces that constrain opportunity to learn are the dominant forces in the achievement gap.

It has always been a great irony in the United States that as a society we do not seem to recognize that we're all in the same boat, that what affects one segment of society will eventually leach into the other segments. It is in this light that I see the persistent achievement gap predicted by race and class as a microcosm of a broader set of dilemmas around how we envision pathways for the development of complex subject matter learning. On the one hand, our folk theories and in some cases our "scientific" theories explain the dilemma as some kids being prepared for such learning and others not (Deutsch & Brown, 1964; Hall & Moats, 1999; R. Hess & Shipman, 1965). On the other hand, our approaches to those students who we think are prepared from home, community experiences, and prior schooling to be ready for complex subject matter learning don't yield the outcomes that our high expectations for these youth would predict (ACT, 2006) . On National Assessments of Educational Progress (NAEP), consistently less than 10% of all youth are able to read with understanding the texts which pose the most complex challenges on the NAEP assessment (Campbell, Hombo, & Mazzeo, 2000; Perle et al., 2005). Patricia Alexander (1997) rightly argues:

Many of the efforts undertaken to promote this goal have appeared overly simplistic or have targeted only cognitive or motivational dimensions of learning. Until we, as educators, recognize that the journey toward competence is not a stroll down a primrose lane but rather a trek through difficult, unknown, and sometimes treacherous terrain, we cannot expect the general public or the students we guide to change their misperceptions. . . . The forces involved in academic development do not operate in isolation but, in effect, feed off one another. Fortunate is the learner who, early in her academic journey, acquires a foundation of subject-matter knowledge, some personal interest in the domain, as well as the strategies for regulating and augmenting her learning. For such a learner, the adventure will likely be more fulfilling and successful. Yet, many others who set out on this pilgrimage lack one or more of these critical dimensions of domain learning. For these individuals, it is simply not enough to hope that the requisite knowledge, interest, or strategic processes will eventually emerge. Educators must labor to ensure that these elements are directly and meaningfully incorporated in the students' instructional experiences. (p. 239)

This observation by Alexander provides a window to illustrate my claims that the problems of the achievement gap predicted by race and class are both a thorny public sore as well as an example of a larger set of scientific issues with which we still need to grapple. First, this "trek through difficult, unknown, and sometimes treacherous terrain" of domain learning to which Alexander refers is made more treacherous when youth must simultaneously learn to manage both the psychosocial and physiological challenges that racism and poverty present as well as the difficult contours of complex subject matter learning. Indeed, cognition and motivation, cognition and emotional states, cognition and phenomenological perceptions act in dynamic tandem. This is the case for all humans. Learning to manage perceptions and thought, emotional states and thinking in relation to particular circumstances is one of the prime developmental tasks that humans face across the life course (Dai & Sternberg, 2004; Graham & Golan, 1991; Spencer, 2006; Steele, 1997, 1998). These challenges and patterned ways of responding to them will differ by communities. Part of our scientific challenge as well as our challenge of practice is to understand that variation and how to help shape that variation for specific ends.

We have differences in our understanding of the antecedents of early foundations of subject-matter knowledge and strategic knowledge in relation to such knowledge. For example, in early reading, some have argued that young children whose parents do not read storybooks to them are missing critical domain knowledge to facilitate early reading (Hall & Moats, 1999). As such, the claim is that such children come to school less prepared to learn to read. Others argue that many of these same children experience rich oral traditions of storytelling that provide them with other models of narrative genres and rhetorical strategies that are not captured in the kinds of stories that their middle-class counterparts may read at home (Baquedano-López, 1997; Bloome, Champion, Katz, Morton, & Muldrow, 2001; Cazden, Michaels, & Tabors, 1985; Champion, 1998; Champion, Seymour, & Camarata, 1995; Heath, 1983; Lee, Rosenfeld, et al., 2003). A broader and more comprehensive view will recognize the breadth of repertoires of practice (Gutierrez & Rogoff, 2003) that students bring to the process of learning to read (Lee, 1997), rather than taking a simplistic either-or stance, with an implicit assumption that one set of repertoires leads to a "stroll down a primrose lane" that leads to reading success, while the other set leads to a "trek through difficult, unknown . . . terrain." Learning to read with understanding across the life course will be a difficult trek for both groups of youngsters as they progress to expand the range of kinds of texts they can and are willing to tackle with some modicum of success.

The process of ensuring that knowledge, interest, and strategic processing "are directly and meaningfully incorporated in the students' instructional experiences" is also contested territory. Direct incorporation of such strategic knowledge for African American, Latino, American Indian, Asian American and students from low-income communities generally is typically translated to mean direct scripted instruction. Witness the number of districts and even whole states, such as California, that now require the Open Court system of direct instruction in reading. Current direct instruction is rooted in earlier forms of scripted instruction that are based on assumptions of inherent language deficits of children who do not speak a so-called mainstream dialect of English. More typically, direct incorporation of strategic knowledge for more affluent students is translated as project-based or inquiry-based instruction in which students work with intelligent artifacts that provide them with opportunities to reason the way scientists or mathematicians do. What makes instructional experiences meaningful is also contested. Many of the efforts to design culturally responsive instruction are intended to make instruction meaningful, but there is often resistance to such efforts in fields like science and mathematics with an underlying implication that everyday experiences of some students are less relevant to these domains, or that experiences associated with historical ethnic communities also bear little import for learning in these domains.

I selected the subtitle of this book from the prophetic poem by poet laureate Gwendolyn Brooks. I present multiple cases of both the whirlwind that too many Black and Brown students face as well as the ways that schools can contribute to their blooming in the midst of their many difficulties. Unfortunately, public education has in too many instances been a

CAGED BIRD

The free bird leaps
on the back of the wind
and floats downstream
till the current ends
and dips his wing
in the orange sun rays
and dares to claim the sky.

But a bird that stalks
down his narrow cage
can seldom see through
his bars of rage
his wings are clipped and
his feet are tied
so he opens his throat to sing.

The caged bird sings
with a fearful trill
of things unknown
but longed for still
and his tune is heard
on the distant hill
for the caged bird
sings of freedom

The free bird thinks of another breeze
and the trade winds soft through the sighing trees
and the fat worms waiting on a dawn-bright lawn
and he names the sky his own.

But a caged bird stands on the grave of dreams
his shadow shouts on a nightmare scream
his wings are clipped and his feet are tied
so he opens his throat to sing

The caged bird sings
with a fearful trill
of things unknown
but longed for still
and his tune is heard
on the distant hill
for the caged bird
sings of freedom.

—Maya Angelou

Notes

Introduction

1. All of these ethnographic field and verbatim notes are from the excellent work of Jan Derrick, the ethnographer and videographer of the Cultural Modeling Project. Jan went above and beyond the call of duty in getting to know students, faculty, and staff in ways beyond anything I could have accomplished. Her rich field notes and interview data revealed a side of the school that I typically did not see with my focus on the classroom. I am immensely indebted to her. The names of all students, teachers, administrators, staff, and the school are pseudonyms.

2. I have taken the liberty of claiming that in the domains of mathematics and science the design principles of the Algebra Project (Moses & Cobb, 2001) and Chéche Konnen (Rosebery, Warren, Ballenger, & Ogonowski, 2005) are consistent with the principles of Cultural Modeling. We have also developed and field tested Cultural Modeling to teach narrative writing at the elementary school level (Lee, Rosenfeld, Mendenhall, Rivers, & Tynes, 2003).

Chapter 1

1. While Asian American students typically score higher than their White counterparts in mathematics on assessments such as the ACT, SAT and NAEP, they do not compare well in reading (Pang, 1995). In addition, Asian American scores vary significantly by country of national origin and class (Lee, 1996).

2. Throughout most of U.S. history, laws have been designed to racially classify persons in order to determine access to legal rights (Stampp, 1953). In the seventeenth century, racial classification was based on matrilineal descent (Brunsma & Rockquemore, 2002; Hollinger, 2003). By the 1700s, states developed blood-fraction laws wherein being Black or White was determined by lineage: one or more Black great-grandparents meant $\frac{1}{8}$ black blood or what were called octaroons; one or more Black grandparents or $\frac{1}{4}$ black blood were called quadroons (Finkelman, 1992; Sollors, 1997; Stephenson, 1969). These blood-fraction laws were used in court cases until the 1940s.

3. Special thanks to Geneva Smitherman (2000c) and Arthur Spears (Spears & Winford, 1998) for clarification of the complex linguistic issues involved in understanding Africanisms in English and other European languages.

189

4. In my conversations with Geneva Smitherman, she raised the complexity of the reference to African Americans. The Americas include Canada, the United States, and Central and South America. There are significant populations of African descent not only within the United States, but also in Central and South America, as well as the Caribbean. Thus, the term African American to refer to Blacks living in the United States masks the Black presence in other parts of the Americas. The term also typically does not privilege the African descent immigrant populations from other parts of the world who currently live within the United States. I will continue to use the term African Americans to refer broadly to Blacks living within the United States, but thought it important to acknowledge the complexity here.

5. *Playing the dozens* is a specialized form of signifying or ritual insult in which the targets of the insult are the mothers of the interlocutors (Smitherman, 1977). Playing the dozens is essentially a game of word play as the content of the insults cannot be true. The point is to respond to an insult creatively playing with the vehicle of the metaphor used for the initial insult.

6. It should be noted that by "scientific," Vygotsky was not limiting himself to the domain of science. Rather, he referred to domains of knowledge that are systematic and generally taught in school.

7. This may be because they use some array of AAE features—syntax, lexicon, phonology, prosody, speech genres, or rhetorical features—totally, in particular circumstances, or at some point in their life course (Geneva Smitherman, personal communication).

8. For example, statements made by teachers that in surface structure are requests may be intended as commands. The sociolinguistic literature has noted instances where students whose home dialects differ from the teacher may interpret statements such as "Please sit down" as requests. When they refuse what the teacher intended as a command, they then become subject to disciplinary actions.

Chapter 3

1. I use the phrase African Holocaust of Enslavement to refer to the 350 years during which people of African descent were held captive in this country and the 100 years of legalized Jim Crow. The term *holocaust* means "an act of mass destruction of human lives." It is used to refer to events in human history so abhorrent as to defy the bounds of morality. It is most often used in relation to the Jewish Holocaust during the Second World War in which 6 million Jews were systematically killed after being placed in captivity in Nazi concentration camps. It is a most unfortunate testimony to the human condition that such systematic efforts to kill or enslave whole groups of people have occurred many times, including the attacks on the indigenous populations of the Americas (Jackson, 1993; Stannard, 1992) and the mass captivity of Africans across the Americas and the Caribbean. I use the term African Holocaust of Enslavement as a public marker of the immensity of these historical acts so that we may all remember.

2. I acknowledge that there are critical stances that do not privilege the idea of coherence. For example, Deconstructionists explicitly aim to deconstruct any notion of coherence within a work of literature (Bloom et al., 1987).

3. Thanks to Moshe Krakowski for the English translation of the Hebrew in "Sax Cantor Riff."

Chapter 4

In this chapter, the following transcription conventions are used:
Speech overlap [
Rising pitch ↑
Falling pitch ↓
Extension of the sound or syllable
   : medium
   :: long
Emphasis _____
Loud CAPS
Quicker pacing >transcript<
No interval between adjacent utterances—utterances are linked together with =
Phonetic transcription /transcription/
Researcher's comments ((comments))
Rise-Fall pitch ^

Chapter 5

1. See "A Cultural Modeling Perspective: The Creation of Opportunity to Learn Through the Cultural Practices of Classroom Instruction" (Lee, in press a) for a critique of state assessments such as the Massachusetts Comprehensive Assesment System that purport to be more rigorous.

References

ACT, Inc. (2006). *Reading between the lines: What the ACT reveals about college readiness in reading.* Iowa City, IA: Author.

Adams, G., & Engelmann, S. (1996). *Research on direct instruction: 20 years beyond DISTAR.* Seattle, WA: Educational Achievement Systems.

Afflerbach, P., & Johnston, P. (1984). Research methodology on the use of verbal reports in reading research. *Journal of Reading Behavior, 16*(4), 307–322.

Alcoff, L. (1995). Mestizo identity. In N. Zack (Ed.), *American mixed race: The culture of microdiversity* (pp. 257–278). Lanham, MD: Rowman & Littlefield.

Alexander, P. A. (1997). Mapping the multidimensional nature of domain learning: The interplay of cognitive, motivational, and strategic forces. In M. L. Maehr &, P. R. Pintrich (Eds.), *Advances in motivation and achievement* (Vol. 10, pp. 213–250). Greenwich, CT: JAI.

Alexander, P. A. (1998). Positioning conceptual change within a model of domain literacy. In B. Guzzetti & C. Hynd (Eds.), *Perspectives on conceptual change: Multiple ways to understand knowing and learning in a complex world* (pp. 55–76). Mahwah, NJ: Erlbaum.

Alexander, P. A. (2003). *The path to competence: A lifetime developmental perspective on reading.* [Policy Brief]. Oak Creek, WI: National Reading Conference.

Alexander, P. A., Kulikowich, J. M., & Jetton, T. L. (1994). The role of subject matter knowledge and interest in the processing of linear and nonlinear texts. *Review of Educational Research, 64,* 201–252.

Allington, R. L., & Woodside-Jiron, H. (1999). The politics of literacy teaching: How "research" shaped educational policy. *Educational Researcher, 28*(8), 4–13.

Alvermann, D., & Moore, D. (1991). Secondary school reading. In R. Barr, M. Kamil, P. Mosenthal, & P. D. Pearson (Eds.), *Handbook of reading research* (Vol. 2, pp. 951–983). New York: Longman.

America, R. F. (1990). *The wealth of races: The present value of benefits from past injustices.* New York: Greenwood Press.

Ancess, J. (2003). *Beating the odds: High schools as communities of commitment.* New York: Teachers College Press.

Anderson, J. D. (1988). *The education of Blacks in the South, 1860–1935.* Chapel Hill: University of North Carolina Press.

Anson, A., Cook, T., & Habib, F. (1991). The Comer school development program: A theoretical analysis. *Urban Education, 26,* 56–82.

Anyon, J. (1980). Social class and the hidden curriculum of work. *Journal of Education, 162*(1), 67–92.

Anyon, J. (1981). Social class and school knowledge. *Curriculum Inquiry, 11*(1), 3–42.

Apple, M. (1979). *Ideology and Curriculum.* New York: Routledge.

Applebee, A. (1996). *Curriculum as conversation: Transforming traditions of teaching and learning.* Chicago: University of Chicago Press.

Applebee, A., Burroughs, R., & Stevens, A. (2000). Creating continuity and coherence in high school literature curricula. *Research in the Teaching of English, 34*(3), 396–429.

Appleman, D. (2000). *Critical encounters in high school English : Teaching literary theory to adolescents.* New York: Teachers College Press.

Asante, M. K., & Welsh-Asante, K. (1990). *African Culture: The Rhythms of Unity.* Trenton, NJ: Africa World Press.

Ausubel, D. (1960). The use of advanced organizers in the learning and retention of meaningful verbal material. *Journal of Educational Psychology, 51*, 267–272.

Bakhtin, M. M. (1981). *The dialogic imagination: Four essays* (M. Holquist, Ed.; C. Emerson & M. Holquist, Trans.). Austin: University of Texas Press.

Baldwin, J. (1974). *If Beale Street Could Talk.* New York: Dial Press.

Ball, A. (1992). Cultural preferences and the expository writing of African-American adolescents. *Written Communication, 9*(4), 501–532.

Ball, A. (1995). Text design patterns in the writing of urban African-American students: Teaching to the strengths of students in multicultural settings. *Urban Education, 30*, 253–289.

Ball, A. (2000). Teachers' developing philosophies in literacy and their use in urban schools. In C. D. Lee & P. Smagorinsky (Eds.), *Vygotskian perspectives on literacy research: Constructing meaning through collaborative inquiry* (pp. 226–255). New York: Cambridge University Press.

Ball, A. (2002). Three decades of research on classroom life: Illuminating the classroom communicative lives of America's at-risk students. In W. Secada (Ed.), *Review of Reseach in Education* (Vol. 26, pp. 71–112). Washington, DC: American Educational Research Association.

Ball, D. L., & Rundquist, S. S. (1993). Collaboration as a context for joining teacher learning with learning about teaching. In D. K. Cohen, M. W. McLaughlin, & J. E. Talbert (Eds.), *Teaching for understanding: Challenges for policy and practice* (pp. 13–42). San Francisco: Jossey-Bass.

Ballenger, C. (1997). Social identities, moral narratives, scientific argumentation: Science talk in a bilingual classroom. *Language and Education, 11*(1), 1–14.

Bamshad, M., Fraley, A. E., Crawford, M., Cann, R., Busi, B., Naidu, J. M., & Jorde, L. B. (1996). mtDNA variation in caste populations of Andhra Pradesh, India. *Human Biology, 68*(1), 1–28.

Bandura, A. (1986). *Social foundations of thought and actions: A social cognitive theory.* Englewood Cliffs, NJ: Prentice-Hall.

Baquedano-López, P. (1997). Creating social identities through *Doctrina* narratives. *Issues in Applied Linguistics, 8*(1), 27–45.

Baron, R., Tom, D., & Cooper, H. (1985). Social class, race, and teacher expectations. In J. B. Dusek (Ed.), *Teacher expectancies* (pp. 251–269). Hillsdale, NJ: Erlbaum.

Bateson, G. (1972). *Steps to an ecology of mind.* New York: Ballantine.

Baugh, J. (1983). *Black street speech: Its history, structure, and survival.* Austin: University of Texas Press.

Baugh, J. (1988). Twice as less: Black English and the performance of Black students in mathematics and science [book review]. *Harvard Educational Review, 58,* 395–403.

Bauman, R. (1977). *Verbal art as performance.* Prospect Heights, IL: Waveland Press.

Bauman, R., & Briggs, C. (1990). Poetics and performance as critical perspectives on language and social life. *Annual Review of Anthropology, 19,* 59–88.

Baumann, J. F. (1984). Effectiveness of a direct instruction paradigm for teaching main idea comprehension. *Reading Research Quarterly, 20,* 93–108.

Bell, C. (2004). *The sanity of survival: Reflections on community mental health.* Chicago: Third World Press.

Bell, D. (1992). *Faces at the bottom of the well: The permanence of racism.* New York: Basic Books.

Bell-Villada, G. (1990). *García Márquez: The man and his work.* Chapel Hill: University of North Carolina Press.

Bennett, L. (1964). *Before the Mayflower: A history of the Negro in America, 1619–1964.* Chicago: Johnson.

Bereiter, C., & Engelmann, S. (1966). *Teaching disadvantaged children in the preschool.* Englewood Cliffs, NJ: Prentice Hall.

Bereiter, C., & Scardamalia, M. (1992). Cognition and curriculum. In P. W. Jackson (Ed.), *Handbook of research on curriculum* (pp. 517–542). New York: Macmillan.

Berliner, P. (1994). *Thinking in jazz: The infinite art of improvisation.* Chicago: University of Chicago Press.

Bernstein, B. (1961). Social class and linguistic development: A theory of social learning. In A. Halsey, J. Floud, & C. Anderson (Eds.), *Education, economy, and society* (pp. 288–314). New York: Free Press.

Bernstein, M. (2007). *At the desk and on the nightstand: Reading as a mediating artifact in teachers' professional and personal lives.* Unpublished doctoral dissertation, Northwestern University, Evanston, IL.

Bloom, H., deMan, P., Derrida, J., Hartman, G., & Hillis Miller, J. (1987). *Deconstructionism and criticism.* New York: Continuum.

Bloome, D., Carter, S. P., Christian, B. M., Otto, S., & Shuart-Faris, N. (2005). *Discourse analysis and the study of classroom language and literacy events: A microethnographic perspective.* Mahway, NJ: Erlbaum.

Bloome, D., Champion, T., Katz, L., Morton, M. B., & Muldrow, R. (2001). Spoken and written narrative development: African American preschoolers as storytellers and storymakers. In J. Harris, A. Kamhi, & K. Pollock (Eds.), *Literacy in African American communities* (pp. 45–76). Mahwah, NJ: Erlbaum.

Boaler, J. (2002). *Experiencing school mathematics: Traditional and reform approaches to teaching and their impact on student learning.* Mahwah, NJ: Erlbaum.

Bond, H. M. (1935). The curriculum of the Negro child. *Journal of Negro Education, 4*(2), 159–168.

Booth, W. (1974). *A rhetoric of irony.* Chicago: University of Chicago Press.

Booth, W. (1983). *A rhetoric of fiction.* Chicago: University of Chicago Press.

Bowles, S., & Gintis, H. (1976). *School in capitalist America.* New York: Basic Books.

Bowman, P. (1989). Research perspectives on Black men: Role strain and adaptation across the adult life cycle. In R. Jones (Ed.), *Black adult development and aging* (pp. 117–150). Berkeley, CA: Cobbs & Henry.

Boykin, A. W. (1982). Task variability and the performance of Black and White school children: Vervistic explorations. *Journal of Black Studies, 12*, 469–485.

Boykin, A. W., & Allen, B. (1988). Rhythmic-movement facilitation of learning in working-class Afro-American children. *Journal of Genetic Psychology, 149*, 335–347.

Bransford, J., Brown, A., & Cocking, R. (1999). *How people learn: Brain, mind, experience, and school*. Washington, DC: National Academy Press.

Brofenbrenner, U. (1979). *The ecology of human development: Experiment by nature and design*. Cambridge, MA: Harvard University Press.

Brophy, J. E., & Evertson, C. M. (1977). Teacher behavior and student learning in second and third grades. In G. D. Borich (Ed.), *The appraisal of teaching: Concepts and process* (pp. 79–95). Reading, MA: Addison-Wesley.

Bruer, J. (1993). *Schools for thought*. Cambridge, MA: MIT Press.

Bruner, J. (1990). *Acts of meaning*. Cambridge, MA: Harvard University Press.

Bruner, J., & Tagiuri, R. (1954). The perception of people. In G. Lindzey (Ed.), *Handbook of social psychology* (Vol. 2, pp. 634–654). Cambridge, MA: Addison-Wesley.

Brunsma, D. L., & Rockquemore, K. A. (2002). What does "Black" mean? Exploring the epistemological stranglehold of racial categorization. *Critical Sociology, 28*(1), 101–121; *28*(2), 106–107.

Byrd, W. M., & Clayton, L. (2000). *An American health dilemma: A medical history of African Americans and the problem of race*. New York: Routledge.

Calfee, R., & Calfee, K. H. (1976). Reading and mathematics observation system: Description and measurement of time usage in the classroom. *Journal of Teacher Education, 27*, 323–325.

Callaghan, M., Knapp, P., & Noble, G. (1993). Genre in practice. In B. Cope & M. Kalantzis (Eds.), *The powers of literacy: A genre approach to teacing writing* (pp. 179–202). Washington, DC: Falmer Press.

Callaghan, M., & Rothery, J. (1988). *Teaching factual writing: Report of the Disadvantaged Schools Programs Literacy Project*. Sydney, Australia: Metropolitan East Disadvantaged Schools Program.

Campbell, J. R., Hombo, C. M., & Mazzeo, J. (2000). *NAEP 1999 trends in academic progress: Three decades of student performance*. Washington, DC: National Center for Educational Statistics.

Carey, K. (2004). *The funding gap, 2004*. Washington, DC: The Education Trust.

Cassidy, S. (2004). Learning styles: An overview of theories, models, and measures. *Educational Psychology, 24*(4), 419–444.

Cazden, C. (2000). *Classroom discourse: The language of teaching and learning* (2nd ed.). Portsmouth, NH: Heinemann.

Cazden, C., John, V. P., & Hymes, D. (1972). *Functions of language in the classroom*. New York: Teachers College Press.

Cazden, C., Michaels, S., & Tabors, P. (1985). Spontaneous repairs in sharing time narratives: The intersection of metalinguistic awareness, speech event, and narrative style. In S. Freedman (Ed.), *The acquisition of written language: Revision and response*. Norwood, NJ: Ablex.

Chaiklin, S., & Lave, J. (1993). *Understanding practice: Perspectives on activity and context*. New York: Cambridge University Press.

Champion, T. (1998). "Tell me somethin' good": A description of narrative structures among African-American children. *Linguistics and Education, 9*(3), 251–286.

Champion, T., Seymour, H., & Camarata, S. (1995). Narrative discourse among African American children. *Journal of Narrative and Life History, 5*(4), 333–352.

Chi, M. T. H., Feltovich, P. J., & Glaser, R. (1981). Categorization and representation of physics problems by experts and novices. *Cognitive Science, 5*, 121–152.

Children's Defense Fund. (2006). *Protect* children, Not guns. Retrieved September, 2006, from http://www.childrensdefense.org.

Civil, M. (2006). Building on community knowledge: An avenue to equity in mathematics education. In N. Nasir & P. Cobb (Eds.), *Improving access to mathematics: Diversity and equity in the classroom*. New York: Teachers College Press.

Clark, C., & Peterson, P. (1986). Research on teacher thinking. In M. C. Wittrock (Ed.), *Handbook of research on teaching* (pp. 255–296). New York: Macmillan.

Clement, J. (1982). Student preconceptions of introductory mechanics. *American Journal of Physics, 50*, 66–71.

Clement, J. (1993). Using bridging analogies and anchoring intuitions to deal with students' preconceptions in physics. *Journal of Research in Science Teaching, 30*(10), 1241–1257.

Clement, J. (2000). Analysis of clinical interviews: Foundations and model viability. In A. Kelly & R. Lesh (Eds.), *Handbook of research design in mathematics and science education* (pp. 547–590). Mahwah, NJ: Erlbaum.

Clement, J., Brown, D., & Zietsman, A. (1989). Not all preconceptions are misconceptions: Finding anchoring conceptions for grounding instruction on students' intuitions. *International Journal of Science Education, 11*, 554–565.

Cohen, D., & Barnes, C. (1993). Pedagogy and policy. In D. K. Cohen, M. W. McLaughlin, & J. E. Talbert (Eds.), *Teaching for understanding: Challenges for policy and practice* (pp. 207–239). San Francisco: Jossey-Bass.

Cole, M. (1996). *Cultural psychology: A once and future discipline*. Cambridge, MA: Belknap Press, Harvard University Press.

Cole, M., Gay, J., Glick, J. A., & Sharp, D. W. (1971). *The cultural context of learning and thinking: An exploration of experimental anthropology*. New York: Basic Books.

Coleman, J. (1966). *Equality of educational opportunity*. Washington, DC: U.S. Department of Education.

Coleridge, S. T. (2000). Biographia literaria. In H. J. Jackson (Ed.), *Samuel Taylor Coleridge: The major works*. New York: Oxford University Press. (Original work published 1816)

Collins, A., Brown, J., & Holum, A. (1991, Winter). Cognitive apprenticeship: Making thinking visible. *American Educator, 15*(3), 6–91.

Collins, A., Brown, J., & Newman, S. (1989). Cognitive apprenticeship: Teaching the craft of reading, writing and mathematics. In L. Resnick (Ed.), *Knowing, learning, and instruction: Essays in honor of Robert Glaser* (pp. 453–493). Hillsdale, NJ: Erlbaum.

Collins, A., & Ferguson, W. (1993). Epistemic forms and epistemic games: Structures and strategies to guide inquiry. *Educational Psychologist, 28*(1), 25–42.

Comer, J. (1988a). Educating poor minority children. *Scientific American, 159*(5), 42–48.

Comer, J. (1988b). *Maggie's American dream: The life and times of a Black family.* New York: New American Library.

Common Sense. (1994). I Used to Love H.E.R. On *Resurrection* [CD]. Santa Monica, CA: Relativity Records.

Conant, F. R., Rosebery, A. S., Warren, B., & Hudicourt-Barnes, J. (2001). The sound of drums. In E. McIntyre, A. S. Rosebery & N. Gonzales (Eds.), *Classroom diversity: Connecting curriculum to students' lives* (pp. 51–60). Portsmouth, NH: Heinemann.

Cook-Gumperz, J. (1986). *The social construction of literacy.* New York: Cambridge University Press.

Cross, W. (1991). *Shades of black: Diversity in African American identity.* Philadelphia: Temple University Press.

Culler, J. (1975). *Structuralist poetics: Structuralism, linguistics, and the study of literature.* New York: Cornell University Press.

D'Andrade, R. (1990). Some propositions about the relationship between culture and human cognition. In R. A. Shweder & G. Herdt (Eds.), *Cultural psychology: Essays on comparative human development* (pp. 65–129). New York: Cambridge University Press.

Dai, D. Y., & Sternberg, R. (2004). *Motivation, emotion, and cognition: Integrative perspectives on intellectual functioning and development.* Mahwah, NJ: Erlbaum.

Dante Alighieri. (1995). *The Inferno* (M. Musa, Ed. & Trans.). Bloomington: Indiana University Press.

Dante Alighieri. (1996). *Dante: De vulgari eloquentia* (S. Botterill, Ed. &Trans.). New York: Cambridge University Press.

Darling-Hammond, L. (1985). *Equality and excellence: The educational status of Black Americans.* New York: College Entrance Examination Board.

Darling-Hammond, L. (1987). Teacher quality and equality. In P. Keating & J. Goodlad (Eds.), *Access to knowledge* (pp. 237–258). New York: College Entrance Examination Board.

Darling-Hammond, L. (1999a). State teaching policies and student achievement. *Teaching Quality Policy Briefs,* No. 2. Seattle, WA: Center for the Study of Teaching and Policy (University of Washington).

Darling-Hammond, L. (1999b). *Teacher quality and student achievement: A review of state policy evidence.* Seattle, WA: Center for the Study of Teaching and Policy.

Dash, J. (Writer/Director). (1991). *Daughters of the dust* [motion picture]. New York: Kino International.

Dash, J. (Director). (1997). Sax Cantor Riff [Television series segment]. In *Subway stories: Tales from the underground.* New York: HBO.

Delpit, L. (1986). Skills and other dilemmas of a progressive Black educator. *Harvard Educational Review, 56*(4), 379–385.

Delpit, L. (1988). The silenced dialogue. *Harvard Educational Review, 58*(3), 280–298.

Delpit, L. (1995). *Other people's children: Cultural conflict in the classroom.* New York: The New Press.

DeMeis, D. K., & Turner, R. R. (1978). Effects of students' race, physical attractiveness, and dialect on teachers' evaluations. *Contemporary Educational Psychology, 3,* 77–86.

Deutsch, M., & Brown, B. (1964). Social influences in Negro-White intelligence differences. *Journal of Social Issues, 20,* 24–35.

Dillard, J. (1972). *Black English.* New York: Random House.

DiSessa, A. (1982). Unlearning Aristotelian physics: A study of knowledge-based learning. *Cognitive Science, 6,* 37–75.

Dostoevsky, F. (1984). *Crime and Punishment* (C. Garnett, Trans.). New York: Bantam. (Original work published 1866)

Dreeban, R., & Gamoran, A. (1986). Race, instruction and learning. *American Sociological Review, 51,* 660–669.

DuBois, J. (1992). Transcription design principles for spoken discourse research. *Pragmatics, 1*(1), 71–106.

DuBois, W. E. B. (1968). *The souls of Black folks: Essays and sketches.* Greenwich, CT: Fawcett.

DuBois, W. E. B. (1973). *The education of Black people: Ten critiques, 1906–1960.* New York: Monthly Review Press.

DuBois, W. E. B., & Dill, A. G. (1911). *The common school and the Negro American.* Atlanta: Atlanta University Press.

Dundes, A. (1972). The strategy of Turkish boys' verbal dueling rhymes. In J. J. Gumperz & D. Hymes (Eds.), *Directions in sociolinguistics: The ethnography of communication* (pp. 130–160). New York: Holt.

Dunn, R., & Griggs, S. (2000). *Practical approaches to using learning styles in higher education.* Westport, CT: Bergin & Garvey.

Eccles, J. S., Wigfield, A., & Schiefele, U. (1998). Motivation to succeed. In W. Damon & N. Eisenberg (Eds.), *Handbook of child psychology* (5th ed., Vol. 3, pp. 1017–1095). New York: Wiley.

Eccles-Parson, J., Adler, T. F., Futterman, R., Goff, S. B., Kaczala, C. M., Meece, J. L., et al. (1983). Expectancies, values, and academic behaviors. In J. T. Spence (Ed.), *Achievement and achievement motivation.* San Francisco: Freeman.

Education Trust. (2004). *Education watch achievement gap summary tables.* Washington, DC: Author.

Education Trust. (2005a). *The funding gap 2005: Low income and minority students short changed by most states.* Washington, DC: Author.

Education Trust. (2005b). *Gaining traction, gaining ground: How some high schools accelerate learning for struggling students.* Washington, DC: Author.

Education Trust. (2005c). *The power to change.* Washington, DC: Author.

Elder, G. (1985). Household, kinship, and the life course: Perspectives on Black families and children. In M. B. Spencer, G. K. Brookins, & W. R. Allen (Eds.), *Beginnings: The social and affective development of black children* (pp. 29–44). Mahwah, NJ: Erlbaum.

Elmore, R. F. (1995). *Getting to scale with successful education practices: Four principles and some recommended actions*: *Harvard Educational Review, 66*, 1–25.

Elmore, R. F., & McLaughlin, M. W. (1989). *Steady work: Policy, practice, and the reform of American education.* Santa Monica, CA.: Rand Corporation.

Erickson, F. (1984). Rhetoric, anecdote, and rhapsody: Coherence strategies in a conversation among Black American adolescents. In D. Tannen (Ed.), *Coherence in spoken and written discourse* (pp. 81–154). Norwood, NJ: Ablex.

Erickson, F., & Shultz, J. (1997). When is a context? Some issues and methods in the analysis of social competence. In M. Cole, Y. Engestrom, & O. Vasquez (Eds.), *Mind, culture and activity: Seminal papers from the laboratory of comparative human cognition* (pp. 22–31). New York: Cambridge University Press.

Farr, M. (1991). Dialects, culture and teaching the English language arts. In J. Flood, Jenson, J., Lapp, D., & Squire, J. (Ed.), *Handbook of research on teaching the English language arts* (pp. 365–371). New York: Macmillan.

Faulkner, W. (1997). A rose for Emily. In *The language of literature: American Literature* (pp. 352–400). Evanston, IL: McDougal Littell. (Original work published 1930)

Ferguson, C., & Heath, S. B. (Eds.). (1981). *Language in the USA.* New York: Cambridge University Press.

Ferguson, R. F. (2002a). Addressing racial disparities in high-achieving suburban schools. *NCREL Policy Issues, No. 13*, 1–11.

Ferguson, R. F. (2002b, November). *What doesn't meet the eye: Understanding and addressing racial disparities in high-achieving suburban schools* [Working Paper]. Retrieved June 13, 2006, from http://www.ncrel.org/gap/ferg/

Finders, M. J. (1998). Raging hormones: Stories of adolescence and implications for teacher preparation. *Journal of Adolescent and Adult Literacy, 42*(4), 252–263.

Finkelman, P. (1992). The crime of color. *Tulane Law Review, 67*(6), 2063–2112, 2085–2086, 2106.

Fish, S. (1980). *Is there a text in this class? The authority of interpretive communities.* Cambridge, MA: Harvard University Press.

Fisher, M. T. (2003). Open mics and open minds: Spoken word poetry in African diaspora participatory literacy communities. *Harvard Education Review, 73*(3), 362–389.

Fisher, M. T. (2004). "The song is unfinished": The new literate and the literary and their institutions. *Written Communication, 21*(3), 290–312.

Flavell, J. H. (1981). *The development of comprehension monitoring and knowledge about communication.* Chicago: University of Chicago Press.

Flesch, R. (1974). *The art of readable writing: With the Flesch readability formula.* New York: Harper & Row.

Flower, L. (1994). *The construction of negotiated meaning: A social cognitive theory of writing.* Carbondale, IL: Southern Illinois University Press.

Flower, L., & Hayes, J. R. (1981a). A cognitive process theory of writing. *College Composition and Communication, 32*, 365–387.

Flower, L., & Hayes, J. R. (1981b). Plans that guide the composing process. In

C. H. Frederiksen & J. F. Dominic (Eds.), *Writing: The nature, development and teaching of written communication* (Vol. 2) (pp. 39–58). Hillsdale, NJ: Erlbaum.

Forman, E., & Larreamendy-Joerns, J. (1998). Making explicit the implicit: Classroom explanations and conversational implicatures. *Mind, Culture, and Activity, 5*(2), 105–113.

Foster, M. (1995). Talking that talk: The language of control, curriculum and critique. *Linguistics and Education, 7,* 129–150.

Foster, M. (1997). *Black teachers on teaching.* New York: New Press.

Frederickson, G. M. (1981). *White supremacy: A comparative study in American and South African history.* New York: Oxford University Press.

Fry, R. (2005). *The higher drop-out rate of foreign-born teens: The role of schooling abroad.* Washington, DC: Pew Hispanic Center.

Fugees. (1996). The mask. On *The score* [Record]. Holland: Ruffhouse.

Gabbin, J. (Ed.). (2004). *Furious flower : African American poetry from the Black Arts Movement to the present.* Charlottesville: University of Virginia Press.

Garcia, G. E. (1998). Mexican-American bilingual students' metacognitive reading strategies: What's transferred, unique, problematic? *National Reading Conference Yearbook, 47,* 253–263.

Garner, R. (1987). *Metacognition and reading comprehension.* Norwood, NJ: Ablex.

Gates, H. L. (1988). *The signifying monkey: A theory of Afro-American literary criticism.* New York: Oxford University Press.

Gates, H. L., & McKay, N. (Eds.). (2004). *Norton anthology of African American literature.* New York: Norton.

Gay, G. (1993). Ethnic minorities and educational equality. In J. A. Banks & C. A. M. Banks (Eds.), *Multicultural education: Issues and perspectives* (2nd ed., pp. 171–194). Boston: Allyn & Bacon.

Gay, G. (1995). Curriculum theory and multicultural education. In J. A. Banks & C. A. M. Banks (Eds.), *Handbook of research on multicultural education* (pp. 25–43). New York: Macmillan.

Gay, G. (2000). *Culturally responsive teaching: Theory, research, and practice.* New York: Teachers College Press.

Gee, J. P. (1990). *Social linguistics and literacies: Ideology in discourses.* New York: Falmer Press.

Gee, J. P. (1994). First language acquisition as a guide for theories of learning and pedagogy. *Linguistics and Education, 6,* 331–354.

Gee, J. P. (2000a). Discourse and sociocultural studies in reading. In M. Kamil, P. Mosenthal, P. D. Pearson, & R. Barr (Eds.), *Handbook of reading research* (Vol. 3, pp. 195–208). Mahwah, NJ: Erlbaum.

Gee, J. P. (2000b). Identity as an analytic lens for research in education. In W. Secada (Ed.), *Review of research in education* (Vol. 25, pp. 99–126). Washington, DC: American Educational Research Association.

Gerima, H. (Writer). (1993). *Sankofa* [motion picture]. United States: Mypheduh Films.

Gersten, R., & Keating, T. (1987a). Improving high school performance of "at risk" students: A study of long-term benefits of direct instruction. *Educational Leadership, 44*(6), 28–31.

Gersten, R., & Keating, T. (1987b). Long-term benefits from Direct Instruction. *Educational Leadership, 44*(6), 28–29.

Gersten, R., Keating, T., & Becker, W. (1988). The continued impact of the Direct Instruction model: Longitudinal studies of Follow Through students. *Education and Treatment of Children, 11*(4), 318–327.

Goffman, E. (1974). *Frame analysis: An essay on the organization of experience.* New York: Harper & Row.

Gonzáles, N., Moll, L. C., & Amanti, C. (Eds). (2005). *Funds of knowledge: Theorizing practice in households, communities, and classrooms.* Mahwah, NJ: Erlbaum.

Goodenow, C. (1993). Classroom belonging among early adolescent students: Relationships to motivation and achievement. *Journal of Early Adolescence, 13,* 21–43.

Goodman, K. (1973). *The psycholinguistic nature of the reading process.* Detroit, MI: Wayne State University Press.

Goodman, Y. (1989). Roots of the Whole-Language Movement. *Elementary school Journal, 90*(2), 113–127.

Goodwin, M. (1990). *He-said she-said: Talk as social organization.* Bloomington: Indiana University Press.

Gopnik, A., Meltzoff, A. N., & Kuhl, P. K. (1999). *The scientist in the crib: Minds, brains, and how children learn.* New York: Morrow.

Gordon, E. W., & Bridglall, B. L. (Eds.). (in press). *The affirmative development of academic abilities.* Boulder, CO: Rowman & Littlefield.

Gould, S. J. (1981). *The mismeasure of man.* New York: Norton.

Graham, S. (1992). "Most of the subjects were White and middle class": Trends in published research on African Americans in selected APA journals, 1970–1989. *American Psychologist, 47*(5), 629–639.

Graham, S. (1994). Motivation in African Americans. *Review of Educational Research, 64,* 55–117.

Graham, S., & Golan, S. (1991). Motivational influences on cognition: Task involvement, ego involvement, and depth of information processing. *Journal of Educational Psychology, 83*(2), 187–194.

Graham, S., & Taylor, A. (2002). Ethnicity, gender, and the development of achievement values. In A. Wigfield & J. Eccles (Eds.), *Development of achievement motivation* (pp. 121–146). San Diego, CA: Academic Press.

Graham, S., Taylor, A., & Hudley, C. (1998). Exploring achievement values among ethnic minority early adolescents. *Journal of Educational Psychology, 90*(4), 606–620.

Graves, B., & Frederiksen, C. H. (1996). A Cognitive Study of Literary Expertise. In R. J. Kruez & M. S. MacNealy (Eds.), *Empirical approaches to literature and aesthetics* (pp. 397–418). Norwood, NJ: Ablex.

Green, J. L., & Dixon, C. N. (1993). Talking knowledge into being: Discursive and social practices in classrooms. *Linguistics and Education, 5*(3 & 4), 231–239.

Green, J., & Harker, J. (1988). *Multiple perspective analysis of classroom discourse.* Norwood, NJ: Ablex.

Greenfield, P. (2004). *Weaving generations together: Evolving creativity in the Maya of Chiapas.* Santa Fe, NM: School of American Research Press.

Greenfield, P. M., & Cocking, R. R. (1994). *Cross-cultural roots of minority child development*. Hillsdale, NJ: Erlbaum.

Greenough, W. T., Black, J. E., & Wallace, C. S. (1987). Experience and brain development. *Child Development, 58*, 539–559.

Griffin, S. A., Case, R., & Capodilupo, A. (1995). Teaching for understanding: The importance of the central conceptual structures in the elementary mathematics curriculum. In A. McKeough, J. Lupart, & A. Marini (Eds.), *Teaching for transfer: Fostering generalization in learning* (pp. 121–151). Hillsdale, NJ: Erlbaum.

Grossman, P. (1990). *The making of a teacher: Teacher nnowledge and teacher education*. New York: Teachers College Press.

Grossman, P. (2001). Research on the teaching of literature: Finding a place. In V. Richardson (Ed.), *Handbook of research on teaching* (4th ed.). (pp. 416–432). Washington, DC: American Educational Research Association.

Grossman, P., Wilson, S. M., & Shulman, L. S. (1989). Teachers of substance: Subject matter for teaching. In M. C. Reynolds (Ed.), *Knowledge base for the beginning teacher* (pp. 23–36). New York: Pergamon.

Guiton, G., & Oakes, J. (1995). Opportunity-to-learn and conceptions of educational equality. *Educational Evaluation and Policy Analysis, 17*(3), 323–336.

Gumperz, J. J., & Hymes, D. (1972). *Directions in sociolinguistics: The ethnography of communication*. New York: Holt.

Gutierrez, K., Baquedano-Lopez, P., & Tejeda, C. (1999). Rethinking diversity: Hybridity and hybrid language practices in the third space. *Mind, Culture, and Activity, 6*(4), 286–303.

Gutierrez, K., & Rogoff, B. (2003). Cultural ways of learning: Individual traits or repertoires of practice. *Educational Researcher, 32*(5), 19–25.

Hall, S., & Moats, L. (Eds.). (1999). *Straight talk about reading: How parents can make a difference during the early years*. Lincolnwood, IN: Contemporaary Books.

Hansen, D. T. (2001a). *Exploring the moral heart of teaching: Toward a teacher's creed*. New York: Teachers College Press.

Hansen, D. T. (2001b). Teaching as a moral activity In V. Richardson (Ed.), *Handbook of research on teaching*(4th ed., pp. 826–857). Washington, DC: American Educational research Association.

Harding, V. (1981). *There is a river: The Black struggle for freedom in America*. New York: Harcourt Brace Jovanovich.

Hawthorne, N. (2000). *The scarlet letter*. New York: Modern Library. (Original work published 1850)

Haycock, K. (1998a). Good teaching matters . . . a lot. *Thinking K–16, 3*(2), 3–14.

Haycock, K. (1998b). Good teaching matters: How well-qualified teachers can close the achievement gap. *Thinking K–16, 3*(2), 1–2.

Haycock, K. (2000). No more settling for less. *Thinking K–16, 4*(1), 3–12.

Haynes, N., & Comer, J. (1993). The Yale school development program: Process, outcomes, and policy implications. *Urban Education, 28*(2), 166–199.

Heath, S. B. (1983). *Ways with words: Language, life, and work in communities and classrooms*. New York: Cambridge University Press.

Heath, S. B., & McLaughlin, M. (1994). The best of both worlds: Connecting schools and community organizations for all day, all year learning. *Educatinal Administration Quarterly, 30*(3), 278–300.

Hemingway, E. (1995). *The snows of Kilimanjaro and other stories.* NY: Scribner. (Original work published 1938)

Hernstein, R., & Murray, C. (1994). *The bell curve: Intelligence and class structure in American life.* New York: Free Press.

Herskovitz, M. J. (1958). *The myth of the Negro past.* Boston: Beacon Press.

Hess, G. A., & Cytrynbaum, S. (1999). *Monitoring the implementation of the CPS design for high school: The second year, 1998–99.* Evanston, IL: Center for Urban School Policy, Northwestern University.

Hess, R., & Shipman, V. (1965). Early experience and the socialization of cognitive modes in children. *Child Development, 36,* 869–886.

Hicks, D. (2002). *Reading lives: Working-class children and literacy learning.* New York: Teachers College Press.

Hill, P., & Roza, M. (2004). *How within-district spending inequalities help some schools fail.* Washington, DC: Brookings Institute.

Hilliard, A. G. (1991). Do we have the will to educate all children? *Educational Leadership, 49*(1), 31–36.

Hillocks, G. (1986). *Research on written composition: New directions for teaching.* Urbana, IL: National Conference on Research in English/ERIC Clearinghouse on Reading and Communication Skills.

Hillocks, G. (1995). *Teaching writing as reflective practice.* New York: Teachers College Press.

Hillocks, G. (1999). *Ways of thinking, ways of teaching.* New York: Teachers College Press.

Hillocks, G., & Ludlow, L. (1984). A taxonomy of skills in reading and interpreting fiction. *American Educational Research Journal, 21,* 7–24.

Holland, J. (1995). *Hidden order: How adaptation builds complexity.* Cambridge, MA: Perseus.

Hollinger, D. A. (2003). Amalgamation and hypodescent: The question of ethnoracial mixture in the history of the United States. *American Historical Review, 108*(5), 1363–1390.

Holt-Reynolds, D. (1999). Good readers, good teachers? Subject matter expertise as a challenge in learning to teach. *Harvard Educational Review, 69*(1), 29–50.

Hughes, L. (1962). Red-headed baby. In *The ways of White folks* (pp. 121–128). New York: Alfred A. Knopf. (Original work published 1934)

Hunter, M. (2005). *Race, gender, and the politics of skin tone.* New York: Routledge.

Hutchins, E. (1995). *Cognition in the wild.* Cambridge, MA: MIT Press.

Hymes, D., & Cazden, C. (1980). Narrative thinking and story-telling rights: A folklorist's clue to a critique of education. In D. Hymes (Ed.), *Language in education: Ethnolinguistic essays* (pp. 126–138). Washington, DC: Center for Applied Linguistics.

Ingersoll, R. M. (2002). *Out-of-field teaching, educational inequity, and the organization of schools: An exploratory analysis* (Research Report No. R-O2-1). Seattle, WA: Center for the Study of Teaching and Policy, University of Washington.

Introduction to the Cyclopedia of Interesting Facts about key people, places, and things in the Holy Bible. (1969). In *The Holy Bible, containing the old and new testaments in the authorized King James version*. Chicago: Timothy Press.

Irvine, J., & York, D. E. (1995). Learning styles and culturally diverse students: A literature review. In J. A. Banks & C. A. M. Banks (Eds.), *Handbook of research on multicultural education* (pp. 484–497). New York: Macmillan.

Irvine, R. W., & Irvine, J. J. (1983). The impact of the desegregation process on the education of Black students: Key variables. *Journal of Negro Education, 52*(4), 410–422.

Jackson, H. (1993). *A century of dishonor: A sketch of the United States government's dealings with some of the Indian tribes*. New York: Indian Head Books.

Jacob, E. (1992). Culture, context, and cognition. In M. LeCompte, W. Millroy, & J. Preissle (Eds.), *The handbook of qualitative research in education* (pp. 293–336). New York: Academic Press.

Jacobson, M. (1999). *Whiteness of a different color: European immigrants and the alchemy of race*. Cambridge, MA: Harvard University Press.

Jean, W. (1998). Gunpowder. On *Gunpowder* [CD]. United States: Sony.

Jefferson, G. (1979). A technique for inviting laughter and its subsequent acceptance/declination. In G. Psathas (Ed.), *Everyday language: Studies in ethnomethodology* (pp. 79–96). New York: Irvington.

Jencks, C. (1972). *Inequality: A reassessment of the effect of family and schooling in America*. New York: Basic Books.

Jencks, C., & Mayer, S. (1990). The social consequences of growing up in a poor neighborhood: A review. In M. McGeary & L. Lynn (Eds.), *Inner city poverty in the United States*. Washington, DC: National Academy Press.

Jensen, A. (1969). How much can we boost IQ and scholastic achievement? *Harvard Educational Review, 39*, 1–123.

Jimerson, S., Egeland, B., & Teo, A. (1999). A longitudinal study of achievement trajectories: Factors associated with change. *Journal of Educational Psychology, 91*, 116–126.

Jones, G. (1991). *Liberating voices: Oral tradition in African American literature*. New York: Penguin Books.

Jones, L., & Neal, L. (Eds.). (1968). *Black fire: An anthology of Afro-American writing*. New York: Morrow.

Jones, R. (Ed.). (1998). *African American identity development*. Hampton, VA: Cobb & Henry.

Joyce, J. (1993). *Ulysses*. New York: Oxford University Press. (Original work published 1922)

Kaufman, P., Alt, M. N., & Chapman, C. D. (2004). *Dropout rates in the United States: 2001*. Washington, DC: National Center for Education Statistics.

Kintsch, W. (1992). How readers construct situation models for stories: The role of syntactic cues and causal inferences. In A. F. Healy, S. M. Kosslyn, & R. M. Shiffrin (Eds.), *From learning processes to cognitive processes: Essays in honor of William K. Estes* (pp. 261–278). Hillsdale, NJ: Erlbaum.

Kintsch, W. (1998). *Comprehension: A paradigm for cognition*. New York: Cambridge University Press.

Kintsch, W., & Greene, E. (1978). The role of culture-specific schemata in the comprehension and recall of stories. *Discourse Processes, 1,* 1–13.

Klausmeier, H. J. (1985). *Educational psychology.* New York: Harper & Row.

Knapp, M., & Shields, P. (1990). Reconceiving academic instruction for the children of poverty. *Phi Delta Kappan, 71*(10), 752–758.

Kozol, J. (1991). *Savage inequalities.* New York: Harper-Collins.

Kuhl, P. K. (2004). Early language acquisition: Cracking the speech code. *Nature Reviews Neuroscience, 5,* 831–843.

Kuhl, P. K., Williams, K. A., Lacerda, F., Stevens, K. N., & Lindblom, B. (1992). Linguistic experience alters phonetic perception in infants by 6 months of age. *Science, 255,* 606–608.

Kuhn, D. (1991). *The skills of argument.* New York: Cambridge University Press.

Kunda, Z. (1999). *Social cognition: Making sense of people.* Cambridge, MA: MIT Press.

Labov, W. (1972). *Language in the inner city: Studies in the Black English vernacular.* Philadelphia: University of Pennsylvania Press.

Labov, W. (1998). Coexistent systems in African-American English. In S. S. Mufwene, J. R. Rickford, G. Bailey, & J. Baugh (Eds.), *African American English: History and use* (pp. 110–153). New York: Routledge.

Labov, W., Ash, S., & Boberg, C. (2006). *The atlas of North American English: Phonetics, phonology, and sound change.* Berlin: Mouton/de Gruyter.

Ladson-Billings, G. (1994). *The dreamkeepers: Successful teachers of African American children.* San Francisco: Jossey-Bass.

Ladson-Billings, G. (2001). *Crossing over to Canaan: The journey of new teachers in diverse classrooms.* San Francisco: Jossey-Bass.

Ladson-Billings, G., & Tate, W. (1995). Toward a critical race theory of education. *Teachers College Record, 97*(1), pp. 47–68.

Lagemann, E. C., & Shulman, L. (Eds.). (1999). *Issues in education research: Problems and possibilities.* San Francisco: Jossey-Bass.

Lampert, M. (1990). When the problem is not the question and the solution is not the answer: Mathematical knowing and teaching. *American Educational Research Journal, 27*(1), 29–64.

Lampert, M. (2001). *Teaching problems and the problems of teaching.* New Haven: Yale University Press.

Langer, J. A. (1990). The process of understanding: Reading for literary and informative purposes. *Research in the Teaching of English, 24*(3), 229–260.

Langer, J. A. (2001). Beating the odds: Teaching middle and high school students to read and write well. *American Educational Research Journal, 38*(4), 837–880.

The language of literature: American literature. (1997). Evanston, IL: McDougal Littell.

Lave, J. (1988). *Cognition in practice: Mind, mathematics and culture in everyday life.* Cambridge: Cambridge University Press.

Lee, C. D. (1991). Big picture talkers/words walking without masters: The instructional implications of ethnic voices for an expanded literacy. *Journal of Negro Education, 60*(3), 291–305.

Lee, C. D. (1992). Profile of an independent black institution: African-centered education at work. *Journal of Negro Education, 61*(2), 160–177.

Lee, C. D. (1993). *Signifying as a scaffold for literary interpretation: The pedagogical implications of an African American discourse genre*. Urbana, IL: National Council of Teachers of English.

Lee, C. D. (1995a). A culturally based cognitive apprenticeship: Teaching African American high school students skills in literary interpretation. *Reading Research Quarterly, 30*(4), 608–631.

Lee, C. D. (1995b). Signifying as a scaffold for literary interpretation. *Journal of Black Psychology, 21*(4), 357–381.

Lee, C. D. (1997). Bridging home and school literacies: A model of culturally responsive teaching. In J. Flood, S. B. Heath, & D. Lapp (Eds.), *A handbook for literacy educators: Research on teaching the communicative and visual arts* (pp. 330–341). New York: Macmillan.

Lee, C. D. (2000). Signifying in the zone of proximal development. In C. D. Lee & P. Smagorinsky (Eds.), *Vygotskian perspectives on literacy research: Constructing meaning through collabative inquiry* (pp. 191–225). New York: Cambridge University Press.

Lee, C. D. (2001). Is October Brown Chinese: A cultural modeling activity system for underachieving students. *American Educational Research Journal, 38*(1), 97–142.

Lee, C. D. (2002). Interrogating race and ethnicity as constructs in the examination of cultural processes in developmental research. *Human Development, 45*(4), 282–290.

Lee, C. D. (2005a). Culture and language: Bi-dialectical issues in literacy. In J. Flood & P. L. Anders (Eds.), *Literacy development of students in urban schools: Research and policy* (pp. 241–274). Newark, DE: International Reading Association.

Lee, C. D. (2005b). Double-voiced discourse: African American Vernacular English as resource in Cultural Modeling classrooms. In A. Ball & S. W. Freedman (Eds.), *New literacies for new times: Bakhtinian perspectives on language, literacy, and learning for the 21st century* (pp. 129–147). New York: Cambridge University Press.

Lee, C. D. (2006). Every good-bye ain't gone: Analyzing the cultural underpinnings of classroom talk. *International Journal of Qualitative Studies in Education, 19*(3), 305–327.

Lee, C. D. (in press-a). A Cultural Modeling perspective: The creation of opportunity to learn through the cultural practices of classroom instruction. In P. Moss, D. Pullin, J. P. Gee, E. Haertel, & L. Young (Eds.), *Opportunity to learn and assessment*. New York: Cambridge University Press.

Lee, C. D. (in press-b). The educability of intellective competence. In E. W. Gordon & B. L. Bridglall (Eds.), *The affirmative development of academic abilities*. Boulder, CO: Rowman & Littlefield.

Lee, C. D., & Majors, Y. J. (2000, April). *Cultural modeling's response to Rogoff's challenge: Understanding apprenticeship, guided participation and participatory appropriation in a culturally respnsive, subject matter specific context.* Paper presented at the annual meeting of the American Educational Research Association, New Orleans.

Lee, C. D., Mendenhall, R., Rivers, A., & Tynes, B. (1999, October). *Cultural Modeling: A framework for scaffolding oral narrative repertoires for academic narrative writing.* Paper presented at the Multicultural Narrative Analysis Conference at the University of South Florida, Tampa.

Lee, C. D., Rivers, A., Hutchinson, K., Bernstein, M., & Dixon, K. (2000, April). *Participatory appropriation and its consequences in a Cultural Modeling classroom.* Paper presented at the annual meeting of the American Educational Research Association, New Orleans.

Lee, C. D., Rosenfeld, E., Mendenhall, R., Rivers, A., & Tynes, B. (2003). Cultural modeling as a framework for narrative analysis. In C. Dauite & C. Lightfoot (Eds.), *Narrative analysis: Studying the development of individuals in society* (pp. 39–61). Thousand Oaks, CA: Sage.

Lee, C. D., & Slaughter-Defoe, D. (1995). Historical and sociocultural influences on African American education. In J. A. Banks & C. A. M. Banks (Eds.), *Handbook of research on multicultural education* (pp. 348–371). New York: Macmillan.

Lee, C. D., & Smagorinsky, P. (Eds.). (2000). *Vygotskian perspectives on literacy research: Constructing meaning through collaborative inquiry.* New York: Cambridge University Press.

Lee, C. D., Spencer, M. B., & Harpalani, V. (2003). Every shut eye ain't sleep: Studying how people live culturally. *Educational Researcher, 32*(5), 6–13.

Lee, S. (1996). *Unraveling the "model minority" stereotype: Listening to Asian American youth.* New York: Teachers College Press.

Lemke, J. (2000). Across the scales of time: Artifacts, activities, and meanings in ecosocial systems. *Mind, Culture, and Activity, 7*(4), 273–290.

Levin, H. M. (1993). Accelerated schools for disadvantaged children. *Educational Leadership, 44*(6), 19–21.

Lewis, C., Perry, R., & Hurd, J. (2004). A deeper look at lesson study. *Educational Leadership, 61*(5), 6–11.

Lewis, C., & Tsuchida, I. (1998, Winter). A lesson is like a swiftly flowing river: Research lessons and the improvement of Japanese education. *American Educator, 22*(4), 14–17, 50–52.

Lipski, J. (2005). *A history of Afro-Hispanic language: Five centuries, five continents.* New York: Cambridge University Press.

Luchins, A. S., & Luchins, E. H. (1970). *Wertheimer's Seminar revisited: Problem solving and thinking* (Vol. 1). Albany: State University of New York.

Ma, L. (1999). *Knowing and teaching elementary mathematics.* Mahwah, NJ: Erlbaum.

Madhubuti, H. (1990). *Black men: Obsolete, single, dangerous?* Chicago: Third World Press.

Madhubuti, H. (2002). *Touch notes: A healing call for creating exceptional Black men.* Chicago: Third World Press.

Majors, Y. (2003). Shoptalk: Teaching and learning in an African American hair salon. *Mind, Culture, and Activity, 10*(4), 289–310.

Makoni, S., Smitherman, G., Ball, A., & Spears, A. (Eds.). (2003). *Black linguistics: Language, society, and politics in Africa and the Americas.* New York: Routledge.

Massey, D. S., & Denton, N. A. (1993). *American apartheid: Segregation and the making of the underclass.* Cambridge, MA: Harvard University Press.

Maupassant, G. de. (1992). *The Necklace and other short stories.* New York: Dover.

McCarty, T. L. (2002). *A place to be Navajo: Rough Rock and the struggle for self-determination in indigenous schooling.* Mahwah, NJ: Erlbaum.

McCoy, M. P. (1999). *Privilege and peril in a Black middle-class neighborhood.* Chicago: University of Chicago Press.

McDermott, R. (1987). Achieving school failure: An anthropological approach to illiteracy and social stratification. In G. Spindler (Ed.), *Education and cultural process* (2nd ed., pp. 173–209). Prospect Heights, IL: Waveland Press.

McLaren, P. (1989). *Life in schools.* New York: Longman.

McLaughlin, M. (1993). Embedded identities: Enabling balance in urban contexts. In S. B. Heath & M. McLaughlin (Eds.), *Identity and inner-city youth: Beyond ethnicity and gender* (pp. 36–68). New York: Teachers College Press.

McLaughlin, M., Irby, M., & Langman, J. (1994). *Urban sanctuaries: Neighborhood organizations in the lives and futures of inner-city youth.* San Francisco: Jossey-Bass.

McLoyd, V. (1998). Childen in poverty: Development, public policy and practice. In I. E. Sigel & A. Renninger (Eds.), *Handbook of child psychology: Social, emotional and personality development* (Vol. 4, pp. 135–210). New York: Wiley.

McLoyd, V., & Randolph, S. (1984). The conduct and publication of research on Afro-American children: A content analysis. *Human Development, 27,* 65–75.

Mehan, H. (1979). *Learning lessons.* Cambridge, MA: Harvard University Press.

Mercado, C. I., & Moll, L. (1997). The study of funds of knowledge: Collaborative research in Latino homes. *CENTRO, Journal of the Center for Puerto Rican Studies, 9*(1), 27–42.

Miller, L. S. (1995). *An American imperative: Accelerating minority educational advancement.* New Haven, CT: Yale University Press.

Miller, P. J., Mintz, J., Hoogstra, L., Fung, H., & Potts, R. (1992). The narrated self: Young children's construction of self in relation to others in conversational stories of personal experience. *Merrill-Palmer Quarterly, 38*(1), 45–67.

Miller, P. J., Wiley, A., Fung, H., & Liang, C. (1997). Personal storytelling as a medium for socialization in Chinese and American families. *Child Development, 68*(3), 557–568.

Mills, C. (1997). *The racial contract.* Ithaca, NY: Cornell University Press.

Mitchell-Kernan, C. (1981). Signifying, loud-talking, and marking. In A. Dundes (Ed.), *Mother wit from the laughing barrel* (pp. 310–328). Englewood Cliffs, NJ: Prentice-Hall.

Moll, L. (2000). Inspired by Vygotsky: Ethnographic experiments in education. In C. D. Lee & P. Smagorinsky (Eds.), *Vygotskian perspectives on literacy research: Constructing meaning through collaborative inquiry* (pp. 256–268). New York: Cambridge University Press.

Moll, L., & Gonzáles, N. (2004). Engaging life: A funds-of-knowledge approach to multicultural education. In J. A. Banks & C. A. M. Banks (Eds.), *Handbook of research on multicultural education* (2nd ed., pp. 699–715). San Francisco: Jossey-Bass.

Moll, L., & Greenberg, J. B. (1990). Creating zones of possibilities: Combining social contexts for instruction. In L. Moll (Ed.), *Vygotsky and education: Instructional implications and applications of sociohistorical psychology* (pp. 319–348). New York: Cambridge University Press.

Morgan, M. (1993). The Africanness of counterlanguage among Afro-Americans. In S. Mufwene (Ed.), *Africanisms in Afro-American language varieties*. Athens: University of Georgia Press.

Morgan, M. (1998). More than a mood or an attitude: Discourse and verbal genres in African-American culture. In S. S. Mufwene, J. R. Rickford, G. Bailey, & J. Baugh (Eds.), *African-American English: Structure, history, and use* (pp. 251–281). New York: Routledge.

Morgan, M. (2002). *Language, discourse and power in African American culture*. New York: Cambridge University Press.

Morrison, T. (1987). *Beloved*. New York: Knopf.

Morrison, T. (1970). *The bluest eye*. New York: Knopf.

Morrison, T. (1977). *Song of Solomon*. New York: Knopf.

Morrison, T. (1984). Rootedness: The ancestor as foundation. In M. Evans (Ed.), *Black women writers (1950–1980): A critical evaluation* (pp. 339–345). New York: Doubleday.

Moses, R. P. (1994). The struggle for citizenship and math/sciences literacy. *Journal of Mathematical Behavior, 13*, 107–111.

Moses, R. P., & Cobb, C. E. (2001). *Radical equations: Math literacy and civil rights*. Boston: Beacon Press.

Moses, R. P., Kamii, M., Swap, S. M., & Howard, J. (1989). The Algebra Project: Organizing in the spirit of Ella. *Harvard Educational Review, 59*(4), 423–443.

Moss, B. (1994). Creating a community: Literacy events in African-American churches. In B. Moss (Ed.), *Literacy across communities* (pp. 147–178). Cresskill, NJ: Hampton Press.

Moss, P. (in press). Using tests and other forms of evidence about learning and teaching In P. Moss, D. Pullin, J. P. Gee, E. Haertel, & L. Young (Eds.), *Opportunity to learn and assessment*. New York: Cambridge University Press.

Mufwene, S. (1993). *Africanisms in Afro-American language varieties*. Athens: University of Georgia Press.

Mufwene, S., Rickford, J. R., Bailey, G., & Baugh, J. (Eds.). (1998). *African-American English: Structure, history, and use*. New York: Routledge.

Munby, H., Russell, T., & Martin, A. K. (2001). Teachers' knowledge and how it develops. In V. Richardson (Ed.), *Handbook of research on teaching* (4th ed., pp. 877–904). Washington, DC: American Educational Research Association.

Murata, A. (2004). Paths to learning ten-structured understanding of teen sums: Addition solution methods of Japanese grade 1 students. *Cognition and Instruction, 22*(2), 185–218.

Murata, A., & Fuson, K. (in press). Teaching as assisting individual constructive paths within an interdependent class learning zone: Japanaese first graders learning to add using ten. *Journal for Research in Mathematics Education*.

Murrell, P. (2002). *African-centered pedagogy : developing schools of achievement for African American children*. Albany: State University of New York Press.

Nasir, N. (2000). "Points ain't everything": Emergent goals and average and percent understandings in the play of basketball among African American students. *Anthropology and Education Quarterly, 31*(3), 283–305.

Nasir, N., Rosebery, A. S., Warren, B., & Lee, C. D. (2006). Learning as a cultural process: Achieving equity through diversity. In K. Sawyer (Ed.), *Handbook of the learning sciences* (pp. 489–504). New York: Cambridge University Press.

Nasir, N., & Saxe, G. (2003). Emerging tensions and their management in the lives of minority students. *Educational Researcher, 32*(5), 14–18.

National Commission on Excellence in Education. (1983). *A nation at risk: The imperative for educational reform.* Washington, DC: Government Printing Office.

Neal, L. (1989). *Visions of a liberated future: Black Arts Movement writings.* New York: Thunder's Mouth Press.

Nelson, K. (1989). *Narratives from the crib.* Cambridge, MA: Harvard University Press.

Newell, A. (1980). Reasoning, problem solving, and decision processes: The problem space as a fundamental category. In R. S. Nickerson (Ed.), *Attention and performance VIII.* Hillsdale, NJ: Erlbaum.

Newell, A., & Simon, H. (1972). *Human problem solving.* Englewood Cliffs, NJ: Prentice-Hall.

Nieto, S. (2002). *Language, culture, and teaching: Critical perspectives for a new century.* Mahwah, NJ: Erlbaum.

Nobles, W. (1974). African roots and American fruit: The Black family. *Journal of Social and Behavioral Sciences, 20*(2), 52–64.

Nobles, W. (1985). *Africanity and the Black family: The development of a theoretical model.* Oakland, CA: Institute for the Advanced Study of Black Family Life and Culture.

Nobles, W., & Adeleke, Z. (in press). Nsaka Sunsum (Touching the spirit): A pedagogy in process of black educational excellence. *Journal of Black Psychology.*

Noddings, N. (1984). *Caring: A feminine approach to ethics and moral education.* Berkeley, CA: University of California Press.

Noguera, P. (2003). *City schools and the American dream: Reclaiming the promise of public education.* New York: Teachers College Press.

Nunes, T., Schliemann, A. D., & Carraher, D. W. (1993). *Street mathematics and school mathematics.* New York: Cambridge University Press.

Oakes, J. (1985). *Keeping track: How schools structure inequality.* New Haven, CT: Yale University Press.

Oakes, J. (1990). *Multiplying inequalities: The effects of race, social class, and teaching.* Santa Monica, CA: Rand.

Oakes, J., Gamoran, A., & Page, R. N. (1992). Curriculum differences: Opportunities, outcomes, and meanings. In P. Jackson (Ed.), *Handbook of research on curriculum* (pp. 570–608). New York: Macmillan.

Orfield, G., Losen, D., Wald, J., & Swanson, C. (2004). *Losing our future: How minority youth are being left behind in the graduation rate crisis.* Cambridge, MA: Civil Rights Project, Harvard University.

Ochsner, K. N., & Lieberman, M. D. (2001). The emergence of social cognitive neuroscience. *American Psychologist, 56,* 717–734.

O'Connor, M. C., & Michaels, S. (1993). Aligning academic task and participation status through revoicing: Analysis of a classroom discourse strategy. *Anthropology and Education Quarterly, 24*(4), 318–335.

Odden, D. (1995). Tone: African languages. In J. Goldsmith (Ed.), *Handbook of phonological theory* (pp. 444–475). Oxford: Basil Blackwell.

Orellana, M., Reynolds, J., Dorner, L., & Meza, M. (2003). In other words: Translating or "paraphrasing" as a family literacy practice in immigrant households. *Reading Research Quarterly, 38*(1), 12–34.

Orr, E. W. (1987). *Twice as less: Black English and the performance of Black students in mathematics and science.* New York: Norton.

Ortony, A. (1979). *Metaphor and thought* (2nd ed.). New York: Cambridge University Press.

Paikoff, R. L., & Brooks-Gunn, J. (1991). Do parent-child relationships change during puberty? *Psychological Bulletin, 110*, 47–66.

Palinscar, A., & Brown, A. (1984). Reciprocal teaching of comprehension-fostering and comprehension-monitoring strategies. *Cognition and Instruction, 2*(2), 73–109.

Pang, V. (1995). Asian Pacific American students: A diverse and complex population. In J. A. Banks & C. A. M. Banks (Eds.), *Handbook of research on multicultural education* (pp. 412–426). New York: Macmillan.

Parenti, C. (1999). *Lockdown America: Police and prisons in the age of crisis.* New York: Verso.

Patterson, O. (1998). *Rituals of blood: Consequences of slavery in two American centuries.* Washington, DC: Civitas Counterpoint.

Pea, R. D., & Gomez, L. (1992). Distributed multimedia learning environments. *Interactive Learning Environments, 2*(2), 73–109.

Pearson, P. D., & Fielding, L. (1991). Comprehension instruction. In R. Barr, M. Kamil, P. Mosenthal & P. D. Pearson (Eds.), *Handbook of reading research* (Vol. 2, pp. 815–860). New York: Longman.

Percelay, J., Ivey, M., & Dweck, S. (1994). *Snaps.* New York: William Morrow.

Perle, M., Moran, R., Lutkas, A., & Tirre, W. (2005). *NAEP 2004 trends in academic progress: Three decades of student performance in reading and mathematics.* Washington, DC: National Center for Education Statistics, U.S.Department of Education, Institute of Education Sciences.

Perry, T., & Delpit, L. (Eds.). (1998). *The real Ebonics debate: Power, language, and the education of African-American children.* Boston: Beacon Press.

Peterson, P., Fenemma, E., Carpenter, T., & Loef, M. (1989). Teachers' pedagogical content beliefs in mathematics. *Cognition and Instruction, 6*(1), 1–40.

Phillips, S. U. (1983). *The invisible culture: Communication in classroom and community on the Warm Springs Indian Reservation.* New York: Longman.

Piaget, J. (1975). *The child's conception of the world* (J. & A. Tomlinson, Trans.). Totowa, NJ: Littlefield Adams. (Original work published 1929)

Poldrack, R. A. (2000). Imaging brain plasticity: Conceptual and methodological issues. *NeuroImage, 12*, 1–13.

Polkinghorne, D. (1988). *Narrative knowing and the human sciences.* Albany: State University of New York Press.

Pressley, M. (2000). What should comprehension instruction be the instruction of? In M. L. Kamil, P. Mossenthal, P. D. Pearson, & R. Barr (Eds.), *Handbook of reading research* (Vol. 3, pp. 545–562). Mahwah, NJ: Erlbaum.

Pressley, M., & Afflerbach, P. (1995). *Verbal protocols of reading: The nature of constructively responsive reading.* Hillsdale, NJ: Erlbaum.

Purves, A. (1991). *The idea of difficulty in literature.* Albany: State University of New York Press.

Quartz, S., & Sejnowski, T. (2002). *Liars, lovers, and heroes: What the new brain science reveals about how we become who we are.* New York: HarperCollins.

Rabinowitz, P. (1987). *Before reading: Narrative conventions and the politics of interpretation.* Ithaca, NY: Cornell University Press.

Rabinowitz, P., & Smith, M. (1998). *Authorizing readers: Resistance and respect in the teaching of literature.* New York: Teachers College Press.

Rajshekar, V. T. (1987). *Dalit: The Black untouchables of India* (3rd ed.). Atlanta, GA: Clarity Press.

Ramirez, M., & Castaneda, A. (1974). *Cultural democracy: Biocognitive development and education.* New York: Academic Press.

Rattaray, J. D., & Shujaa, M. (1987). *Dare to choose: Parental choice at independent neighborhood schools.* Washington, DC: U.S. Department of Education.

Resnick, L. (1987). *Education and learning to think.* Washington, DC: National Academy Press.

Reynolds, R., Taylor, M., Steffensen, M., Shirey, L., & Anderson, R. (1982). Cultural schemata and reading comprehension. *Reading Research Quarterly, 17*(3), 353–365.

Richardson, V. (Ed.). (2001). *Handbook of research on teaching* (4th ed.). Washington, DC: American Educational Research Association.

Rickford, J., & Rickford, A. (1976). Cut-eye and suck teeth: African words and gestures in new world guise. *Journal of American Folklore, 89*(353), 194–309.

Rickford, J., & Rickford, A. (1995). Dialect readers revisited. *Linguistics and Education, 7,* 107–128.

Rist, R. (1970). Student social class and teacher expectations: The self-fulfilling prophecy in ghetto education. *Harvard Educational Review, 40*(3), 411–451.

Roderick, M., Byrk, A. S., Jacob, B. A., Easton, J. Q., & Allensworth, E. (1999). *Ending social promotion: Results from the first two years.* Chicago: Consortium on Chicago School Research.

Roderick, M., & Camburn, E. (1999). Risk and recovery from course failure in the early years of high school. *American Educational Research Journal, 36*(2), 303–343.

Rogoff, B. (1990). *Apprenticeship in thinking: Cognitive development in social context.* New York: Oxford University Press.

Rogoff, B. (1995). Observing sociocultural activity on three planes: Participatory appropriation, guided participation, and apprenticeship. In J. Wertsch, P. del Rio, & A. Alvarez (Eds.), *Sociocultural studies of mind* (pp. 139–164). New York: Cambridge University Press.

Rogoff, B. (2003). *The cultural nature of human development.* New York: Oxford University Press.

Rogoff, B., & Lave, J. (1984). *Everyday cognition: Its development in social context.* Cambridge, MA: Harvard University Press.

Rogoff, B., Paradise, R., Mejía-Arauz, R., Correa-Chávez, M., & Angelillo, C. (2003). Firsthand learning through intent participation. *Annual Review of Psychology, 54,* 175–204.

Rose, M. (2004). *The mind at work.* New York: Viking Penguin.

Rose, T. (1994). *Black noise: Rap music and Black culture in contemporary America.* Hanover, NH: Wesleyan University Press.

Rosebery, A. S., Warren, B., Ballenger, C., & Ogonowski, M. (2005). The generative potential of students' everyday knowledge in learning science. In T. Romberg, T. Carpenter, & D. Fae (Eds.), *Understanding mathematics and science matters* (pp. 55–80). Mahwah, NJ: Erlbaum.

Rosebery, A. S., Warren, B., & Conant, F. R. (1992). Appropriating scientific discourse: Findings from language minority classrooms. *Journal of Learning Sciences, 2*(1), 61–94.

Rosenshine, B. (1970). Evaluation of classroom instruction. *Review of Educational Reseach, 40,* 279–300.

Rosenshine, B. (1971). Teaching behaviors related to pupil achievement: A review of research. In I. Westbury & A. A. Bellack (Eds.), *Research into classroom practice.* New York: Teachers College Press.

Rosenshine, B. (1976). Recent research on teaching behaviors and student achievement. *Journal of Teacher Education, 27,* 61–64.

Rossi, R. (2004, February 24). Nearly half of schools face probation threat. *Chicago Sun Times,* p. 9.

Salomon, G. (1993). *Distributed cognitions: Psychological and educational considerations.* New York: Cambridge University Press.

Saracho, O. N., & Spodek, B. (1984). *Cognitive style and children's learning: Individual variation in cognitive processes.* Urbana, IL: ERIC Clearinghouse on Elementary and Early Childhood Education.

Sarich, V., & Miele, F. (2004). *Race: The reality of human differences.* Cambridge, MA: Westview Press.

Saxe, G. (1991). *Culture and cognitive development: Studies in mathematical understanding.* Hillsdale, NJ: Erlbaum.

Saxe, G. (1999). Cognition, development and cultural practices. In E. Turiel (Ed.), *Culture and development: New directions in child psychology* (pp. 19–35). San Francisco: Jossey-Bass.

Saxe, G., & Esmonde, I. (2005). Studying cognition in the flux: A historical treatment of FU in the shifting structure of Oksapimin mathematics. *Mind, Culture and Activity, 12*(3–4), 171–225.

Saxe, G., & Gearhart, M. (1990). The development of topographical concepts in unschooled straw weavers. *British Journal of Developmental Psychology, 8,* 251–258.

Scardamalia, M., Bereiter, C., & Steinbach, R. (1984). Teachability of reflective processes in written composition. *Cognitive Science, 8,* 173–190.

Schank, R. C., & Abelson, R. P. (1977). *Scripts, plans, goals, and understanding: An inquiry into human knowledge structures.* Hillsdale, NJ: Erlbaum.

Schoenfeld, A. H. (1985). *Mathematical problem solving.* Orlando, FL: Academic Press.

Schoenfeld, A. H. (1988). When good teaching leads to bad results: The disaster of "well-taught" mathematics courses. *Educational Psychologist, 23*(2), 145–166.

Schoenfeld, A. H. (1998). Making mathematics and making pasta: From cookbook procedures to really cooking. In J. G. Greeno & S. V. Goldman (Eds.), *Thinking practices in mathematics and science learning* (pp. 299–320). Mahwah, NJ: Erlbaum.

Scholes, R. (1985). *Textual power, literary theory, and the teaching of English.* New Haven, CT: Yale University Press.

Scollon, R., & Scollon, S. B. K. (1981). *Narrative, literacy, and face in interethnic communication.* Norwood, NJ: Ablex.

Scribner, S. (1984). Studying working intelligence. In B. Rogoff & J. Lave (Eds.), *Everyday cognition: Its development in social context* (pp. 9–40). Cambridge, MA: Harvard University Press.

Scribner, S., & Cole, M. (1981). *The psychology of literacy.* Cambridge, MA: Harvard University Press.

Sentencing Project. (1997). *Analysis of the survey of inmates in state and federal correctional facilities, 1997.* Washington, DC: Author.

Shade, B. (1982). Afro-American cognitive style: A variable in school success. *Review of Educational Research, 52,* 219–244.

Shange, N. (1997). *For colored girls who have considered suicide when the rainbow is enuf.* New York: Simon & Schuster.

Shulman, L. (1986). Those who understand: Knowledge growth in teaching. *Educational Researcher, 15*(2), 4–14.

Shulman, L. (2004). Professing the liberal arts. In L. Shulman (Ed.), *The wisdom of practice.* San Francisco: Jossey-Bass.

Shulman, L. (2005). Signature pedagogies. *Daedalus, 134*(3), 52–59.

Shuman, R. B. (1995). Carol D. Lee's "Signifying as a scaffold for literary interpretation": The pedagogical implications of an African American discourse genre. *African American Review, 29*(4), 693–695.

Siddle-Walker, E. V. (1993). Caswell County Training School, 1933–1969: Relationships between community and school. *Harvard Educational Review, 63*(2), 161–182.

Siddle-Walker, E. V. (1996). *Their highest potential: An African-American school community in the segregated South.* Chapel Hill: University of North Carolina Press.

Silva, C. M., Moses, R. P., Rivers, J., & Johnson, P. (1990). The Algebra Project: Making middle school mathematics count. *Journal of Negro Education, 59*(3), 375–392.

Simpkins, G., Holt, G., & Simpkins, C. (1977). *Bridge: A cross-culture reading program.* Boston: Houghton Mifflin.

Singley, K., & Anderson, J. R. (1989). *The transfer of cognitive skill.* Cambridge, MA: Harvard University Press.

Sizemore, B. (1985). Pitfalls and promises of effective schools research. *Journal of Negro education, 54,* 269–288.

Sizemore, B. (1987). The effective African American elementary school. In G. W. Noblit & W. T. Pink (Eds.), *Schooling in social context: Qualitative studies* (pp. 175–202). Norwood, NJ: Ablex.

Sizemore, B. (1988). The Madison school: A turnaround case. *The Journal of Negro Education*, 243–266.

Sizemore, B. (1995). *Ten routines for high achievement*. Chicago, IL: School Achievement Structure, DePaul University.

Sizemore, B. (2007). *Walking in circles: The Black struggle for school reform*. Chicago: Third World Press.

Slavin, R. E., Madden, N. A., Dolan, L. J., & Wasik, B. A. (1996). *Every child, every school: Success for all*. Newbury Park, CA: Corwin.

Smagorinsky, P., & Smith, M. (1992). The nature of knowledge in composition and literary understanding: The question of specificity. *Review of Educational Research, 62*(3), 279–305.

Smethurst, J. E. (2005). *The Black Arts Movement: Literary nationalism in the 1960s and 1970s*. Chapel Hill: University of North Carolina Press.

Smith, M. (1989). Teaching the interpretation of irony in poetry. *Research in the Teaching of English, 23*(3), 254–272.

Smith, M. (1991). Constructing meaning from text: An analysis of ninth-grade reader responses. *Journal of Educational Research, 84*(5), 263–271.

Smith, M., & Hillocks, G. (1988, October). Sensible sequencing: Developing knowledge about literature text by text. *English Journal, 77*, 44–49.

Smitherman, G. (1977). *Talkin and testifyin: The language of Black America*. Boston: Houghton Mifflin.

Smitherman, G. (1981). "What go round come round": King in perspective. *Harvard Educational Review 51*, 40–56.

Smitherman, G. (1992). Black English, diverging or converging? The view from the National Assessment of Educational Progress. *Language and Education, 61*(1), 47–61.

Smitherman, G. (1995). Students' right to their own language: A retrospective. *English Journal, 84*(1), 21–27.

Smitherman, G. (1999). CCCC's role in the struggle for language rights. *College Composition and Communication 50*(3), 349–376.

Smitherman, G. (2000a). African American student writers in the NAEP, 1969–1988/89 and "The Blacker the berry, the sweeter the juice." In *Talkin that talk: Language, culture, and education in African America* (pp. 163–194). New York: Routledge.

Smitherman, G. (2000b). Ebonics, King, and Oakland: Some folks don't believe fat meat is greasy. In *Talkin that talk: Language, culture, and education in African America* (pp. 150–162). New York: Routledge.

Smitherman, G. (2000c). *Talkin that talk: Language, culture, and education in African America*. New York: Routledge.

Smitherman, G., Daniel, J. L., & Jeremiah, M. (1987). "Makin a way outa no way": The proverb tradition in the Black experience. *Journal of Black Studies, 17*(4), 482–508.

Smitherman, G., & Dijk, T. A. van (Eds). (1988). Discourse and discrimination. Detroit, MI: Wayne State University.

Snow, C., Burns, M. S., & Griffin, P. (1998). *Preventing reading difficulties in young children*. Washington, DC: National Academy Press.

Sollors, W. (1997). *Neither Black nor White yet both*. Cambridge, MA: Harvard University Press.

Sophocles. (1977). *The Oedipus Cycle: Oedipus Rex, Oedipus at Colonus, Antigone* (D. Fitts & R. Fitzgerald, Trans.). New York: Harcourt, Brace, Jovanovich.

Spears, A. (Ed.). (1999). *Race and ideology: Language, symbolism, and popular culture*. Detroit, MI: Wayne State University Press.

Spears, A., & Winford, D. (Eds.). (1998). *The structure and status of pidgins and creoles: Including selected papers from the meetings of the Society for Pidgins and Creole Linguistics*. Philadelphia: Benjamins.

Spencer, M. B. (1987). Black children's ethnic identity formation: Risk and resilience in castelike minorities. In J. Phinney & M. Rotheram (Eds.), *Children's ethnic socialization: Pluralism and development* (pp. 103–116). Newbury Park, CA: Sage.

Spencer, M. B. (1995). Old issues and new theorizing about African American youth: A phenomenological variant of ecological systems theory. In R. L. Taylor (Ed.), *Black youth: Perspectives on their status in the United States* (pp. 37–70). Westport, CT: Praeger.

Spencer, M. B. (1999). Social and cultural influences on school adjustment: The application of an identity-focused cultural ecological perspective. *Educational Psychologist, 34*(1), 43–57.

Spencer, M. B. (2000). Identity, achievement orientation, and race: "Lessons learned" about the normative developomental experiences of African American males. In W. H. Watkins, J. H. Lewis, & V. Chou (Eds.), (Ed.), *Race and Education*: Allyn & Bacon.

Spencer, M. B. (2006). Phenomenology and ecological systems theory: Development of diverse groups. In W. Damon & R. Lerner (Eds.), *Handbook of child psychology* (6th ed., Vol. 1, pp. 829–893). New York: Wiley.

Spencer, M. B., Harpalani, V., Cassidy, E., Jacobs, C., Donde, S., Goss, T., et al. (2006). Understanding vulnerability and resilience from a normative development perspective: Implications for racially and ethnically diverse youth. In D. Chicchetti & E. Cohen (Eds.), *Developmental psychopathology* (pp. 627–672). Hoboken, NJ: Wiley.

Spencer, M. B., Swanson, D. P., & Cunningham, M. (1991). Ethnicity, ethnic identity, and competence formation: Adolescent transtion and cultural transformation. *Journal of Negro Education, 60*(3), 366–387.

Sperry, L., & Sperry, D. E. (1996). Early development of narrative skills. *Cognitive Development, 11*, 443–465.

Spillane, J. P. (2006). *Standards deviation: How schools misunderstand education policy*. Cambridge, MA: Harvard University Press.

Spratley, A. (2005, April). *Figuring out the figurative: Understanding and teaching symbolism*. Paper presented at the annual meeting of the American Education Research Association, Montreal, Canada.

Stahl, S., & Miller, P. (1989). Whole language and language experience approaches for beginning reading: A quantitative research synthesis. *Review of Educational Research, 59,* 87–116.

Stampp, K. (1953). *The peculiar institution.* New York: Random House.

Stannard, D. E. (1992). *American holocaust: Columbus and the conquest of the new world.* New York: Oxford University Press.

Stanton, W. (1960). *The leopard's spots: Scientific attitudes toward race in America, 1815–59.* Chicago: University of Chicago Press.

Steele, C. M. (1997). A threat in the air: How stereotypes shape intellectual identity and performance. *American Psychologist, 52,* 613–629.

Steele, C. M. (1998). Stereotyping and its threat are real. *American Psychologist, 53,* 680–681.

Steffensen, M., Joag-Dev, C., & Anderson, R. (1979). A cross-cultural perspective on reading comprehension. *Reading Research Quarterly, 15*(1), 10–29.

Steinberg, L., & Silverberg, S. B. (1986). The vicissitudes of autonomy and early adolescence. *Child Development, 57,* 841–851.

Stephenson, G. (1969). *Race distinctions in American law.* New York: AMS Press.

Stevenson, H. W., & Stigler, J. W. (1992). *The learning gap: Why our schools are failing and what we can learn from japanese and chinese education.* New York: Simon & Schuster.

Stotsky, S. (1999). *Losing our language: How multicultural classroom instruction is undermining our children's ability to read, write, and reason.* New York: Free Press.

Stylistics (Musical Group). (1990). People make the world go round. On *The best of the Stylistics* [CD]. Buffalo, NY: Amherst.

Sullivan, W. (2005). *Work and integrity* (2nd ed.). San Francisco: Jossey-Bass.

Super, C. M., & Harness, S. (1986). The developmental niche: A conceptualization at the interface of child and culture. *International Journal of Behavioral Development, 5,* 545–569.

Swift, J. (1995). *A modest proposal and other satires.* Amherst, NY: Prometheus Books. (Original work published 1729)

Tannen, D. (1979). *Ethnicity as conversational style.* Austin, TX: Southwest Educational Development Laboratory.

Tannen, D. (1989). *Talking voices: Repetition, dialogue, and imagery in conversational discourse.* New York: Cambridge University Press.

Taylor, O. (Ed.). (1986). *Nature of communication disorders in culturally and linguistically diverse populations.* San Diego: College-Hill Press.

Taylor, O., & Lee, D. (1987). Standardized tests and African-American children: Communication and language uses. *Negro Educational Review, 38*(2/3), 67–80.

Teasley, S. D., & Roschelle, J. (1993). Constructing a joint problem space: The computer as a tool for sharing knowledge. In S. P. Lajoie & S. J. Derry (Eds.), *Computers as cognitive tools* (pp. 229–260). Hillsdale, NJ: Lawrence Erlbaum.

Thorne, B. (2003). The sociology and anthropology of childhood. In P. Fass (Ed.), *Encyclopedia of children and childhood in history and society* (Vol. 3, pp. 772–776). New York: Macmillan.

TLC. (2004). Waterfalls. On *Now and forever: The hits* [CD]. New York: Arista.

Tompkins, J. (1980). *Reader-response criticism: From formalism to poststructuralism.* Baltimore, MD: Johns Hopkins University Press.

Toulmin, S., Rieke, R., & Janik, A. (1984). *An introduction to reasoning.* New York: Macmillan.

Traub, J. (1999, January 16). What no school can do. *New York Times Magazine,* pp. 52–56.

Turner, M. (1996). *The Literary Mind.* New York: Oxford University Press.

Urban League. (1999). *The state of Black America.* New York: Author.

Urban League. (2005). *The state of Black America.* New York: Author.

Valdés, G. (1996). *Con respeto: Bridging the distances between culturally diverse families and schools.* New York: Teachers College Press.

Valdés, G. (2002). *Expanding the definitions of giftedness: The case of young interpreters from immigrant countries.* Mahwah, NJ: Erlbaum.

Van Sertima, I. (Ed.). (1987). *African presence in early America.* New Brunswick, NJ: Transaction Books.

Van Sertima, I., & Rashidi, R. (Eds.). (1985). *The African presence in early Asia.* New Brunswick, NJ: Transaction Books.

Varenne, H., & McDermott. R. (1998). *Successful failure: The school America builds.* Boulder, CO: Westview Press.

Vass, W. (1979). *The Bantu-speaking heritage of the United States.* Los Angeles: Center for Afro-American Studies, University of California.

Verga, G. (1997). The wolf. (A. Alexander, Trans.). In I. Howe & I. W. Howe (Eds.), Short stories: An anthology of the shortest stories (pp. 33–38). New York: Bantam.

Vygotsky, L. (1978). *Mind in society: The development of higher psychological processes.* Cambridge, MA: Harvard University Press.

Vygotsky, L. (1981). The genesis of higher mental functions. In J. Wertsch (Ed.), *The concept of activity in Society psychology.* Armonk, NY: M.E. Sharpe.

Vygotsky, L. (1987). *Thinking and speech.* New York: Plenum. (Original work published 1934)

Walker, A. (1982). *The color purple.* New York: Simon & Schuster.

Walker, A. (1983). *In search of our mothers' gardens: Womanist prose.* San Diego: Harcourt Brace Jovanovich.

Walker, A. (1994). Everyday use. In B. M. Christian (Ed.), *Everyday use* (pp. 23–38). New Brunswick, NJ: Rutgers University Press.

Walters, R. W. (2003). *White nationalism, Black interests: Conservative public policy and the Black community.* Detroit, MI: Wayne State University Press.

Warren, B., Ballenger, C., Ogonowski, M., Rosebery, A. S., & Hudicourt-Barnes, J. (2001). Rethinking diversity in learning science: The logic of everyday sensemaking. *Journal of Research in Science Teaching, 38,* 529–552.

Warren, B., & Ogonowski, M. (1998). *From knowledge to knowing: An inquiry into teacher learning in science.* Newton, MA: Education Development Center.

Warren, B., & Ogonowski, M. (2001, April). *Embodied imagining: A study of adult learning in physics.* Paper presented at the annual meeting of the American Educational Research Association, Seattle, WA.

Warren, B., & Rosebery, A. S. (1996). "This question is just too, too easy!":

Perspsectives from the classroom on accountability in science. In L. Schauble & R. Glaser (Eds.), *Innovations in learning: New environments for education* (pp. 97–125). Hillsdale, NJ: Erlbaum.

Warren, K. (1993). *Black and White strangers: Race and American literary realism.* Chicago: University of Chicago Press.

Wasley, P. A., Fine, M., Gladden, M., Holland, N., King, S., Mosak, E., et al. (2000). *Small schools, great strides: A study of new small schools in Chicago.* New York: Bank Street College.

Weaver, C. (1996). *Teaching grammar in context.* Portsmouth, NH: Heinemann.

Weisner, T. (2002). Ecocultural understanding of children's developmental pathways. *Human Development, 45*(4), 275–281.

Wells, G. (1995). Language and the inquiry-oriented curriculum. *Curriculum Inquiry, 25,* 233–269.

Wertsch, J. (1985). *Vygotsky and the social formation of mind.* Cambridge, MA: Harvard University Press.

Wertsch, J. (1991). *Voices of the mind: A sociocultural approach to mediated action.* Cambridge, MA: Harvard University Press.

White, K. R. (1982). The relation between socioeconomic status and academic achievement. *Psychological Bulletin, 91,* 461–481.

White, S., & Clement, J. (2001). *Assessing the lexile framework: Results of a panel meeting. Working paper No. 2001-08.* Washington, DC: U.S. Department of Education, Office of Educational Research and Improvement.

Whitehead, A. N. (1929). *The aims of education.* New York: MacMillan.

Wideman, J. E. (1998). *Damballah.* New York: Mariner Books.

Wilson, W. J. (1987). *The truly disadvantaged: The inner city, the underclass, and public policy.* Chicago: University of Chicago Press.

Wineburg, S. (1998). Reading Abraham Lincoln: An expert-expert study in the interpretation of historical texts. *Cognitive Science, 22,* 319–346.

Wineburg, S., & Grossman, P. (1998). Creating a community of learners among high school teachers. *Phi Delta Kappan, 73,* 684–689.

Wineburg, S., & Wilson, S. M. (1988). Peering at history through different lenses: The role of disciplinary perspectives in teaching hisory. *Teachers College Record, 89*(4), 525–539.

Wineburg, S., & Wilson, S. M. (1991). Subject matter knowledge in the teaching of history. In J. Brophy (Ed.), *Advances in research on teaching* (Vol. 2, pp. 305–347). Greenwich, CT: JAI Press.

Winner, E. (1988). *The point of words: Children's understanding of metaphor and irony.* Cambridge, MA: Harvard University Press.

Wolf, D. (1995). *Reading reconsidered: Literature and literacy in high school.* New York: College Entrance Examination Board.

Wolf, D., Bixby, J., Glenn, J., & Gardner, H. (1991). To use their minds well: Investigating new forms of student assessment. In G. Grant (Ed.), *Review of research in education* (pp. 31–74). Washington, DC: American Educational Research Association.

Wolfram, W. (1981). Varieties of American English. In C. Ferguson & S. B. Heath

(Eds.), *Language in the USA* (pp. 44–68). New York: Cambridge University Press.

Wolfram, W., Adger, C. T., & Christian, D. (1999). *Dialects in schools and communities*. Mahwah, NJ: Erlbaum.

Wolfram, W., & Christian, D. (1976). *Appalachian speech*. Arlington, VA: Center for Applied Linguistics.

Wolfram, W., & Schilling-Estes, N. (1998). *American English: Dialects and variation*. Oxford: Basil Blackwell.

Woodward, C. V. (1974). *The strange career of Jim Crow* (3rd ed.). New York: Oxford University Press.

Wossmann, L. (2003). Schooling resources, educational institutions and student performance: The international evidence. *Oxford Bulletin of Economics and Statistics, 65*(2), 117–170.

Zancanella, D. (1991). Teachers reading/readers teaching: Five teachers' personal approaches to literature and their teaching of literature. *Research in the Teaching of English, 25*(1), 5–32.

Index

SUBJECTS

About the Author

Carol D. Lee is Professor of Education and Social Policy in the Learning Sciences Program of the School of Education and Social Policy and of African American Studies at Northwestern University. She is a founder of an African-centered independent school that has been in existence since 1972 and a founder of three charter schools in Chicago. Dr. Lee is the former president of the National Conference on Research in Language and Literacy, Co-Chair of the Research Assembly of the National Council of Teachers of English (NCTE), Chair of the Standing Committee on Research of NCTE, and Residential Fellow at the Center for Advanced Studies in the Behavioral Sciences. She is currently Vice President of Division G—Social Contexts of Education—of the American Educational Research Association. Her research efforts have been funded by the McDonnell Foundation's Cognitive Studies for Educational Practice, the Spencer Foundation, and the National Science Foundation, among others. She is also a former high school English teacher, primary grade teacher, school director, and community college instructor.